Praise for Waiting Wives

"Donna Moreau deserves a medal for rescuing a lost chapter of the history of the Vietnam War."

—Patricia O'Toole, author of *When Trumpets Call*

"A tragically timely and overdue book. Moreau is more than a chronicler. Her fine writing and sense of tension leaves us with the indelible after-image of the wives of men fighting an unpopular war overseas herding their children into their rooms and holding their collective breaths as an official car moves slowly down the street past bicycles on the front lawn looking for the house at which it will stop with the words: 'It is my duty to inform you . . .'"

—Kate Webb, co-author of *War Torn: Stories of War from the Women Reporters Who Covered Vietnam*

"Donna Moreau's lovely book carries us into a world defined by the exquisite longings of the heart, teaching us that a certain dignity and holiness attend those who wait bravely for the return of love."

—Don J. Snyder, author of *Of Time and Memory: My Parents' Love Story*

"*Waiting Wives* casts light on one of the most overlooked aspects of all wars—the anxiety, loneliness, and resilience of the military wives on the homefront. Donna Moreau, who knows this world from personal experience, illuminates this story with great candor, humanity, and humor. This is a timeless book, and, thanks to Moreau's gifts as a writer, an unforgettable one as well."

—Andrew Carroll, editor of the *New York Times* bestseller *War Letters: Extraordinary Correspondence from American Wars*

"In the Vietnam War men volunteered and were also drafted. Today we have an 'all-volunteer' military. One thing has not changed. When our soldiers go to war they still take the hearts of their families with them. In this moving book Donna Moreau illumines the soul of the American military family. As the father of a Marine who recently deployed to the Middle East, I identify deeply with the brave women and children of Schilling Manor who lived through days that felt like lifetimes."

—Frank Schaeffer, author of *Faith of Our Sons: A Father's Wartime Diary* and *Keeping Faith: A Father-Son Story About Love and the United States Marine Corps*

"So much of what we know about women during wartime comes from contrived, one-dimensional images of dutiful wives left behind, making do, while their husbands are off performing the brave, important work of war. In the stories of her own mother and the other wives of Schilling Manor, Donna Moreau erases those stock characters, replacing them with surprising portraits of women and their children finding ways to live for years and even decades through an often-ignored kind of hell of war. *Waiting Wives* gives voice to the struggles, heroism, and transformations just below the surface, as these American women endure the minute-by-minute, day-by-day, slow torment of waiting, hoping, and not knowing, during the Vietnam war."

—Emily Yellin, author of *Our Mothers' War: American Women at Home and at the Front During World War II*

WAITING WIVES

———ɱ———

The Story of Schilling Manor, Home Front to the Vietnam War

DONNA MOREAU

ATRIA BOOKS

New York   London   Toronto   Sydney

ATRIA BOOKS
Rockefeller Center
1230 Avenue of the Americas
New York, NY 10020

Library of Congress Cataloging-in-Publication Data
Moreau, Donna.
Waiting Wives : the story of Schilling Manor,
home front to the Vietnam War / by Donna Moreau.—
1st Atria Books trade pbk. ed.
p.   cm
ISBN 0-7434-7077-X (pbk.)
1. Vietnamese Conflict, 1961–1975—Women—United States.
2. Military spouses—United States. 3. Schilling Manor (Kan.)
I. Title.
DS559.8.W6M67 2005
959.704'3'082—dc22   2004062348

First Atria Books trade paperback edition May 2005

10 9 8 7 6 5 4 3 2 1

ATRIA BOOKS is a trademark of Simon & Schuster, Inc.

Manufactured in the United States of America

For information regarding special discounts for bulk purchases, please contact Simon & Schuster Special Sales at 1-800-456-6798 or business@simonandschuster.com

For Beverly, Bonnie, Lorrayne
and for all who have waited on the other side of war

Contents

CONTENTS

CONTENTS

CONTENTS

When our country is at war, hers is the unhappy lot of remaining behind. All the responsibilities of family and family affairs, with all the fears, are in her hands. There can be no greater admiration than that of a husband on war service to return and find, as he had hoped, that his own wife has met the test of keeping up her end of things. She must become a "good soldier," and her sense of Duty, Honor, and Country will be those of the Army itself.

—*The Officer's Guide*, 22nd Edition

Preface

At the heart of the three million square miles that form the contiguous United States is the town of Salina, Kansas. In the early days of World War II, the U.S. government carved out four thousand of its flattest acres and constructed the Smokey Hill Air Base, a fortress charged with training young men in the art of aerial warfare. The military closed the base in 1948 and reopened it in 1951 as Schilling Air Force Base. Ironically, the government shut down the base again in 1964 as the first B-52 took flight in what would become America's longest combat mission, the Vietnam War.

But that is not the end of the story.

What was once Schilling Air Force Base, one of the hundreds of military strongholds created for brave men and their mighty weapons, became Schilling Manor: The Home of the Waiting Wives of the United States Armed Forces.

Schilling Manor was remarkable in that it was the only base in the history of the United States set aside for the wives and children of soldiers assigned to Vietnam; a Brigadoon community emerging from the breast of the prairie at the first sign of war, then disappearing with only a handful of people knowing that it had ever existed. I know about this exclusive settlement because I lived there with my mother and two sisters for thirteen months while my father served in Vietnam. My family was one of only seven thousand military families that called Schilling Manor home.

Schilling Manor existed when death tolls were a part of a military family's daily language, when Walter Cronkite and Huntley and Brinkley became virtual uncles to wives desperate for information about their husbands. It was a time when it was normal to see flag-draped coffins, sometimes dozens of them at once, resting on tarmacs across the country, waiting for wives and children and mothers and fathers to claim the remains of those inside. These young men perished for a country that was being ripped apart with every sortie flown into North Vietnam, with each report of another village destroyed, with the photographs of American soldiers weeping beside their dead buddies, and with the perpetual sound of taps carried on the wind to every military base, town, city, or college campus across our country.

No one escaped the melancholy refrain that became America's national anthem.

The sixties generation blossomed with flower power and free love, wilted from protests and rebellion, drugs and confusion, and ended with disillusionment and deep mistrust in our government. And through it all, the wives of the Vietnam War, like Penelope, the loyal wife of Odysseus who waited twenty years for him to return from Troy, struggled to pass the infinite minutes until their husbands returned from war.

Some wives waited successfully, others floundered under the pressure. Many of the women living at Schilling Manor thought their survival depended upon the return of their husbands. Yet these same women held together single-parent households and made important financial decisions long before the women's movement. They traveled across the country and across the world by themselves, some with as many as eight small children in tow. Often they organized and held together entire communities where none existed before.

Waiting Wives is the first book to focus on this other, hidden side of the Vietnam War. It is a narrative investigation of an extraordinary group of women who lived in an incomparable community located in the heart of America during its most tur- bulent decade. Military wives fought on the emotional front of the war. Their enemies were fear, loneliness, depression, isola- tion, destitution, lack of information, and the slow tick of time. In his book *Dispatches*, Michael Herr writes, "We came to fear something more complicated than death, an annihilation less final but more complete. . . ." For the women of Schilling Manor, that annihilation could destroy dreams and devastate futures. It threatened to unravel families and cancel the lives they had with the men they had promised to love forever. For some wives, fac- ing that enemy entailed a quiet day-to-day struggle to maintain a status quo. For others, it triggered change and independence. Whether it was learning how to pay bills, publish a newsletter, or write a petition, most of the wives came away from Schilling with a better sense of themselves and of their roles in a world that had changed forever because of the Vietnam War.

Waiting Wives: The Story of Schilling Manor, Home Front to the Vietnam War is part memoir, part history, and part portrait of three women—Lorrayne, Bonnie, and my mother, Beverly. These women were members of the last generation of hat-and- glove military wives called upon by their country to pack without question, to follow without comment, and to wait quietly with a smile. The stories of these waiting wives begin in the period immediately before their arrival at Schilling Manor and end when they drive out of the gate for the last time—stories gra- ciously shared with me by the women, children, husbands, com- manders, teachers, and other personnel who lived at or were involved with Schilling Manor.

Their personal memories and anecdotes, along with those of my family's, are the foundation for the book.

In addition to Lorrayne's, Bonnie's, and Beverly's story, I have created chapters called "The Committee" that I thread through the book to tell the many heroic, funny, and tragic tales involving other women. The stories, told in different versions by many people, are based on actual incidents that occurred at Schilling Manor, and have become Schilling lore. The anecdotes are impossible to corroborate with the people involved, but are essential in animating the internal life of the home for waiting wives.

The Committee is composed of a group of five waiting wives who volunteer to put on a fashion show as a fund-raiser for Schilling Manor's day-care center. Each woman is a composite of the many military wives I have met during my life. They are a chatty group who, once they have dealt with the business of the fashion show, always has a story to tell about what they heard or saw since their last meeting. I refer to the women by the ranks of their husbands—for example, the lieutenant's wife, warrant officer's wife—because the group could have lived at Schilling Manor during any of the years it was open as the home for waiting wives.

If geography determines destiny, then living at Schilling Manor became a defining experience for many of the women. It was rumored to be the "lucky place" because of a myth that had traveled around the military community suggesting that if a man's family lived there, then he was sure to come home. There was some truth to the myth, as most of the husbands and fathers returned to their families, but as in all reaches into the imagination, reality eventually diminishes myth. Life at Schilling was intense; the memories everlasting. The construct of people, place, and events never happened before, nor will it happen again. Almost all of the women interviewed for this book agreed: Schilling Manor was a place of light during the darkest, most terrifying time of their lives.

Introduction

Thirty-four years ago I pleaded with my father to take me with him to fight in Vietnam.

My father, then a lieutenant colonel in the U.S. Army, drove himself to the Schilling airfield on the first leg of his journey to war. I sat in the backseat, behind my mother, and pleaded my case: Why not? The war was slowing down. It's a right-on cause. I was sure I had heard of other families going to Vietnam. Besides, wouldn't it be great to have me around to help out? I can't remember his part of the conversation. He was not a man of words and, thinking back, I suspect he more or less dismissed me to the snickers of my mother and two sisters.

My elder sister, Gail, sat in the backseat behind my father and clucked her tongue, a sure indication that anything I said made her sick. My younger sister, Lynn, sat in the middle and sucked her thumb, seemingly oblivious to the deathly consequences of war. My mother snapped at me without ever turning around: Are you crazy? Why in the hell do you want to go to that godforsaken jungle? What do you think you can do?

Fight?

I was an Army brat born in 1955. On the day that I was born the United States had already committed over $100 million in military aid to South Vietnam and Cambodia, then a part of French Indochina, and a U.S. Military Assistance Advisory Group had been in country since the early 1950s. When I was four years old, before the decade turned, guerrillas felled the first American soldiers twenty miles northeast of Saigon. I went from training wheels to a two-wheeler as total U.S. military equipment and economic aid approached $2 billion. While I prepared for my graduation from kindergarten, the U.S. Air Force prepared to dump the first of nineteen million gallons of Agent Orange over Vietnam. Nightly news images of soldiers fighting in Vietnam inspired my friends and me to play war with lifelike guns in the woods behind our quarters.

I watched my mother starch Army greens so stiff that when my dad pulled them on in the quiet dawn the sound ripped through the house, alerting us to the start of another day. Every Saturday afternoon, I loyally stood ready to assist my father while he spit-shined his combat boots. If I was lucky he allowed me to help him smear the black cream over his boots with damp cotton balls. I was in awe as he buffed the dull black surfaces to gleaming leather.

The first forty-five record I spent my fifty-cent-a-week allowance on was "The Ballad of the Green Berets," Staff Sergeant Barry Sadler's tribute to his fallen Special Forces brothers. One morning, after Bantam league bowling, I went to the Post Exchange and bought the record. Without stopping to play with friends, I hurried home to my room, closed the door, and played the song over and over again on my plastic record player until I had memorized every word. The next morning at breakfast I impressed my family as I sang along when Sadler's voice came on the radio.

I was ten.

As I grew, the war grew. At dinner, kindly looking news anchors announced death tolls as often as they reported weather

forecasts. *My Favorite Martian* and *The Flintstones* were interrupted with news of firefights, protests, and assassinations.

I saw the enemy commit atrocities against U.S. soldiers on
television. On posters I saw the cages where they kept POWs. I
saw hundreds of flag-draped coffins unloaded from cargo
planes. I saw weeping mothers faint in despair over a lost child.
I saw MedEvac choppers fly over my house in Japan with
wounded soldiers inside. War was as familiar to me as reveille at
dawn and taps at dusk. I heard the mournful timbre signaling
the approach of dusk every day for my entire life. No longer did
the music represent the lowering of the flag at the end of the
day. The somber tune became Odin's call to the Valkyries to
bring forth the souls of the heroes slain in battle to the halls of
Valhalla. Taps heralded the death of men, the death of freedom.

Yes, I told my mother as we drove my father to the airport. I
will go fight in that godforsaken jungle.

I did not know anything back then.

The month before my father left us for Vietnam in December
1970, while Americans were being assured that the government
was seeking a just peace and that the war was slowing down, U.S.
bombers attacked targets in North Vietnam in response to the
continued attacks on U.S. reconnaissance planes by the NVA—the
North Vietnamese Army. The Allied command announced an
increase in battlefield activity. The North Vietnamese high command called for the armed forces to heighten their determination
"to fight victoriously." President Richard Nixon requested an
additional $250 million in assistance to aid Cambodia's fight
against the North Vietnamese. Lieutenant William Calley,
ordered by his commanders to "kill every living thing in My Lai,"
went on trial. On December 24, two hours before the Allied
Christmas cease-fire, U.S. artillery fired a shell into a group of
American soldiers, killing nine and wounding nine others.

American soldiers were killing their superior officers, fragging them while they slept in their tents or in the jungle on a mission. United States forces in country were down to 280,000, but casualties were increasing due to booby traps, mortar attacks, and sniper fire.

This was the slowed-down war I thought my father was flying into one day after Christmas.

On reflection, I guess I did not want to know the truth about America and Vietnam in 1970—or for many years after. I was an Army brat and war was a path to freedom. For the duration of my father's tour I hung a map of Indochina on my bedroom wall. I had rendered my own Peter Max version of the American flag—alternating yellow and blue stripes with Day-Glo pink stars—and mounted it on the Cambodian side of the map. I placed a round black bomb like the kind tossed around by the Roadrunner on Saturday-morning cartoons in the middle of the flag. Red-topped tacks dotted South Vietnam, marking the places where I thought my dad was or had been. In the middle of Vietnam, slightly north of the DMZ, I mounted a metal peace sign inscribed with boldfaced black words: PEACE HELL BOMB HANOI.

When my father returned from Vietnam the day before Christmas in 1971, I took down my peace sign. I hid the emblem deep inside a scrapbook, a memento never to lose, and never, ever to brag about.

The symbol represented my patriotism. My belief in my country. I refused to acknowledge any complicity with the government in the disappointment and betrayal many Americans felt toward our country's leaders. The Pentagon Papers and other revelations that surfaced in the ensuing years in the newspapers, on television, within the covers of tell-all books, or in conversations never penetrated my deliberate ignorance. I was an Amer-

ican. I was proud of my father. To protect those things I held
dear, I buried my childhood patriotism, like my peace symbol,
away.

I pretended that the Vietnam War had no effect on my life.

One year after we left Schilling Manor, the Paris Peace Treaty
was signed and America ended its physical involvement in Vietnam. I left for college soon after. The war and my childhood went
away—innocence lost on a battlefield between protest and patriotism, trust and betrayal—not so much buried in my unconscious
as a retreat to a quiet zone where the war still existed in a foggy
border between denial and acceptance.

One day, when I was older than my parents were when my father
was in Vietnam, I thought of Schilling Manor. Long-buried
memories descended like an old-fashioned slide show. Women
listening to Walter Cronkite tell them about the war. Casualty
reports. A friend weeping because her father had gone to heaven.
She would never see him again. A sedan with soldiers in dress
uniform, one with a cross on his collar, parked at a neighbor's
house. Empty mailboxes. Moving vans. Jungle fatigues. Children
dressed in black. Barry Sadler's voice in the background lament-
ing the loss of his comrades while an ice storm blistered the
Kansas prairie.

The wives demanded attention.

Needless to say, my pleas in the car that day so many years ago
were ignored. My dad walked onto the tarmac, climbed the
portable stairs to the threshold of the Frontier Airline turboprop,
turned and waved good-bye, alone, without his middle daughter
to protect him. As he took his seat by the window, my sisters
raised the homemade signs we had designed on neon poster
board adorned with crepe paper streamers and Magic Marker
wishes for his safe return. My mother, dry-eyed, waved back and

stood firm, like a seasoned military wife who had long before resigned herself to a life where she and her children were often placed second to her husband's duty to our country. The engines revved and the plane lifted off.

I burst into tears, certain that my father would never return.

I was fifteen when we drove my father to the airport. Now, over thirty years later, I wonder if I ever stopped crying over the Vietnam War.

The last generation of hat-and-glove military wives

THE BEGINNING

Now this story's ending of what this base has been
The Army's taking over, their wives are moving in
They'll called the place a Manor, and this once mighty base
Will become the only one that's all decked out in lace.

—WRITTEN AND SUNG BY CAPTAIN DAVID NELSON
AT COLONEL MIKE SCANLAN'S FAREWELL PARTY,
SCHILLING AIR FORCE BASE, DECEMBER 1965

735 WHITE ELEPHANTS

(1965)

By the time Kansas Congressman Bob Dole announced the closing of Schilling Air Force Base (SAFB) in November 1964, the U.S. military death toll in Vietnam hovered around four hundred. Dole was unhappy about the decision to close the base. He pondered the implications; SAFB represented twenty percent of Salina's population and twenty percent of its income. The city might fall to its knees. Despite the protestations and appeals of the community, SAFB would be deactivated by the summer of 1965. With no plans for future military occupation, the base might have been left to bleed out into the prairie had it not been for a shrewd military wife and a compassionate Air Force commander.

Colonel John (Mike) Scanlan, 310th Strategic Aerospace Wing Combat Support Group Commander based out of Schilling Air Force Base, was given six months to deactivate the base and turn over the four thousand acres, seven hundred buildings, and mile-long airstrip to the U.S. General Service Administration, the government's property administrator.

At forty-eight, with twenty-six years of military service, Scanlan had already developed a full head of wavy silver hair. It was impossible not to notice his azure blue eyes. His wife, Margaret, thought them more distinctive than Frank Sinatra's legendary eyes. At first glance one might have thought Scanlan a distinguished elder statesman. The premature lines and thoughtful countenance were the medallions awarded a man fated to solve problems others could barely comprehend. Colonel Mike Scanlan gave one hundred percent to his Air Force, and the soldiers who outranked him never underestimated his contribution to their glory. He was, by all measures, what the military thought of as a good man. And Scanlan, by whatever means, always got the job done.

In the early months of 1965, Scanlan filled his days dismantling the military mission at Schilling. The missiles and bombers came off alert, equipment was transferred to active bases, and the combat crews and support personnel deployed daily to places around the world. Each day the housing office cleared and boarded up quarters until the U.S. Office of Economic Development and the Schilling Development Council could figure out what to do with the homes, the buildings, and the acres they sat on.

Sometimes in the evening, Colonel Scanlan would leave the base, traveling north toward Salina through a chilly Kansas landscape. Cars were rare on these nightly ventures into the civilian world; farm equipment that traveled the same roads during the growing season was holed up in barns scattered throughout the flat, lifeless county. Once inside the city limits, about a mile or so from the base, Scanlan would drive down Ninth Avenue, a stretch of road that cut through the heart of the city. He often took a short detour onto Santa Fe Avenue, the center of Salina's retail district. The avenue paralleled Ninth for half a mile or so. Although still a handsome part of town with the remnants of Norman Rockwell–like shops, the city's downtown had begun to display the signs of a less enchanting American dream. Life in Salina was most visible on Santa Fe. Local folks gathered to shop, to talk, or sometimes to stroll on the sidewalks, looking for bargains or picking up snatches of gossip.

Occasionally, before the winter passed, when a sizable number of troops still remained on the base, Scanlan would see one of his airmen walking toward the Fox movie house with a miniskirt-clad local gal. He always hoped the girl's parents didn't mind that their daughter was on a date with one of his boys. He never drove fast on the city's narrow streets, but when he rode by the bus station he always slowed down to take a closer look inside. In the waning days of winter at least one serviceman with a jam-packed duffel bag would be waiting to board the next bus. To home, he hoped.

Scanlan's ritual always led to the railroad tracks on the north side of town. Sometimes he would park in the Gooch Grain Company's lot and watch the trains pass through the city. Warm spring breezes eventually replaced icy winter wind, and as summer approached the commander noticed cargo other than farmland commodities being transported on the rails. Trainloads of military equipment heading west from Fort Riley rumbled by nearly every day for weeks. Olive-drab jeeps and heavy artillery, things too big to pack inside railcars, were locked down onto flatbeds. Hundreds passed.

It didn't take long for the career soldier to surmise that the government decided that crushing communism in Southeast Asia depended on greater U.S. involvement. One night in early summer, after he returned from town, Scanlan told his wife that it looked like the First Infantry out of Fort Riley was headed for Vietnam. Margaret remembers thinking, *Headed where?*

By midsummer the air base was almost completely shut down. On the drive home after another farewell party, Mike Scanlan mentioned to Margaret that he had had a meeting with an Army wife from Fort Riley. The woman was looking for a place for her and her children to stay while her husband served in Vietnam.

"Imagine," he said to Margaret, "she presented me with a plan to reopen the base housing to military families."

Scanlan added that he had also received a phone call from the commander of a couple of GIs up at Riley a few days before. They, too, were looking for a place for their families to stay after their Division shipped out.

Every week the exodus of friends leaving the base became more apparent. Houses emptied. Traffic stilled. Windows were bare. The grass grew tall, out of control, and flourished in the sidewalk cracks. The last of the military police officers had transferred out, leaving the front gate deserted and the base unprotected from outsiders. Within a few months the sadness of a few departures had turned to depression as the vacancy rate approached one hundred percent. Margaret knew that Mike wondered what might happen to the empty quarters once he closed the base.

Both thought it a shame to let such nice homes go to waste.

Scanlan parked the station wagon in the driveway of their quarters. He sat for a moment. Dozens of fireflies appeared in the darkness after he turned off the headlights. Without a soft wind for their wings to light on, the tiny lanterns floated on air, as if gravity excluded them from its grip. Margaret watched them blink on and off, like yellow caution lights, oblivious to the changes taking place in the world they shared with men.

Before long her husband said, "You know what I think, Margaret? I think I can find a way to give those homes to the families of soldiers going to Vietnam. And not just for the Army boys out of Riley. At the rate we're going, the Air Force will need a place to bring their families. The Marines, too, and maybe even the Navy."

By the time they got out of the car, Margaret knew her husband had taken off on his next mission.

Within a day or two, Scanlan met with the commander of the First Infantry Division—the Big Red One—at Fort Riley. "I've got an idea on how to take care of military families and I think it can start right now, with your people." The commander of the Big Red One had been readying his men for war since receiving the call to arms in March 1965. An advance party had already landed at Qui Nhon. The other fifteen thousand troops, at least half of them with wives and children, were scheduled to ship out in mid-September. The general was preparing to lead his soldiers into battle and had given little thought to where the families might go when his men left Fort Riley. Traditionally, wives and children waited in their hometowns or moved off post into civilian housing. Where the families ended up was not a military priority.

The general leaned back in his chair. "Mike, that's a nice idea, and I tell you what, you take care of the families if you can, but as you can see, I've got all these classified documents on my desk and I've got to keep my full attention to the war in Southeast Asia and my First Infantry. Why don't you talk it over with the deputy commander and see how we can make this fine idea happen for our men."

Before Scanlan left the general he said, "Let me talk to your first sergeants, too, and I'll make this thing happen."

The general arranged for his first sergeants to meet with Scanlan at Schilling. The eighteen-to-twenty-years-in-service Army lifers visited the commander over the next days for briefings in groups of five or ten. All agreed that Scanlan had an outstanding idea.

Before Scanlan began work on the broader plan to open the housing with Fort Riley's deputy commander and the Division's first sergeants, he recognized the desperate situation of some families. He was so enthusiastic about the plan's success that he decided to let twelve families move into housing immediately. The first waiting wife to move in was Lorrayne, the Army wife from Fort Riley who had come to see him.

* * *

Colonel Scanlan had put his eagle on the line when he allowed the first twelve families to move into the shuttered quarters. He had gone ahead with the plan without authority. One day in early fall, as more and more service families requested housing, his deputy came into his office and said, "Boss, I think we're going to get you sent to Leavenworth because of what you're doing." The commander thought his deputy might be right. After Margaret voiced her own concerns he thought about it and told her, "The sun is setting on this colonel's career. I don't think the brass will do much to me as long as what I'm doing is good."

Just the same, he sat down with one of his lawyers, wrote up a wire, and sent it to his boss at division headquarters, to his boss's boss, the three-star general of the Fifteenth Air Force, and to the boss of them all—the commander of the Strategic Air Command at Offutt Air Base in Omaha, Nebraska. The wire covered the details of his plan. His last words were: "Please advise."

Within a few days, he heard from his Division commander who was "all for the plan." The leader of the Fifteenth Air Force called a day or so later and said, "Mike, I think it's a good plan. I'm going to back you and see what I can do to make this a viable thing in the Air Force." The SAC commander still needed to come on board.

Time drifted on while more First Division families moved to Schilling. The only thing Scanlan was hearing from headquarters was "close the base, close the base, close the base." The base was closed. The missiles were gone, the silos were filled, and the aircraft had already relocated. Everything closed on schedule. Everything, that is, except for the housing.

Cool fall winds had replaced the summer's tense heat when Scanlan's secretary, visibly excited, entered his office to announce that the general from SAC headquarters was on the telephone. He asked the general's secretary, "Is the general in a good mood?"

"Colonel, he's in a good mood," she answered. "I think you are going to like what he's got to say."

The general addressed the commander, "You know, Scanlan, I don't know you from a pile of hay, but I'll tell you right now that we are going to back your whole plan on that housing project. By the time the sun goes down tonight you are officially supported out of Washington by the United States Air Force, the United States Army, and the Department of Defense."

A couple of years later, during one of his radio broadcasts, Paul Harvey called Scanlan a "gallant base commander" who went ahead and instituted the Waiting Wives program and got permission afterward. Retrospective newspaper articles lauded him as courageous, compassionate, and nervy. But on that cool afternoon in 1965, Scanlan was happy he still had a job.

Beverly

ORDERS

(1970)

My family's journey to Schilling Manor began in the summer of 1970 when we were stationed at Momote Village, an American military housing area located forty miles outside of Tokyo. The world outside the barbed-wire fence that enclosed the post was in chaos. The U.S. military death toll had reached epic proportions. Battles raged in Vietnam, Cambodia, and Laos. The war was part of our lives in Japan. Its effects on the community, normal. Several friends had fathers in country; two had fathers who had already died in battle. They went to slumber parties and football games, acting just like those of us who had fathers. Several boys who hung around the teen club eventually graduated, enlisted, and went to Vietnam. Everyone wished them good luck. It was normal for boys to go to Vietnam. We would not have thought it unusual never to hear from them again.

MedEvac choppers with wounded troops flew over Camp

Drake Middle School several times a day en route to the Army hospital about a mile down the road where my sister Gail worked as a candy striper. They roared by. We never even looked up. Helicopters zooming overhead were as common as birds flitting about in the sky. They were expected and mostly ignored.

What seemed abnormal was everything going on in the States. American citizens were protesting against the war. I did not understand draft dodgers. Flag burners? How could Americans turn their back on America? How could one American spit on another American because he wore a uniform?

None of it made sense.

Every day, for as long as I could remember, I watched my father leave the house in the morning wearing a starched and polished United States military uniform. By doing so, he proved his allegiance to our country, setting a subtle, nearly impalpable example for me to follow. It was a faith I absorbed slowly, the foundation for how I would think for the rest of my life.

During the two years that my family lived in Japan I was a chubby thirteen-, then fourteen-year-old. I only scanned the military newspaper, *The Stars and Stripes,* on the way to the comics. I had an addiction to fifteen-cent packs of vending-machine cigarettes. I rolled up my skirts once I had left the house. I obsessed about boys and wrote poems about dead soldiers. My main objective was figuring out how to wedge my way into the in-crowd. I ached for the kind of popularity that would cause boys a little older than me to shuffle shyly in my presence and girls my age to vie for my friendship. But I had crooked teeth, could not do cartwheels, and early on in my career as an Army brat I had acquired a protective *I don't need anyone* facade.

My elder sister, Gail, had graduated with fifty-four other

military brats from Narimasu High School in June. She had taken modeling lessons in Tokyo during her senior year and was booked to shoot a Japanese Cheerios ad in September. Nine-year-old Lynn exists in my memory as little more than a whiney tattletale who wore thick, blue eyeglasses, and sucked her thumb.

One afternoon at the beginning of summer, my father arrived home early from work and asked my mother to join him in the backyard. As the commander of the Army Security Agency/Communications Unit Japan, he rarely came home before dusk. My father was a man of average height, with a tendency to carry ten or fifteen extra pounds. He had stubby, workingman's fingers, thin lips, and rich brown eyes that rarely displayed emotion. He was averse to relying on small talk to break the ice among strangers or to soften the effects of bad news. He would stay silent until he had chosen the appropriate words to explain a situation.

My mother went on alert as she followed him to the garden behind our house. She had a sixth sense about things and clearly remembers her anxiety as my father quietly surveyed his maturing vegetables. While she waited for him to speak, she wondered if something had happened to one of our family members in the States, or if one of us were in trouble. She could not imagine what he had to tell her. We still had another year to go before reassignment to the Army War College at Carlisle Barracks, Pennsylvania, yet she sensed something profound was about to take place. My father had looked uncomfortable, and she knew that she was not going to like whatever it was he had to tell her. When she couldn't stand the silence another moment, she asked, "What is it?"

My father told her that we had to leave Japan earlier than anticipated. Orders had come down from headquarters: By the end of December he was to report to his next permanent duty station, Military Assistance Command, Vietnam. My father was not going to the war college. He was going to war.

My mother asked if he had volunteered.

He said, "No."

She did not believe him.

Before they left the garden my father told my mother he had to attend a three-month course in Vietnamese at the language school out of Fort Bliss, Texas. The course started in September. We had only a few weeks to prepare for the move. My mother voiced her concern as they walked into the kitchen, "Well, this is great. Where in the hell are me and the girls going to live while you're in Vietnam?"

My family's move began with the first ritual of departure— sorting through our stuff, saving treasures to help us remember our time in Japan, and throwing out mementos of people and places once important but now long forgotten.

I spent hours in my room digging through my drawers and closet, studying everything I owned, sometimes trying to remember why something had once meant so much to me. Choosing what stayed and what went began with questions and answers. Is that poster of The Monkees too worn out to make another move? *I don't even like them anymore. Toss.* Should I pack my Archie comics? *No, but I think I'll take the last few issues of my* 16 *magazines.* Do I need all of these stuffed animals? *Yes, save.* I hate that blouse my mother bought me. Will she notice if I throw it away? *Take the chance—toss it and everything else that makes me look fat.* What about the stack of letters written years before by old friends? *We don't stay in touch anymore. Toss.* White go-go boots? *Yes, save, no matter what Gail says.* What about that ugly charm bracelet? *Toss—no, give it to Lynn.* Peacenik collection? *Save.*

It took days to go through everything.

My mother spent most of her time in the dining room and kitchen. Lynn wanted to pack everything until my mother insisted that she did not need a doll without arms or a game without all its pieces.

Gail was miserable. Every box she sealed represented the end of her future as a glamour girl. The new assignment meant missing the modeling opportunity of a lifetime. In a way, I sympathized with her. The military brat formula of popularity-by-attrition never failed as long as you stayed somewhere long enough. By the ninth grade I had already attended thirteen different schools. We had finally lived somewhere long enough for me to acquire the social positioning I only dreamed about during the hundreds of meals I ate alone in lunchrooms around the world. But, we had to leave.

While my mother, sisters, and I were categorizing our belongings—save and pack or toss out—my father was sorting through piles of papers at work. Beneath a stack of government forms he noticed a flyer circulated by the Department of the Army announcing the existence of a military post in Kansas set aside for the wives and children of soldiers on hardship tours. My father decided to find out more information after a friend told him his family had lived there and had liked it. The base had everything a regular base had, including activities available to anyone who wanted to participate. He discussed it with my mother. It sounded like a great place to her. She did not want to go back home to Lynn, Massachusetts. They decided Schilling Manor would be our home while my dad was in Vietnam.

That was that.

Gail and I gagged at the supper table when our parents told us that we were moving to what they described as a home for waiting wives somewhere in the middle of Kansas. A military base with only women and children? We could not imagine a base without soldiers marching in formation down the streets. We did not believe an Army post existed where no one wore a uniform. Would the theater play "The Star-Spangled Banner" before the movie? No military police? No jeeps, no deuce and a halves, and no men driving them around the neighborhood? Is a military base without men still a military base?

Schilling Manor occupied our entire dinner conversation until my younger sister asked if we could buy a little dog and call it Toto. Gail and I laughed at her uncharacteristic display of humor until Lynn, irate to the point of tears, informed us that she was not joking. My mother glared at us and commanded Lynn to eat her peas.

In the long run, my sisters and I really didn't care where we moved. Kansas. Timbuktu. The moon. Moving was an inevitable part of our lives. We never had a choice of where we were going, when we were going, or how long we were going to stay. Schilling Manor was as foreign to us as Siberia, but we would live there if that's what we had to do.

The movers came at the beginning of September. My mother is at her best when there is a lot of action around the house. She gave orders, directed the room-by-room traffic, pointed out delicate objects that needed special attention, made everyone lunch, yelled at us to get a move on with our own packing, and worried if everything would arrive in the States in one piece.

For days our quarters buzzed with activity from early morning until the early evening when my parents were required to drop what they were doing to attend farewell parties given on their behalf. Except for the parties her close friends threw, my mother always resented going to mandatory military social events. She despised what she sensed were phony smiles and was disgusted by the endless displays of ass-kissing by some lower-ranked men and their wives toward the higher-ranked couples. She rarely attended parties when my father was a junior officer because she never wanted to leave my sisters and me with babysitters. As my father achieved rank and acquired commands that demanded her presence at social functions, her ability to stay home became less of an option. So, despite the fatigue that accompanied a major move, on her last two evenings in Japan, my mother cleaned up, put on a dress, applied her brightest red lipstick and a dab of perfume, and, with my father, left us girls within the echo of our nearly empty house to perform her duty as an Army wife. While they were gone, Gail and I fought over the phone so that we could call our friends to say good-bye.

On the day we left Japan, papa-sans lugged our material lives onto a steel moving van and hauled it to the Yokohama shipyards. A middle-aged Japanese driver, smoking a chain of nonfiltered cigarettes that he never touched with his fingers, grabbed my father's extra set of car keys, hopped into the driver's seat of our gold, 1967 Chrysler Newport, told my dad in broken English not to worry, and trailed the van to the docks.

Immediately after our household goods and car left, a government sedan moved in to pick us up. Fifteen minutes later we drove through the front gate of Momote Village, leaving the ripening vegetables in our backyard for the next family to feast upon.

Two hours remained for us to experience things unique to Japan. The pungent smell of diesel fuel and fish oil wafted into the car. Final images of the country that had been our home for two years sped by: iridescent green rice paddies; crowded, narrow streets bordered by *benjo* ditches; ancient men and women wearing silk kimonos and wooden gaiters; pagodas and toriis; noisy Pachinko parlors; plastic sushi displays in restaurant windows; YANKEE GO HOME signs; the front gate of Yokuska Air Force Base; then the island below, shrinking from view as we flew northeast toward America.

We left Japan on September 3, 1970, the morning of my fifteenth birthday. Twenty-four hours later we arrived in California on the same date, hours after our neon green Braniff International jet made an emergency landing in Washington State. An engine had blown out at the point of no return over the Pacific, at the place where we could not turn back, only forward into another unknown.

Lorrayne

THE THIRTEENTH MOVE
(1965)

Long before my father got orders for Vietnam, when he was a major teaching courses in cryptology at the Army Security Agency School at Fort Devens, Massachusetts, and I was ten and singing verses to "The Ballad of the Green Berets" at the breakfast table, Lorrayne, the wife of a soldier assigned to the Post Exchange system out of Fort Riley was about to receive news, setting her on an urgent mission to find a place for her and her two children to live.

Early in the year President Johnson had declared in his Inaugural Address that

> *The American covenant called on us to help show the way for the liberation of man. And that is today our goal. Thus, if as a nation there is much outside our control, as a people no stranger is outside our hope.*
>
> *Change has brought new meaning to that old mission.*

We can never again stand aside, prideful in isolation. Terrific dangers and troubles that we once called "foreign" now constantly live among us. If American lives must end, and American treasure be spilled, in countries we barely know, that is the price that change has demanded of conviction and of our enduring covenant.

* * *

America was at the ebb of innocence. It was a time when most Americans were unaware that our government was about to make a giant leap from several thousands of advisers to hundreds of thousands of fighting men in Vietnam; a time when over one thousand U.S. troops had died and over five thousand were wounded; a time when one hundred and fifty were already missing or captured in a remote country that most U.S. citizens had never heard of. A time when the unquestioning, blind faith in our leaders began to unravel.

In late summer, Lorrayne's husband, Bob, asked her to join him at the kitchen table. Although skirts were quickly rising and bright flowers were beginning to pop up on all sorts of clothing and accessories, Lorrayne looked as she had nearly every day since they were married in 1952. She wore a classic, sensibly patterned dress, girded at the waist and hemmed slightly below the knee. A double strand of pearls decorated her neckline, and a local beautician maintained her short hairstyle on a weekly basis. Lorrayne had amassed a fine collection of hats and gloves during her years as a military wife. She never left her house without something on her head or encasing her hands. It was a hard habit to break, even after the glossy pages of women's fashion magazines showed women with bare heads and naked hands.

The dinner dishes were washed and dried, bedtime prayers

were recited, and her children, Terry and Robbie, were in bed. Lorrayne removed her apron. The moon slid above the horizon and a whisper of hot Kansas wind slipped through the open windows of their quarters. The homes on Fort Riley had been around since the time of Geronimo, tack room and all. They were notorious for holding the heat. Lorrayne may not have been grateful for the sticky August heat, but she had promised God she would never complain about the weather if He got her out of their last assignment in Fairbanks, Alaska, alive.

Lorrayne had already moved twelve times in her thirteen years as a military wife. She knew what her husband wanted to tell her. They had lived at Fort Riley seventeen months; rarely had their assignments lasted more than a year and a half.

It was time for another move.

His next assignment. Vietnam. A hardship tour.

He would go alone.

Fort Riley was the home of the Army's First Division, the Big Red One. Many of her friends were the wives of soldiers who had shipped out earlier that summer. The men were to lay the groundwork for the Division's arrival. Lorrayne had heard rumblings. Fort Riley would be a ghost town by the end of September. She had known America was involved in some sort of police action in Southeast Asia, but when she thought about it, where was Vietnam, anyway?

Lorrayne took in the news. She calculated its effects on her family. "How much time do we have?"

"I have to leave before the bulk of the First Division arrives in Vietnam."

Less than two weeks to move.

The former Lorrayne Tollefson, farm-raised on the North Dakota frontier, close to the Canadian border, was thirty-eight years old and utterly fearless when faced with change. When Bob told her the news she took off her cat's-eye glasses and fiddled with the pearls he had brought her from Korea. Her mind sorted through challenges with the logic of a mathematician, leaving very little room for intemperate emotion. Lorrayne's compassion and generosity were manifest in her ability to solve problems. If a neighbor had a crisis, she left the hand-holding to others. She resolved the situation.

Lorrayne had to figure out where she and the boys would live for the next year. "I'll call the airlines in the morning and make a reservation to Fargo." She hoped to buy a house in her husband's hometown. There, her family would wait for Bob to come home.

Before bed she looked in on her children. Terry, a stocky preteen with a comfortable smile, was not as tough as he looked. Her eldest son was logical and even-tempered. Once she had to intervene when she found the neighborhood kids, some of them smaller and younger than he was, pounding the daylights out of him. When she would ask him if he was going to do something about it, he replied, "It takes a better man not to fight than it does to fight." She hung up his camouflage shirt knowing that the year without his dad would be hard, but that he was old enough to understand that his father had a duty to perform, and that he would not be gone forever. Terry would be fine.

Lorrayne worried about her youngest child, Robbie. He was quiet. Sensitive. It did not take much to bring the little boy to tears. Her nine-year-old had recently suffered through a series of surgeries to correct the near total deafness caused by a bout with the measles when he was younger. Robbie was at the age where he needed his dad and she told her husband so that night. The statement was a fact, not a challenge. No argument followed. Bob was a captain in the U.S. Army. Duty called. Her family had to live with it and she would do what she had to do until her husband returned home. It was not so much a resignation as it was a call to arms. Lorrayne steeled herself to the inevitable and began mental preparations for her family's thirteenth move in as many years.

Bonnie

AIR KISSES GOOD-BYE
(1964–1967)

Since 1964, before the U.S. military death toll in Vietnam had reached three hundred, Bonnie had lived near her family in Harbor Beach, Michigan. It was familiar and she felt safe living by herself while her husband, Bruce, was in Vietnam. Harbor Beach was on the tip of the thumb that reached into Lake Huron. Fishing was popular in the summer; ice fishing in the winter. It was the kind of town where grannies whispered beauty tips in granddaughters' ears, gave them advice on how to behave like young ladies, and warned them never to tell their age or friends would never trust them with their private thoughts.

Like many small towns in America, Harbor Beach was a place teenagers hoped to escape from when they got old enough to decide where and how to live their lives. The same teens would often return as adults after starting their own families. It was a fine place to live, a peaceful town where everyone knew everyone else and their business, sometimes before they knew it themselves.

Bonnie, born Kathleen Bonelle Weiss, and Bruce Johnson had been born a few months apart in the same hospital. They were sweethearts throughout high school. With her homespun beauty and his tall, muscular, good looks, they made a striking couple walking hand in hand through the school's halls. Bruce loved sports. He played basketball in the winter, baseball in the spring, and football in the fall. Bonnie was always there, on the sidelines, cheering. Bruce would ask her to the sock hops and she would go, dressed in her flared poodle-skirt and saddle shoes. Bonnie would ask him to the Sadie Hawkins dance, and he would go, willingly costumed as L'il Abner to her Daisy Mae. Bonnie was Bruce's girl and when they got married in 1958, during his final year at Billy Graham's alma mater, Wheaton College, and after her graduation from nursing school, they planned to have a long life together.

While at Wheaton, Bruce enlisted in the ROTC program. After graduating with a teaching degree in physical education, the young husband, now with a new baby, joined the army to fulfill his ROTC obligation. Bonnie and Bruce, Jr., followed the new recruit to Fort Benning, Georgia, and to Fort Knox, Kentucky, during his months of training. Thirteen months after their first child was born, their second child, Bryan, joined the growing family and in 1962, during the Cuban Missile Crisis, Colleen Joy came into the world. Bruce and Bonnie had remained close to their families and had taken every opportunity to visit home in between assignments to show off their growing little ones. When Bruce received orders in October 1963, just weeks before President John F. Kennedy's assassination, for an unaccompanied tour of duty in Vietnam, Bonnie and Bruce decided that she and the children would return to Harbor Beach to wait for him.

He would only be gone for a year.

Bruce left one morning in July 1964. It was the kind of sticky summer day that families spend at the lake to keep the kids cool and out of trouble. Even the breeze off Lake Huron did not relieve the thick, dense heat that sometimes bodes electrical storms. The air smelled of garden flowers and the heat bugs had started early with the hypnotic swell and fade of their mating calls. Outside of their home the town was waking up. Bruce finished packing; Bonnie readied the children. She had decided to let them go to the airport to say good-bye. They were so young—only four, three, and not quite two. Bonnie worried that they might forget their father during the year he was away. Allowing them to watch him leave might give them a memory that would last until he came home.

At the airport Bruce hugged his two boys and then Bonnie, who held her arms tight around Colleen Joy, a sprightly, blond toddler with a contagious smile. As they said their good-byes, Bonnie was certain her husband would return home in a year. Vietnam was not at war in 1964. The U.S. military was on an advisory mission. American soldiers were there to train the army of the Republic of Vietnam how to counter the Communist influence leaking out of North Vietnam. It was not supposed to be a dangerous mission.

Bruce was well prepared for his assignment. He went east for jungle survival training—just in case he became lost or had to hide inside Vietnam's verdant terrain. He went west to study Vietnamese—to learn how to communicate with the soldiers he was sent to advise. Bonnie would miss him terribly.

A year was not too long; the little ones would keep her busy.

Bruce let go of his family. The children waved good-bye. They blew air kisses. He never turned back to glance at his high school sweetheart and their three beautiful babies. Bonnie watched her tall, athletic husband—dressed in his crispest khakis and wearing a new pair of black-framed, Army-issue glasses—and wondered why he did not turn around for a last wave good-bye. Then, he was gone.

During Bruce's tour the U.S. military death toll doubled in Vietnam. Bonnie missed her husband, but the children kept her busy.

Bruce's letters, filled with hopefulness and expressions of love, and the almost daily tapes he sent home, kept him close to Bonnie's heart and comforted her during the long, lonely nights. The months passed slowly, but the assignment was almost over. Bruce was due home in less than a month.

On the morning of June 10, 1965, fourteen helicopters from the 118th Assault Helicopter Company flew in on the second wave to rescue American and South Vietnamese soldiers ambushed and pinned down the day before by the Viet Cong at Special Forces Detachment A-342 outside of the Thanh Loi Rubber Plantation, six kilometers from the village of Dong Xoia. No sooner had their skids hit the landing zone and the troops disembarked than a tremendous explosion ignited a hailstorm of automatic-weapons fire.

From behind rubber trees the VC, concealed in foxholes and bunkers and on the roofs and in the windows of the plantation's mansion, maintained a barrage of bullets and mortar fire directed at the company. They were surrounded. Door gunners burned up the barrels of their machine guns to suppress enemy fire. Bullets ripped holes through American steel as the commander, fearing annihilation, ordered the formation's retreat to the battle's staging area at Phou Vinh.

Thirteen of the fourteen helicopters flew out of the hot zone.

Helicopter UH-1B, tail number 63-08557, four crew, two passengers—call sign Blue Thunderbird 2—crashed during liftoff after a mortar exploded outside of the cockpit. The commander of the 118th, Major Harvey Stewart—code name Thunderbird 6—had remained behind circling the crash site. He eventually established contact with the sole survivor of the downed chopper.

Grapevine 6, a Military Assistance Command, Vietnam (MACV) adviser to the South Vietnamese Army's Fifth Infantry Division reported to the pilot that "The crew and all others on board are dead. Situation hopeless. Pull up. Abort. They've got us. Abort. Pull up now. They have us." The major pulled up from the landing zone. He noticed an opening for possible evacuation and transmitted pickup coordinates to Grapevine 6. He told him to get to the site and he'd try to land his chopper and pull him out. Grapevine 6 acknowledged the coordinates. At that point the helicopter was hit. All hell broke loose while Stewart struggled to keep his vehicle airborne. Moments later he watched as a round of mortars exploded at the point he had estimated to be Grapevine 6's last location. He hoped the soldier was able to escape and was moving toward the rescue coordinates. Thunder-bird 6 lingered in the air until things settled down. He attempted radio contact but received no further transmission. Major Stewart left the combat zone believing that mortars had killed the lone survivor on the ground.

A follow-up search of the crash site was conducted when the area was secured. No American remains were found. Sometime later, a captured Vietnamese reported that the Viet Cong had carried away and buried the bodies of several of the downed servicemen. He also told his captors that a big American who spoke Vietnamese had been captured. Subsequently, the report of the big American landed in Grapevine 6's service file. Until they could prove otherwise, the Army assumed that the big American who spoke Vietnamese was Bonnie's husband. He was the fifth U.S. military soldier reported missing in Vietnam.

Bonnie was home with Bryan and Colleen, and Bruce, Jr., was in school when the telegram arrived on Friday, June 11, 1965. The people in the telegraph office, located in the back of the corner drugstore, were horrified when they saw the yellow envelope addressed to Bonnie. Everyone at the store knew Bruce and Bonnie, their parents, their brothers and sisters, aunts and uncles. Both families had lived in the area for generations. Most families had.

The office manager called Bruce's dad. *Bonnie got a telegram.*

Bruce's mom and dad went to Bonnie's home to tell her the news. It was a terrible task they had to perform that afternoon. Bonnie read the message.

Missing.

The telegram said that her husband was missing.

Not killed. Not lost. Missing.

Not even missing in action, though there had been lots of action in Dong Xoia. Bruce was a MACV adviser. If he was missing in the jungle he would eventually find his way out. As soon as he found a phone he'd call. He had less than a month to go in Vietnam; she had started preparing for their next assignment. Bonnie assured her in-laws: "Don't worry. Bruce will come home."

Bruce and Bonnie had written each other almost every day. In one of his first letters he explained that he could not look at her and the babies when he left them at the airport. He was so sad to leave that he could not bear to see them blowing him kisses. He wrote that he missed her and the children, but she was not to worry, his tour was only a year and then he'd be home. Bruce's letters were a guarantee to her and the children. Her favorite line was "there is no doubt in my military mind that I'll be back home in July." With that, Bonnie was able to think about their future.

In the days that followed the arrival of the telegram, Bonnie remained certain Bruce was alive. Her phone would ring at any minute. Sometimes, she could almost hear it ring. If his unit had told him that his family had been erroneously informed of his missing status, she knew he would get to a phone sooner or later to tell them that he was fine. He'd tell her that he'd had a little trouble up Route 13, but that he was safe.

If the phone did not ring today, it would ring tomorrow. If he did not walk through the door today, then he would next week. She was as sure of it as she was sure her eyes were brown.

Summer turned to fall—no call from Bruce. In the meantime, the Army had assigned Bonnie a casualty officer, a kind of a military godfather whose duty was to help the families whose men were lost or had died in war. Bonnie's officer worked out of Washington, D.C. He assured her that her military benefits would continue. She would receive her husband's pay. He kept Bonnie informed of any developments in Bruce's case and was available to answer all of her questions.

Bonnie eventually unpacked the things she had packed before Bruce disappeared. The boys started school in Harbor Beach. Bonnie never lost faith, maintaining her belief that Bruce would return.

Months passed.

Then years.

No call from Bruce. Yet.

After a while Bonnie wondered what lay beyond Harbor Beach. Her family was dear to her, and her hometown had wrapped its arms around her and the children, but life during the two years since Bruce went missing had become complex. She was in frequent contact with the government, making trips to Washington for updates on Bruce's status. In a way, she became more involved with and knowledgeable about the Army than when her husband was around. Bonnie's world had widened. She began to feel somewhat isolated from the normal life her old friends and classmates lived in Harbor Beach. She yearned to be with other young wives like her, military wives with husbands in Vietnam.

Bonnie read about Schilling Manor in *The Army Times*. She called her casualty officer in Washington and asked, "Are we eligible for housing at the base?" The officer called John Kindlesparger, Schilling Manor's housing officer. He explained Bonnie's situation. Mr. K., a retired Air Force colonel who believes that he was the pilot on the C-47 Sky Train that flew

Bob Dole from Naples to Algiers after the future senator was wounded, felt compassion for Bonnie. His superiors up at Fort Riley had advised against admitting MIA and POW wives on Schilling because of the emotional impact they might have on the community of wives waiting for their husbands to return home.

Mr. K. pondered the consequences. Should he allow Bonnie and her children to live at Schilling? *How in the world can I turn this woman away?* What better place is there for the wife and children of one of our missing boys than Schilling Manor? Without hesitation he told the officer, "You send her on down here. We'll take real good care of her and the children."

Millions of minutes had passed between the time the telegram from the casualty office of the Department of the Army arrived and Bonnie's subsequent journey to Schilling Manor in the summer of 1967. She was not yet thirty. The young wife thought her stay would last no longer than a year. She clung to the vague memory of hearing the Chairman of the Joint Chiefs of Staff, General Maxwell Taylor, report that American involvement in Vietnam would not last more than a few years. That was back before Bruce left for Vietnam, when she had hardly paid attention to the developments in the war.

The few years had passed. If General Taylor were right, maybe Bruce would be home by Thanksgiving. If not Thanksgiving, then Christmas. It was simply a matter of time. She was as sure of it as she was sure Bruce would call one day from out of the blue and say, "Hey, Bon, I finally got out. I can hardly wait to get back home and start living again."

Bonnie's life was no longer divided between days and nights or months and years. To her, the years following Bruce's disappearance became one long day.

Beverly

_____

133 PHOENIX STREET

(1970)

Texas for my father meant three months of intensive study. One night, after living in El Paso for several weeks, he enlisted me as a study partner. I said yes, but wondered why he hadn't asked Gail. She had a relationship with him that excluded my younger sister and me. I retreated with him to a quiet place in the apartment. Over the next few months we practiced the musical language of a people at war. *Trungh uy*—Colonel. *Ong mahn yoi khong*—Mister, how are you? *Thoi khong viet*—I do not know. *Ba moui ba*—Beer. *Camh anh ong*—Mister, thank you. I helped him prepare for future conversations with Vietnamese friendlies and Vietnamese enemies. I remember asking if he would know the difference between the two.

After some thought he said, "I'm sure it will be impossible to tell the difference."

I had no idea of the weight my father's answer carried. What mattered to me during those study sessions was that my father came out of the secret world of the Army Security Agency. The bridge that connected us was the Vietnam War. A war that would never end.

My father graduated from the language school on a warm morning in December 1970. Later that day we loaded our belongings into the car and headed north toward Kansas. We had taken dozens of road trips, traveling from one military post to another. The journeys were treated like family vacations, and in between sisterly conflicts we usually had fun. But this trip was different. My dad had to leave for Vietnam in less than two weeks. Before he left we needed to move in, unpack, organize, decorate, and celebrate Christmas. No sightseeing side trips were planned. We traveled for hours a day tied in with seat belts like prisoners. My mother sat in the front seat. Silent. Arms and legs crossed. Her shoulders so tense they almost touched her ears. She remained convinced that my dad had volunteered for Vietnam. Her anger lived between them for the duration of the trip.

My sisters and I sat in our assigned positions. Gail behind my father. Me in back of my mother. Lynn in the middle. I had no use for either of them. One was stuck-up and the other was a spoiled brat. We hated one another. We fought.

Don't touch me. Stop sucking your thumb so loud. You're such a jerk. So are you. Make her stop looking at me. You're fat. Well, you'll never be a model, Miss Cheeriohead. Mom, she's touching me again.

We antagonized one another until my father would reach his arm around and try to hit one of us—usually Lynn because she was in the middle—causing my mother to scream at him to ignore us and watch the road. We would quiet down for a little while, until one of us touched the other, then we would go at each other again. Too many years separated us, we were too big to be cramped in the backseat, and our personalities were as different as the places we were born.

The air grew colder and the sky grayer the farther north we traveled. At one point we had to stop, relinquishing short sleeves and sandals for sweaters and socks. In Wichita we turned northeast and drove the remaining ninety miles to Schilling Manor. We were less than two hours away from starting our lives over—one more time—on a new post in the middle of nowhere.

The last few miles before we arrived at Schilling Manor were like driving through quilted land, our family traveling along a seam of hibernating cornfields. Nothing but undulating fields of winter wheat and a gentle drizzle of rain landing on the closed windows interrupted the monochrome, dormant landscape. No hills or trees intruded upon the vast expanse of the prairie's horizon. Kansas's slate-gray sky enveloped our car, sealing us inside like captives with an uncertain future. In the distance thunder cracked, disrupting our solitary thoughts as we approached our exit.

A winter storm was coming—the first of the season—and despite our change of clothes, we were not ready.

From an eagle's view, Schilling Manor resembled most military fortresses. A sign stood sentinel at the entrance, warning that only authorized personnel were allowed into the community.

Nearly identical family quarters were built on either side of Schilling Road, the base's central artery. Enlisted houses were to the right, officers to the left. At least two American flags waved high on flagstaffs: one fluttered above Command Headquarters, the other received or discharged travelers at the airfield. Disarmed weapons served as lawn decorations on the ground below the flags. A decrepit cannon lazed at a split in the road and a tired

B-17 rested at the mouth of a rusting hangar. The airstrip designed to accommodate the extraordinary weight and size of the B-52 framed the western edge. Wheat and milo fields bounded the south and east side of the base. Salina stretched for about eight miles north. The base was smaller than when it once sprawled over four thousand acres. Now only empty administration buildings and deserted barracks remained as a testament to the existence of a once mighty fortress for men and their machines.

I knew from the moment we drove through the front gate that Schilling was unlike any other post. It was like Gail and I had imagined it at the dinner table in Japan four months earlier. Not one convoy of military vehicles carrying soldiers to maneuvers clogged the roads. Women drove cars with children in the front seat. Homemade signs hung on the front windows: WELCOME BACK DAD! GLAD YOU'RE HOME! THE WAIT IS OVER! A worn MIA/POW flag languished on a makeshift pole. The wind had whipped at it for so long that it looked like it had been around since WWII. GIs in starched khakis or olive-drab fatigues, marching in perfect formation, singing cadence, were nowhere to be seen. Salutes were replaced with casual waves from across the commissary parking lot. We didn't see any men until we got to the housing office to pick up the keys to our new quarters. Only then did we see a few soldiers in uniform and a couple of military sedans parked outside of the building.

My family completed the worst road trip we had ever taken. We were tired. Hungry. Anxious. What would it be like for the next year? Sleet pelted our car as we drove around the base. Schilling Manor had all the markings of a government installation; the layout was regimented, planned according to a code that disapproved of individuality. Only the starched, stand-at-attention cadre of military life was missing.

The post gave me the same weird, creepy feeling that I got

when I looked at an Edward Gorey drawing. Everything, even the sparse, stick-shaped trees, seemed a study in black and white. And a little unreal.

My dad turned down Phoenix Street. *There it is.* Number 133, a single-unit, four-bedroom ranch with a garage. We sat in the car, surveying the outside of the house. My mother worried out loud—that house better be spic-and-span if it isn't we can just turn around and return the keys I'm not living in someone else's filth.

Long rectangular windows reached from the ground to the roof in the front room. Would our curtains fit? An evergreen to the right of the door rose about four feet higher than the roof. Four little flowerless bushes looked like presents beside its trunk. It was identical to every other house on the block. After we shrugged our shoulders and noncommittally agreed that it looked okay from the outside, my father got out of the car, slipped his nameplate into the slot on the front of the house, pulled out the keys, and opened the door.

We were home.

Lorrayne

---

308 HELENA COURT
(1965)

Lorrayne's trip to Fargo proved fruitless. Not one house was available on such short notice. The evening after she returned from North Dakota, she attended a promotional party at the Officer's Club. The talk had turned to politics—how the Republicans treated the military versus how the Democrats treated the armed forces—when someone mentioned that the recent base closings appeared to fall primarily in Republican territory. The party klatch had found it hard to believe that the government would close Schilling Air Force Base, a strategic air command base filled with war-ready intercontinental ballistic missiles (ICBMs) and a runway long enough to land a B-52. It did not make sense. Besides the cold war, a build-up of American forces was taking place in Southeast Asia. The politics did not interest Lorrayne. What caught her attention was that hundreds of quarters were vacant.

She enlisted the willing support of Bob who telephoned

Colonel Scanlan the next morning, asking him for an appointment. That afternoon Lorrayne recruited her best friend, Pat, to keep an eye on the boys while she and Bob drove to Schilling. Lorrayne reviewed her argument. A house that sits empty deteriorates. Quickly. Instead of making money, it loses money. It becomes a white elephant, eventually draining the pockets of its owner. If the government did not have plans for the empty houses, she would argue, why not allow the families of men assigned to Vietnam live in them. Lorrayne added a clincher. The government would make money. Every soldier is given a housing allowance and separation pay if it is necessary for his family to live off post. If the families were allowed to live on the base, the government would keep the allocations. Keeping the Schilling Air Force Base quarters occupied would not cost the government anything; it would pay for itself.

The meeting lasted an hour. When she and Bob left his office, Scanlan told them to give him a couple of days to see what he could come up with. Two days later he called Bob and said, "I have a house for you and twelve other military families."

Not two weeks had passed since Bob had told Lorrayne that he was going to Vietnam. During that time she had traveled to and from Fargo, presented a case for opening empty homes before a colonel in the U.S. Air Force, packed up her house, arranged for movers, said good-bye to friends—a couple of them she hoped to see in a few weeks since she had clued them in on Scanlan's decision—and was on her way to her new home.

Lorrayne noticed few signs of military life when she and Bob drove down Schilling Road, she in her Chevelle convertible with the boys and their bull terrier, Tuffy, he towing a boat behind his Opel station wagon filled with suitcases and boxes. Most of the houses had been empty for some time. Only seven Air Force families, including Colonel Scanlan's and the base's doctor's, remained; all seven were awaiting departure orders.

Except for an occasional gust of wind that blew through the branches of the sparse trees, the base was as still as an oil painting. In a way, it looked like a dying town, the kind depicted in old black-and-white westerns, waiting for the last residents to move out so that the tumbleweeds could take over and the ghosts could move in.

---

138 Denver Street

(1967)

August is the hottest month of the year in Salina. Plains winds wrap the heat around Salinans like desperate suitors. Women struggle to hold down flipping skirts and perspiring men pull at their shirts. Local beauticians sometimes joked that Clairol invented hair spray for the women of Kansas. Between trickling sweat and fervent gusts, a woman's hairdo doesn't have a chance without a good blast every morning.

And every August is the same. As the community prepares for the annual Tri-Rivers Rodeo and 4-H Fair, unimpeded winds sweep over the land and a heat wave hotter than the one before takes over the town.

It was that way when Bonnie turned off the highway on her way to Schilling Manor with her three children, Bruce seven, Bryan six, and Colleen Joy almost four. She headed south through north Salina. Ancient pickups, faded and pockmarked from years of exposure to the sun and the wind, were parked beside ramshackle homes with rusted bicycles tumbled over on dirt lawns. The townies stopped short of calling the north side of the tracks the ghetto part of town. There might have been a little prostitution going on in earlier years when the air base was in full swing. Soldiers liked to raise a little prairie dust every now and again.

The north side wasn't dangerous. Just forgotten. The two-mile stretch of land between the highway and the railroad tracks had been left behind when the city's neighborhoods and businesses moved south. A few months before Bonnie moved to Kansas, radio commentator Paul Harvey had stopped by Salina for a visit. Harvey was so impressed, in spite of its shadier north side, that he proclaimed to all Americans listening to his broadcast that Salina was a "first-class town."

Bonnie gently navigated her station wagon over the bumpy double set of railroad tracks set into the landscape sometime in the late 1800s. The tracks were the city's rugged terrain. Salina's share of the thousands of miles of rails that ran east to west across America was laid beside six elevators owned by the Gooch Grain Company. The one hundred foot-tall landmark jutted up against the horizon for a hundred miles. At least on a clear day. Three generations of locally grown grain was hauled here, there, and everywhere by the Union Pacific Railroad Company. The great white silos towered over the city. As Salina developed during the thirties and forties they became the official boundary separating the north side of town from the south.

Bonnie and Bruce had been stationed at Fort Riley before receiving orders for Vietnam. There, someone had told them that Salina was a quiet little town. Bonnie had never thought anything about it. Funny how life works. Four years later her husband was missing in Vietnam and there she was, on her way to live in one of Schilling's quarters. The death toll had risen to an astonishing fifteen thousand. Public opinion about the war had changed. Americans disapproved of President Johnson's handling of it. Many thought the United States had made a mistake sending troops. Over half thought the United States was losing.

Did the criticism about the war bother Bonnie? Yes, very much so. Vietnam was as real to her as it was to Bruce. She had walked down Route 13 a hundred times with her husband in his letters and tapes. When she closed her eyes she could visualize the villages located along the road with all the little children running this way and that way, looking for attention from Bruce when he passed. How could helping people fight for freedom against communism be wrong? How could America lose? It was not possible.

But Bonnie was neither hawk nor dove, just a mother who desperately wanted her children's father to come home.

Bonnie continued her journey southward on Ninth. Homes lovelier than the ones north of the tracks stood behind a sidewalk bordered by sturdy ash trees. She veered right onto Broadway. She passed a couple of car dealerships. A plumber offered twenty-four-hour emergency service. Bonnie checked the gas gauge when she spotted the Skaggs 66 Service Station at the corner of Crawford and Ninth. The Skaggs family had pumped thousands of gallons of gas into Salina's cars every year for as long as anyone could remember. About halfway between the highway and Schilling Road were a couple of dozen family-owned shops that satisfied the needs of the town's residents. A pharmacy filled hundreds of prescriptions every week and a furniture store professed to have sold thousands of dinettes and couches since it opened its doors in 1946.

Farther south all signs of life grew scarce. The Kansas landscape turned to flat, endless acres of maturing crops. On the left, a little beyond Magnolia Road, the Starlight Roller Rink resembled a man vs. nature diorama set against a backdrop of endless wheat fields. Neon-colored bulbs had lured generations of the county's youth to roll around in circles on steel skates nearly every Friday and Saturday night. It was a place where many Salina and Schilling preteens stumbled into their first kiss, often cloaked in a subtle brush against the cheek after an upending turn in the rink.

Mr. K. at the housing office had told Bonnie the rink was the final landmark before she was to look for Schilling Road. *Ahead, on the right. Look for the sign.*

SCHILLING MANOR:
THE HOME OF THE WAITING WIVES
OF THE U.S. ARMED FORCES

Bonnie followed the directions to the housing office. Mr. K. gave her the key to 138 Denver.

It's a real nice house. Has a big yard for the children. Lots of women in the same boat.

Unlike her friends in Harbor Beach, they, at the very least, would understand what it's like to raise three children with a husband thousands of miles away from home.

The Committee

SOMETIMES

Their children were finally off to school, the babies down for morning naps. The five women had volunteered to plan Schilling Manor's first fashion show. The post nursery desperately needed cots and blankets and the membership had voted unanimously to organize the show to raise money at the last Waiting Wives Club meeting. The women arrived at the warrant officer's wife's house, greeting and chatting in pairs as they poured and dressed their coffee and nibbled on homemade cinnamon twists provided by their hostess.

The warrant officer's wife was from the Deep South; she was in her early thirties, had four children, and had been a military wife for ten years. She had been her high school's head cheerleader. A princess in the homecoming queen's court. The likable, well-manicured wife had won the Miss Sparkle beauty pageant in her hometown. She had hoped for a modeling career, but then came an unplanned pregnancy. Marriage. Hope had turned to a lost dream.

The warrant officer's wife had jumped at the chance to work

on the show. She subscribed to all of the fashion magazines, wore all the latest styles—multicolored A-line dresses that freed her from the confines of waist-cutting girdles, mid-thigh miniskirts for fun, and plenty of panty hose, the new rage for legs. She had five differently styled wigs to match her mood and her outfit. The warrant officer's wife loved fashion. And keeping up with the latest gossip.

Before the women settled down to business, the lieutenant's wife addressed her hostess, "I don't know. I'm about ready to yank that boob tube right out of the living room."

At twenty-three, the lieutenant's wife was the least experienced of the group. After she graduated from twelfth grade, her high school sweetheart, who was a year ahead of her, returned to their hometown in the Midwest from Officer's Candidate School. *Marry me.* She did.

Nine months, nearly to the day of her wedding, she gave birth to her first daughter. Eleven months later she delivered her second daughter. She was alone, fifteen hundred miles away from friends or relatives. Her pilot husband was out on a helicopter-training mission, preparing for his next assignment.

She tried to keep up her figure, her looks, but found it increasingly difficult to maintain her *That Girl* hairstyle. Too much work. Wedding-day size-four hips had expanded to a size eight. She liked Mars Bars. They were cheap and easy to unwrap while running after toddlers. The lieutenant's wife did not care about the war or politics. She wanted Vietnam to go away so that her husband could come home and take care of her and the girls.

The warrant officer's wife asked her why she wanted to get rid of her TV.

"Because the news is always so scary."

"I know what you mean," agreed the warrant officer's wife. "You know what my six-year-old said to me the other day after watching Huntley and Brinkley?"

By now all the women were seated around the dining room table.

"He came over and crawled right up on my lap like he did when he was two or three," she continued. "At first I thought he was sick. But then he looked up at me with a big old worried look on his face and said, 'Mommy! Is Daddy going to die in the war?' and I thought, my goodness, what am I going to say to this child?"

The lieutenant's wife was curious. "What did you tell him?"

"I said the first thing that came into my mind. I told him no, only bad people die in war and that he shouldn't worry about his daddy coming home because his daddy was a good person and would be home to tuck him into bed in no time."

"What he say then?" asked the captain's wife, who was Japanese and still learning the English language.

"He asked me to make him a fluffer-nutter and that was the end of that."

The captain's wife was from Narimasu, Japan. She had met and married her husband while working as a civilian in the PX at Grant Heights, the army base next to her town. English had been an easy subject in school. Still, she had a tendency to drop key words in sentences and to replace the letter *l* with the letter *r*. Her little boy was in elementary school and her young daughter liked to stay at a friend's house when she had military duties to attend to.

The captain's wife was approaching thirty, had a petite frame, happy eyes, and a round face surrounded by jet-black hair that she often coiled up with a single chopstick—a Japanese version of a French twist that many of the other wives on her block had taken to wearing.

Another wife offered an opinion. "I think, out of everything, this war is hardest on the children." She was a sergeant major's wife. Her five children ranged in age from four to fifteen. At nearly forty, distinct lines radiated from compassionate eyes and offset her graying hair. Her sweet disposition and forgiving nature were the earnest result of her belief that good could be found in every situation. The sergeant major's wife never wore makeup, but she set her hair in pin curls every night and styled it each morning. She had met her husband after he had been wounded in Korea. The government sent him to Virginia to recover in the hospital where she volunteered after school.

They were married in the hospital chapel the day after she graduated from high school. Since then, the family had moved fourteen times. Three of the moves were from one continent to another. One happened when she was eight months pregnant, by herself, with her four eldest children in tow. The sergeant major's wife was a great committee member. *No* was not in her vocabulary. She continued, "The things these kids say are so unsettling. The other day my teenage son Bobby came into the kitchen when I was having coffee with a neighbor. He blurted out, right there in front of my friend, 'How can you sit around and drink coffee when Dad is killing babies?'"

The women gasped as the sergeant major's wife finished.

"Then he stormed out of the room."

The colonel's wife spoke up. "Did you do anything to him?"

"What could I do? Or say? I was stunned. I made excuses about how all the antiwar protests he sees on TV, and his father being in Vietnam, and how much he hates living here has had a terrible impact on him."

The colonel's wife had six children, was the oldest member of the committee, and a seasoned veteran of everything having to do with being a military wife. She was New England bred, born into a family with a history of military service dating back to the Revolutionary War. She unabashedly assumed the rank of her husband, a graduate of West Point, no matter what the assignment, and particularly enjoyed her role as her husband's career advanced to full-bird colonel. The colonel's wife had the look of a well-dressed, perfectly coiffed, thick-ankled woman from peasant stock. She was her husband's biggest asset, her children's primary disciplinarian, and her church's most enthusiastic catechism teacher. She told the sergeant major's wife, "I wouldn't put up with that. Take his allowance away for being so disrespectful. If that doesn't work, tell him to pack his bags and look for a better place to live."

"He hatesu riving here?" asked the captain's wife.

"Hates it. All he wants to do is go back to Germany to be with his friends. You're probably right," the sergeant major's wife directed her comment to the colonel's wife. "Sometimes I think I should buy him a ticket and send him overseas until his father comes home."

The women debated what effect the news was having on their children before getting down to the business of the fashion show.

The warrant officer's wife volunteered to do makeup and to ask local stores to donate stylish ensembles. The lieutenant's wife would help the warrant officer's wife with matching shoes and accessories. The captain's wife chose decorations and refreshments. Invitations and announcements became the responsibility of the sergeant major's wife. The colonel's wife thought she could be most useful finding volunteers to model the new styles, write the script, and secure the master of ceremonies.

Before adjourning, the ladies finished another pot of coffee as they discussed the theme of the show. They decided on "The Mix-and-Match Wardrobe: Adaptable Styles for Today's Busy Women" because it gave them plenty of material to put on a great show.

A cry from one of the babies signaled the end of the meeting. Before leaving they agreed to meet at the colonel's wife's house in a week to report on their progress.

Beverly

CHRISTMAS

(1970)

Our evergreen was burdened with color. Its limbs sagged, wearied by the role it played in our Christmas celebration. The golden star placed on the top weighed down the single fragile branch, bending it in resignation. Dagger-sharp needles shed at the slightest whisper. Colored lights twinkled throughout the day, an effort at cheer. During the gift-giving and the dinner and the naps when no one really slept, holiday music played on the reel-to-reel: Burl Ives enlivened us with "Rudolph the Red-Nosed Reindeer," Jim Nabors, sounding astonishingly different from Gomer Pyle, crooned "White Christmas," and Nat King Cole soothed us with "Oh Holy Night."

My mother never took off her apron, the one she had decorated with felt poinsettias and silver sequins. She fussed with her teased and lacquered hair. Although only forty-one, the gentle displays of middle age had deepened on her face. Hundreds of thousands of cigarettes—first butt at thirteen—and years of baking in the sun with baby oil had aged her.

For as long as I can remember my mother was the general of the family, the order-giver, and the schedule-keeper. No matter how many times my father was promoted, he never outranked her. But on Christmas day at Schilling Manor things were different. My mother relinquished command of our household, allowing the holiday to evolve slowly, without the pressure of time. The turkey roasted in the oven, taking forever to cook. Gail and my mother posed in front of the wilting tree. I took their snapshot with my new Polatoid. The pair wore Thai silk maxiskirts made the year before by our Japanese dressmaker. Gail—in green, arms poised prettily at her side, breasts out, long brown hair parted in the middle, and blessed with perfect teeth— flashed her model's smile. She was eighteen and bitter. She had so wanted to be Japan's Cheerios Girl. My elder sister was born domesticated. Sewing, cooking, and dating popular boys came naturally. Gail kept her room clean, saved her babysitting money, subscribed to the Book of the Month Club, said the right things, and never brought anybody home our parents didn't like.

Behind her my mother stood erect in pink silk, hands behind her back correcting her slouched posture. She lifted her chin unnaturally to avoid being captured for eternity with a double chin. A sticky Aqua Net mist had set every one of her carefully teased and frosted hairs in place. My mother was several inches taller than Gail and zipper thin from a diet of instant coffee, cereal, and cigarettes.

It was likely that we went to Mass in the morning because we always went to church on Sundays and holidays.

Lynn played with her new Liddle Kiddle dolls throughout the day. She dressed and undressed her tiny playmates, got bored, then abandoned them half-naked on the living-room floor. Exhausted from rising at dawn, she sought the comfort of her thumb. Cuddling her Mrs. Beasley doll, she lay on a *zabuton* pillow in front of a muted TV. My younger sister was born with severe vision problems. Her lenses were thicker than the frames. Bony knees knocked when she walked—a result of polio. In her first ten years she was in and out of hospitals for the treatment of one infection after another. My mother doted on Lynn, worried about her, and did everything for her. Any gentleness she had was reserved for her youngest daughter.

I waited for Lynn to doze, then, for no particular reason, yanked her thumb out of her mouth. She wailed as if I were killing her. Everyone ran to her rescue, yelling at me to leave her alone. I flopped in the chair by the front window and began pulling tinsel off the tree. I experimented with the thin silver strands, stretching them until they ripped in half, then threw the damaged threads on the floor.

Gail announced that dinner was ready.

If an attempt at cheer was made during dinner, I don't remember. Perhaps my parents asked Lynn and me about our new schools. Or asked if we had made any friends yet. Lynn might have gone on about something; I probably told them everything was fine.

Salina High South was no different from the thirteen other schools I had attended since first grade. I saw no point in telling them that the first couple of weeks in a new place meant being alone, friendless. My mother would have felt sorry for me if she knew that I ate lunch at an empty table, staring purposefully at my food, too shy to ask anyone if I could sit with them. Besides, I was an officer's daughter. Who needed friends?

My parents could not have done anything to help ease the transition from one school to another. Had I told them about the trials of a new school during dinner they would have offered some useless advice that I would not have heeded. The best thing to do was to respond to their questions with one word. Fine. Okay.

Yes. No. Besides, even though they did not talk about it, they had bigger things to worry about, like my father going to war and maybe never coming home.

No one in my family can really say for sure what we talked about that day. We can only be certain, because it's what we had every Christmas, that we ate turkey with stuffing and gravy, canned yams with marshmallows, potatoes mashed with generous amounts of butter and whole milk, rutabaga, green bean casserole, jellied cranberry sauce, biscuits, and canned peas, whatever kind were on sale at the commissary because my dad was the only one who ate them and he didn't care what brand they were. Lynn would have grossed us out by putting mayonnaise on everything, including the cranberry sauce. Other than indulging in the luxury of swabbing their rolls in warm gravy, my mother and Gail would have picked at their plates, moving the white meat and dollops of potatoes around, afraid to eat too much because they could never be too thin. My dad and I were the hearty eaters. We always went back for seconds.

Maybe my family forgot that it was Christmas, because despite the holiday music and the turkey and the new toys and clothes, the mood was as somber as a requiem mass. Even though we had lived with Vietnam, it had never come so close to home.

After I finished my part of the kitchen cleanup I was on my way to my room when I noticed my father sitting alone in the living room on the hassock. I stood at the edge of the hall watching him stare at the carpet. He did not look like an important officer in charge of U.S. Army Security. He wore civilian clothes—no silver leaf clusters rested on his shoulders to define him as anyone other than my father. His body was unbalanced, one arm rested awkwardly across his thighs, the heel of his other hand held up his chin. His face resembled mine—a square frame with a small chin, a high forehead, serious eyes, thin lips, and dark, nearly black hair. Sideburns conformed to military regulation, ending at the middle of his ear.

Silently, I watched my father. I thought about asking him if he wanted to practice some Vietnamese phrases, but I never did. I wanted to ask him how he liked the Joan Baez tape I got him for Christmas, but I never did. I wanted to ask him if he was afraid to go to war, but I never did. I wanted to hug him but Gail came in from the kitchen and announced that the dishes were done and everything finally put away. He smiled and they talked about her future.

I fell back to my room and closed the door. Lynn went to bed, no doubt carrying Mrs. Beasley. Soon after, Gail went to her room, probably to read. I lay on my bed, not sure what I was feeling, if I was feeling anything at all. I heard my mother and father walk past my door on the way to their bedroom. Only a few hours remained for him to pack his duffel bag before he had to leave the next morning. Their door closed. The quiet day turned into a still night.

In Vietnam, a twenty-four-hour Christmas truce had ended. The U.S. military death toll had risen to more than fifty thousand. In Paris, the peace talks were once again at a stalemate.

Lorrayne

MOTHER AND SONS ALONE

(1965)

The sky was blue, billowed with clouds. The wind was warm and, at least for a little while, tame. The airfield was not more than a five-minute drive from the family's new house. Bob pulled the Opel into a parking spot. This routine was not unlike the one they followed when they went to church or to a restaurant. The only difference was that one of the family would not be returning home.

Lorrayne had dressed in one of her two-piece suits, probably the one with the oversized buttons and three-quarter-length sleeves that she wore for special occasions. She had on her hat and gloves and matching high heels and purse and she had paid special attention to the application of her lipstick. The boys wore their Sunday suits, had fresh haircuts, and polished shoes. Lorrayne had not allowed them to go out and play in the morning, lest they get dirty and spoil the last image their father would have of them for the next year. Bob wore his khaki-colored summer uniform, starched and pressed the evening before. He carried his bag in one hand. The other held on to his wife. The boys led the way into the terminal.

Inside, the building looked more like the waiting room of a small-town bus depot than a passenger-holding terminal where, not long before, Air Force pilots had taken off in and landed American bombers. A couple of people were walking around the grounds. Lorrayne and the boys were the only ones saying good-bye to a loved one.

September 8, 1965: time for Bob to leave for Vietnam.

Little did he know that two U.S. soldiers, held captive since 1963 as war criminals, had been executed in the days leading up to his departure. The North Vietnamese claimed, as they did for many years after, that the 1949 Geneva agreements on war prisoners did not apply to what was happening in their country. The two soldiers brought the death toll to nearly twelve hundred. It was better that he not know.

Lorrayne had no time to sit in the waiting area making small talk with her husband. The plane was on the tarmac when they arrived. Uncomfortable minutes when everyone waits around, not knowing what to say next, were avoided. The terminal was so quiet their footsteps echoed in the hollow of the building as they walked toward the door that led outside to the airstrip. Silence was broken when the pilot fired up the twin engines and engaged the propellers. Then the hatch opened and their final moments as a family were over. At least for the next year.

Lorrayne and the boys walked Bob to the chain-link fence that divided those leaving from those staying. Farewells were brief. Lorrayne had said good-bye to her husband five or six times during their marriage. Still, tears welled, spilling down her cheeks. She kissed her husband one last time before he went through the gate, alone. Terry and Robbie noticed their mother's tears. They had never seen her cry.

Bob climbed the portable stairway, turned to his family, and waved good-bye. He entered the aircraft.

Gone.

Lorrayne and her sons watched through the links. Terry wondered if it was the last time he would see his father. Robbie, his hands stuffed inside his pants pockets, scuffled his feet back and forth. What was racing through his mind? If everything was going to be okay like his parents said, then why was his mother crying? Why did his dad have to leave? Was he ever coming home?

In the midst of all the internal confusion and fear, Robbie watched his mother wipe her cheeks with the handkerchief she kept stuffed up her sleeve. He obeyed when she told him it was time to go home.

When they got home Terry tacked up a map of Vietnam, which his dad had left behind, inside the pantry door. He explained to his mother and brother that they could put pins on the map whenever their dad wrote and told them where he had traveled in the country. They all thought it was a good idea, then the boys changed their clothes and went outside to play while Lorrayne fixed dinner. She looked at the map inside the cupboard, wondering how many pins would be on it before Bob returned home.

Bonnie

RITUAL

(1967)

Leaving Harbor Beach had been difficult for the children, but by the time Thanksgiving arrived they had made many new friends. Bonnie missed the family but her neighbors were welcoming. A pot of coffee was always percolating on someone's stove. Thanksgiving would be celebrated without their husbands, but the wives knew that the situation would eventually change. No one's husband or father would be gone forever. Besides, Bonnie's neighbors told her, Schilling was known as the lucky place. One day, though not all on the same day, every husband and father would return to his family. The men would again sit at the head of the table, say grace, and carve the turkey into perfect slices.

The women believed it. The children believed it.

Bonnie had held out hope that Bruce would be home by Thanksgiving. The holiday arrived with no word. Not yet. Earlier in the month the North Vietnamese had released three U.S.

Army prisoners to Tom Hayden, an antiwar protestor who had entered Vietnam with the goal of bringing men home. In a way he succeeded—three families would celebrate Thanksgiving with their freed loved ones. Bruce was not among them. Neither were the hundreds of other men still missing or captured. No one knew for sure how many. The North Vietnamese Army (NVA) refused to provide a list of imprisoned men so it was hard to determine who was captured, missing, or dead. Some hoped that freeing the prisoners at Thanksgiving time signaled the beginning of a greater plan by the enemy to release American soldiers. Christmas was coming; more soldiers might come home. One of them might be Bruce. Bonnie could not help but look forward to the coming year. In the meantime she and the children marked their first holiday at Schilling with their new friends.

Bonnie called everyone to the table. After giving thanks for the wonderful meal and all of the good things in their lives, dishes were passed around the table, gravy was poured, forks were raised, and everyone talked of pleasant things. Bonnie sat down to dinner, joined the conversation, and began a holiday ritual she had started the first year Bruce had gone missing. If her husband could not be with his family during the celebration then she would share the day with him by fasting. She would do it alone. No one would ever know. It was an intimate expression reserved only for Bonnie and the man she loved who was so far away.

With no one the wiser, Bonnie nudged her mashed potatoes under a slice of turkey. She made sure that everyone had plenty to eat and drink. During the discussion, she scooped the potatoes out again, repositioning the small, gravy-slathered mound closer to the cranberry sauce. After a little laughter and a few more shifts and swirls with her fork, she finally lifted a film of the starchy vegetable, now slightly tinged with small streams of pink from the cranberry sauce, to her mouth. One of the children might have told a story about school. Bonnie cut the thin slice of turkey on her plate into little bites, pieces so small that piercing them with one prong of her fork was the only way to pick up the tiny morsels. They talked of the weather. Bonnie raised the meat to her mouth then put it down again. She ran for a forgotten condiment in the kitchen. She had many duties to perform during the meal. A glob of cranberry on the linen or a dribble of gravy on a chin needed wiping. More butter needed retrieving from the refrigerator. *More cold milk, please.* When she returned to the table the bit of turkey finally made it into her mouth. She nibbled on it for several minutes, continuing to push and gently pulverize the food on her plate. And no one at her table ever realized what she shared with her husband during dinner.

But where was Bruce at that moment? Where was he when Bonnie sat with their children at a table laden with piping hot food? Where was he when she coaxed everyone else to eat as she played with her meal and silently asked God for strength?

Where was Bruce? She didn't know. The only thing she was certain of—as certain as she was of the color of his eyes—was that he was alive. Amid the table clatter and casual chatting, without anyone knowing, Bonnie sent another plea to heaven for the safe return of her children's father.

After the meal had ended and the neighbors had left, the children wrote a letter to their father. Bonnie cleaned up and as darkness settled on Kansas, morning broke in Vietnam as it did every day, holiday or not. What was on her mind as she tidied up her kitchen? If only Bruce could send a message to her. Few letters from POWs were allowed out of Vietnam. Even the International Red Cross could not convince the North Vietnamese that the Geneva Convention permitted the exchange of packages and letters during wartime. Bonnie dried the dishes, whispering lines from a favorite Psalm:

> *The LORD is my light and my salvation; whom shall I fear? the LORD is the strength of my life; of whom shall I be afraid?*
>
> *Though an host should encamp against me, my heart shall not fear: though war should rise against me, in this will I be confident.*
>
> *And now shall mine head be lifted up above mine enemies round about me: therefore will I offer in his tabernacle sacrifices of joy; I will sing, yea, I will sing praises unto the LORD.*
>
> *Wait on the LORD: be of good courage, and he shall strengthen thine heart: wait, I say, on the LORD.*

Bonnie sent the prayer to Bruce on the wings of faith from Kansas to Southeast Asia, over lands familiar and strange, and waters rough and calm, knowing that somehow her husband would hear her.

Wait on the Lord. Be of good courage. Wait.

The children gave the letter to their mother to mail. Sending a letter to their father was like sending a letter to Santa Claus. The notes were filled with fervent wishes that they would get everything they asked for. But, like letters to Santa Claus, the envelopes never left the custody of the U.S. Postal Service. Still, sometimes wishes came true.

Before Bruce, Bryan, and Colleen went to bed, they gathered around their mother. They had a very important question. It's hard to remember who asked her the question, each one had probably asked her at one time or another, but they all had concerned looks when one of them spoke up, "Mommy, what if Daddy is dead?"

Bonnie was prepared for their question. "You know, some people believe that daddy *is* dead."

"They do?"

"Yes, some people are certain that Daddy died that day. But you know what? I don't believe Daddy is dead. I believe he is alive somewhere, waiting to come home to us." And Bonnie always reassured them, "Daddy's not here now, but he may be home by Christmas, if not then, maybe by Easter."

Bryan asked, "Where would Daddy be if he died that day, Mommy?"

"Well, Bryan, if he had died that day, where do you think Daddy would be?"

Bryan thought for a moment. Bruce and Colleen pondered the question. Bryan answered his mother, "Daddy would be in heaven with Jesus."

"That's right. Daddy would be with Jesus if he had died, but I believe we will see Daddy again." It was important to Bonnie that the children felt free to express all of their fears and it was just as important that they knew she believed that their father was alive.

Later, after the children were asleep, Bonnie's night began. She had news to catch up on and little things to do around the house. Put the china away. Wash the good linen. Think about what to do with the children over the long weekend. She and Colleen could bake a raspberry pie. Maybe they could drive to one of the old cowboy towns. The boys would like that. So would Colleen. She knew the children were happy to stay home playing with friends. Schilling was safe.

The clock passed midnight. Then one o'clock. Then two. Everything was quiet as the moon slipped toward the horizon.

Bonnie had nothing left to do. She sat at the piano and played quietly, mostly hymns that she had learned and played as a child. One of Bruce's favorites, the one that soothed her was "Let the Lower Lights Be Burning," a century-old hymn inspired by sailors trying to find the harbor at night in the midst of a storm. Sometimes Bonnie hummed along, or sang a favorite phrase or two as her fingers tumbled over the keys.

> *Dark the night of sin has settled,*
> *Loud the angry billows roar;*
> *Eager eyes are watching, longing,*
> *For the lights along the shore.*
>
> *Let the lower lights be burning,*
> *Send a gleam across the wave!*
> *Some poor fainting struggling seaman*
> *You may rescue, you may save.*

The music filled her with the hope that Bruce was hanging on somewhere. She knew he would never give up until he found his way home. And the day that began so long ago would finally end.

She believed. It was important that she believe.

Bonnie fell into the twilight sleep of one holding vigil over the lower lights. It was not unlike the trance of a soldier on night watch, sent to the edge by his commander. *Wait for your buddies. Stay quiet. Help them find their way back to camp. If you don't, they might die out there, alone in the jungle.* In the dark, when eyes want desperately to close, staying awake becomes essential to life. And so a deal is made. The body rests, but the mind remains alert, listening for signs of movement.

Bonnie listened, too, ever vigilant, for the echo of a prayer sent in answer to hers.

Beverly

FEAR

(1971)

My mother once told me she feared darkness more than anything. As a child growing up in Maine in the 1930s and 1940s, after the house quieted and her four brothers and sisters were asleep, she often called out to her father in the deepest time of night. Malevolent shadows with silvery eyes pinpointed her as she lay shivering in bed. They hovered above her, swooping down to torment her when she closed her eyes tight and whispered for her savior. "Pa. Pa. Come. I'm afraid."

Whenever she needed her father, he was there. Always. And so he rose from his bed to protect his Bell from the monsters he knew were real to his slim, redheaded daughter. When he walked into her room one of her slender fingers—her relatives said they were piano fingers—would point to a place on the wall, "There, Pa. There." But the shadows had already slid behind the bureau, hidden under the bed, and retreated to the closet. She held his hand to make sure he did not leave until she was fast asleep.

The next thing she saw after her father's face was a halo of morning light around the blinds on her window. No one else in the family understood, and so she and her father alone fought the baleful shadows. Theirs was a battle fought against a covert enemy and my mother had faith that her father would always protect her.

Two weeks had passed since my father had left for Vietnam. Almost every night since then my mother had sat alone at the kitchen table drinking cups of coffee. Smoking cigarettes. Packs of cigarettes. *What am I doing in the middle of nowhere without any friends? Who are these girls who constantly fight over the bathroom, clothes, housework, and the television?* Only God could make matters worse. He did.

The first ten days of 1971 were the worst Salina had seen in years. Five people had died from the cold. Four hundred hogs smothered to death seeking shelter at a local farmyard. Sub-zero temperatures kept us inside and a blizzard had dumped more than fifteen inches of snow on the county. Gale winds blew roof-high drifts in our front yard. *Where in the hell is the shovel?*

And there we were, four females with nothing to do except get on one another's nerves.

In the time between my father's departure and the blizzard, my mother sometimes saw the lady across the street check her mail. They would wave to each other, then go about their business. The camaraderie that usually developed among military wives had been curtailed by the lousy weather. My mother's welcoming luncheon had been postponed and the men were not around to break the ice among the women. She was frustrated and began to think she had made a mistake. Hooking rugs and beading sweaters helped pass the time during the day. At night she kept busy breaking up the fights between my sisters and me. Once, she even had to save my life.

We sisters had taken a casual approach to dining since my father left, usually opting to eat on TV trays in the living room. One evening I decided that the chair where Gail usually sat had a better view of the TV. I sat down and made myself comfortable. She came into the living room carrying a plate of pancakes and a bottle of Log Cabin syrup.

It's a sight to see, my elder sister freaking out.

"Get out of my chair or I'll kill you." Her face contorted.

I ignored her.

Again, she was ready to explode. "Get your fat body out of my seat."

I sat there. She mentioned something about watching *Star Trek*.

"Yeah. So what? I want to watch it, too."

"It's my chair."

"I don't see your name written on it."

"Move. Now."

"What makes you so special?"

"I said, MOVE."

"Why don't YOU watch it from the couch?"

Gail, enraged, raised the glass bottle of Log Cabin syrup over her head. "I'll kill you if you don't move."

I didn't move.

My mother arrived from the kitchen just in time to grab the bottle from Gail's plummeting arm. She screamed, "What are you trying to do, kill your own sister over a lousy TV program?" My turn. "And you. What are you trying to do? Start trouble?"

Disgusted, our mother turned off the television. Lynn started to cry. She liked *Star Trek*, too. Gail ran to her room. Slam.

I remained in her chair eating my pancakes.

My mother stayed in the kitchen long after we had gone to our rooms. Her family was falling apart. I had not made any friends so I moped around the house or antagonized my sisters.

When Gail wasn't reading, she, too, moped around the house looking bored and unhappy.

When Gail and I weren't at each other's throats we found reasons to complain about Lynn: her noisy thumb sucking, her eating habits, her whiny voice. My mother resented my father for leaving us in what she referred to as "this godforsaken place" without friends, family, or even a damned shovel. *It would serve him right if he came home to find we had killed one another.*

Prank phone calls had added to my mother's misery. The telephone had rung several times during the evening and when my mother picked it up her hellos were answered by heavy breathing.

My mother was tired, but sleep offered little relief from her anxiety. She rinsed her cup and looked outside, straining to catch any movement in the houses that mirrored ours across the back lawn. She turned off the kitchen and porch lights to see better in the dark. The world was lifeless beyond the ten-by-ten-foot cement patio. Every house had its floodlight turned on. A Schilling commander had thought the lights would offer the women comfort against the dark while making it easier for the deputy patrolling the post to see what was happening around the quarters.

Nothing moved but the second hand on the wall clock. Night filled the kitchen; shadows drifted onto the walls. Shapes familiar to my mother in childhood suddenly appeared. *Pa, make them go away. Close your eyes, Bell. Turn on the light.* My mother flipped on the lights and rechecked the lock on the back door. Don't forget the floodlight. She bolted the front door, peeking out of one of the tiny rectangular windows. Everything was still; the snow had stopped and the wind had quieted. She switched on all of the nightlights on her way to her bedroom.

* * *

My mother's bedtime ritual included tending to her hair. She had classified it as an ever-loving mess since arriving at Schilling. The only beautician she tried did not know how to tease her hair so that the style lasted for at least a week. The snow had prevented her from giving anyone else a chance. Out of habit she reached for her protective hair bonnet, but after looking in the mirror, thought to hell with it and threw it on the sink. Who cared how her hair looked anyway? When she crawled into bed she felt as frightened as she did when she was a child in Maine. She might have cried herself to sleep if she were the crying type. Instead she lay awake with the nightstand light turned on, thinking about prank calls, fighting children, and what my father was doing until the picture of Mount Fuji hanging on the wall in her bedroom went blurry and disappeared.

The doorbell rang.

My mother's already tense body seized up. Mount Fuji reappeared. *Is it one of the deputies coming to tell her to turn the floodlight on?* She was certain she had turned it back on before she went to bed. Piano fingers held the edges of the blanket. Knuckles turned white.

The doorbell rang a second time.

My mother forced herself out of bed, fearing the noise might wake us up. Her midnight cup of coffee gurgled in her stomach. She hoped whoever it was could not hear her tiptoeing down the hall.

Again. The bell rang again. And again.

Okay. Okay. Bile flooded her throat. Who could it be? Shadow monsters? A sedan? They might go away if she did not answer the door. In the hazy glow of shin-high lights my mother, terrified, crept toward the door. She peeked through the window.

Oh my God! My mother unbolted and opened the door.

"Pa. Pa. What are you doing here?"

Her father. He was wearing his tired blue work pants and the tank-top undershirt he wore around the house. Great bubbles of sweat poured off of him in the way it does on nervous cartoon characters.

"Hello, Bell. Can I come inside?"

It was her father. The one she remembered before he had his leg amputated. The one who had held her hand in the dark when she was young and who had promised to always protect her. My mother opened the screen door.

"But Pa, you look so young."

"Come on, Bell, let me tuck you in."

He followed her to the bedroom. When his daughter got under the covers he sat beside her on the bed and held her hand.

"Pa, I'm so afraid."

"I know, Bell. But I'm here now. Don't be afraid. I'll always watch over you."

My mother awoke the next morning, made a pot of coffee, and had a cigarette. Before my sisters and I got up, she rearranged the living-room furniture. Every chair had a good view of the television. The sun was out. Temperatures promised to climb out of the teens. Phoenix Street had been plowed. Wives and kids were outside shoveling their driveways.

The doorbell rang.

It was the woman from across the street. She held a shovel in one hand. In the other, a cup of coffee. My mother reached for the bolt. The door had already been unlocked.

Lorrayne

SILENCE

(1965)

Thanksgiving was a bittersweet day for Lorrayne. Fall was her favorite time of year and the holiday signaled its end. Soon icy winds would howl throughout the plains. Deep snow would cover everything. Winter in Kansas would not last as long as it did in Alaska, but for a time, Lorrayne knew it would be as fierce. Robbie's ear infection might reoccur if she wasn't vigilant about making him keep a hat on. The last thing she wanted was for him to have to go through more surgeries.

Since Bob left in early September, Robbie had grown quieter. Lorrayne missed her husband, but his father's absence was having a profound effect on her youngest son. He and Terry and their friends played outside all the time. When Robbie wasn't outside playing, Lorrayne often found him in his room, quietly building model airplanes. Bob was good about writing; sometimes he even sent home reel-to-reel tapes, but hearing from his father had not been a comfort to Robbie. He read or listened to his father's messages without enthusiasm.

Since her arrival at Schilling, Lorrayne's days had become increasingly overloaded with organizing the growing community. In a way she felt responsible for the families moving into the neighborhood. Before leaving Riley, she had spread the word about the available quarters to her friends. Thousands of families needed homes. Most had chosen to return to their hometowns. Many had moved off base into Junction City so they could be close to the commissary, PX, and dispensary at Fort Riley. Twelve or so of Lorrayne's friends, including her best friend, Pat, followed her to Schilling a few weeks after her arrival. Twenty more families moved in soon after. By the end of September a small, energetic group of women with no less than one hundred children among them occupied a block of houses in and around Helena Court. Bicycles, tricycles, and skateboards were soon careening down the sidewalks and into the streets. A few dogs had moved in with their families, free to run after and bark at anything that moved. Hula hoops dangled on tree limbs. Forts were popping up in backyards. Tonka trucks began excavating sandboxes and little girls swapped Barbie doll clothes on front stoops. The boys liked to play war. Robbie always made sure it was one of the world wars or Korea before he agreed to chase his enemies around the fields and gullies behind the housing area. He refused to play Vietnam War. The kids told him all the wars were the same, but he never believed them.

In late October final approval for the Waiting Wives experiment came down from General Staff Headquarters in Washington. Schilling would be run on an austere basis. Only the most basic of services would be provided to the families. The brass had to be certain that a military post composed of women and children would not present a public relations problem for the U.S. government. The report recommended that Fort Riley take over the administration of the base on January 1, 1966. Lorrayne was relieved. She would finally have a place to make appeals on behalf of the families.

By the time Thanksgiving arrived families were moving in on a daily basis. The women, many with impossibly meager allotments, needed more services than those the government was providing the families. Scanlan had managed to keep open a small commissary and a dispensary manned by one Air Force doctor and a couple of leftover corpsmen waiting for orders to their next assignment. The families needed a PX and a larger dispensary with permanently assigned doctors. The children needed athletic leagues and scout troops and Lorrayne wanted to open the movie theater and the swimming pool before summer started. Teenagers needed a place to gather or they would start finding places to hang out on their own. Lorrayne convinced Colonel Scanlan to open one of the base houses to use as a teen/tween club. Before the colonel left in early November he offered Lorrayne another one of Schilling's quarters to use as the official community center and meeting place for the women. Lorrayne was on her own after Scanlan left because, although an Air Force major was assigned to command the transition of the base over to the Army, his position was temporary. In fact, he was so unavailable to her that she never realized he existed.

Some wives didn't have cars. Most of the women did not have the necessary tools or experience to maintain a house. Many of the foreign-born wives were uncertain as to how to change a lightbulb or how to turn on the stove. Lorrayne figured the community would not succeed without a housing officer, maintenance men, and other services military families were used to. She had set out on a personal quest to acquire some of those amenities from the government as well as from the town of Salina.

Lorrayne had gone to Salina's Chamber of Commerce, asking what they could do to help the military families. The Chamber came up with a plan whereby local merchants would give the wives a ten percent discount provided they could prove they were from the base. Lorrayne had small charms engraved with the initials WW that she presented to the wives when they moved in, explaining that they should show it to the shopkeepers in town to receive the discount.

As Lorrayne prepared for Thanksgiving, casualties neared the two thousand mark as a result of intensified fighting in the Ia Drang Valley and the Central Highlands. A record number of American troops had been killed in the first large-scale battle involving U.S. soldiers and North Vietnam regulars. Two hundred and fifty U.S. soldiers died. Five hundred were wounded. Luckily, Bob was nowhere near the fighting.

Thanksgiving Day's chilly weather did not hinder the celebration at Lorrayne's house. Sunbeams shone through the windows, warming the kitchen long before she turned on the oven. Earlier in the week she had replaced the screens on the front and back doors with storm windows, allowing her to open the big, wooden outer doors to let in more sun.

In the morning, Lorrayne puttered around the kitchen, preparing the turkey and all the accompaniments. She was grateful to live at Schilling while Bob was in Vietnam. The schools were good. Town folk were friendly and helpful. Quarters were the nicest they had had in the military, with a spacious kitchen, plenty of cupboards and counter space, and a good-sized dining room that fit the large dinner table that she had set with her best linen and china earlier in the morning.

She never worried about Bob. He was a soldier for the United States of America, and she knew when she married him that there would be separations. She accepted it, and as far as she was concerned, her job was to do whatever she could to keep things normal until he returned. And Bob had always come home.

In 1965, Vietnam had not yet swelled to epic proportions, although network news executives had expanded their coverage of the simmering conflict. Black-and-white images of war were available for viewing in living rooms. The U.S. military death toll, reported during every broadcast, increased daily. Nevertheless, as Lorrayne basted the turkey and peeled potatoes in preparation for the family's feast, it never occurred to her that what was happening in Southeast Asia would leave a lasting mark on her family. She was about to find out.

Sitting around the house trying to find something to do had gotten to the boys. *Please, can we go outside and play? We promise we won't get our good clothes dirty before dinner.* She relented. Around midmorning they joined the other kids on the block trying to figure out what to do that did not involve cruddying up their clothes.

Terry and his friend Mitch took their trumpets out to the field and practiced the cavalry charge. The kids might have had a scavenger hunt, an activity that didn't require tackling, or having to roll around in the dirt after being shot by a toy gun, but could occupy hours of searching in an effort to find weird things hanging around in the grass, under the rocks, up in the trees, or in someone's garage. At some point, Robbie came home. He sat on the steps outside the front door, watching the others play.

Pat and her newly adopted daughter, four-month-old Cricket, arrived early to help. Lorrayne insisted that she didn't need any help, but for Pat to go ahead and sit down to a cup of coffee while she put the final touches on dinner. Pat had lost a child to brain cancer several years earlier. Months before her husband received orders for Vietnam, they had started the process of adopting a baby from Catholic Family Services. Pat and Lorrayne had chatted endlessly as to whether or not her husband's assignment in Vietnam might hurt their chances of getting a baby. They convinced each other over many cups of coffee that it would not matter—and it hadn't.

One day in October Pat received a call telling her to be at the Salina Airfield the next day to pick up her little girl. She was so excited that she ran over to Lorrayne's to tell her the news. The friends spent the afternoon shopping for baby clothes and accessories. The next day they went to pick up the baby. Pat was dressed in her best outfit and Lorrayne, having some fun, donned one of Bob's military hats so that when Cricket saw her, the little girl would have an idea what her father looked like.

Lorrayne announced that dinner was almost ready. Pat called the boys in from outdoors. Robbie walked in the front door. Terry flew in from the kitchen door, followed by a gust of wind that refreshed the steamy room with the last smells of autumn. Lorrayne was grateful for the cool air, wishing that fall would linger a few days more before winter blasted in.

Robbie looked a little tired when he came inside for dinner. Lorrayne prayed that he was not coming down with something. Lately he always looked exhausted, as if he had something on his mind. She asked if anything was wrong.

No, nothing's the matter.

Lorrayne and Pat carried bowls and platters of steaming food to the dining room table. The friends sat down to a traditional Thanksgiving dinner complete with large glasses of cold milk, thick gravy, home-baked buns, and baby food for Cricket. Lorrayne remembers that the bird was especially moist that year; as she carved through the crispy skin down through the meat, clear juice flowed onto the platter.

Lorrayne recalls only one part of the dinner conversation on Thanksgiving Day in 1965. Robbie had not said much during the meal. He had poked and pushed his food around without eating much of anything. The little boy put his fork down, as if to take a break. Terry had eaten with gusto and was into his second helping when Robbie's tentative voice rose from the clatter of knives and forks scraping on dishes and the light chatter around the table. As if from out of the blue, with earnestness, Robbie asked, "Mom, what is eternity?" The table quieted. Everyone focused on Robbie.

Bob's leaving had upset Robbie longer than Lorrayne had anticipated and she was not sure what to do about it. He seemed more sensitive since his ear operations, more vulnerable, as if he had felt something darker in life, something that little boys are not suppose to feel. She had hoped that going to school and making new friends would help him through whatever turmoil was going on inside of him. It hadn't. Her son could not tell her what was wrong. It was as if too many complicated thoughts were darting around in the little boy's head.

Robbie had asked about eternity with such sincerity that it took a moment to think about an answer. "Eternity," she told him, "is something that goes on forever. It has no end."

Robbie thought for a moment, then turned to his mother. "No, Mom. Eternity is when your dad is in Vietnam and you are nine years old."

Lorrayne asked why he felt that way. He did not answer. Robbie turned his attention to his plate. He sat as if he were alone. He did not ignore the people at the table—that would suggest defiance. It was more like they were not there or that if he were to talk he might explode.

By the time the dishes were cleared Lorrayne was as close to panic as she would ever get. Robbie's earnestness had transformed into stoicism. It was as if after he spoke his last words he placed the final brick in an invisible wall that he had been building for months to protect him from things he could not understand—like why his dad had gone away and might never come home.

Bonnie

___

St. Valentine's Day
(1968)

When Bonnie and the children had lived at Schilling for five months the worst fighting of the war was taking place in South Vietnam. Soon after her arrival at the base, Bonnie had joined the Schilling Manor bowling league and had become involved with the Protestant Women of the Chapel. Bruce was in third grade, Bryan was in second grade, both were involved with sports. Colleen had begun taking dance lessons and was eagerly awaiting her first dance recital in the spring. Everyone would come. Her mother and brothers. Her grandparents from Michigan. Maybe even her father would show up and surprise her.

Schilling Manor was brimming with women and children, so much so that the housing office had a long waiting list of families wanting quarters. Bonnie enjoyed the company of the other wives and the base housed so many children that doors were constantly swinging open and slamming closed with the arrival or departure of one friend after another. It was still winter and blustery outside, so the children would play at one another's houses with dolls or matchbox cars, passively listening to the drone of the television set while entertaining themselves with their toys or one another.

Bonnie left the TV on from the moment the local stations signed on the air until they signed off at night. It was her primary source of information about the war. Interruptions in regularly scheduled programs were viewed with concentrated interest, not as an excuse to run a household errand or to grab a snack. One evening on the nightly news a truce was announced in honor of Tet, the Vietnamese Lunar New Year. But the next morning reports of a massive offensive taking place in South Vietnam filled the airwaves. The attacks raged for several weeks.

Bonnie watched the television coverage, witnessing strikes against well-fortified U.S. compounds from her living room. All of it happening in the south, maybe somewhere close to where the Viet Cong were holding Bruce. Hundreds of men went missing during the Tet Offensive—Bonnie could not help but think about their families, especially their little ones now left alone to wonder, as her children did, when or if their father would ever come home.

In the weeks leading up to St. Valentine's Day, twenty-three hundred American soldiers died in Vietnam. It was hard for Americans not to notice. And it was hard for the children not to notice, especially when they lived at Schilling Manor and their fathers were somewhere in the middle of the mayhem. Fear simmered in everyone, and every day that fear boiled over in some small or large way.

In early February, while the offensive was quieting down—but not over—Bruce, Jr.'s class at Schilling's elementary school embarked on a new project: making St. Valentine's Day cards to send to their fathers in Vietnam. The children did not know or care about the legend of St. Valentine, and even though it was a saint's day, no one went to church unless the holiday fell on a Sunday. Pastel-colored, sugary hearts with flirty words like "Be Mine" or "You're Cool" were something the children looked forward to around Valentine's Day. So, too, were fresh-baked, heart-shaped sugar cookies topped with red frosting and crystalline sprinkles.

For the children it was a day to exchange miniature cards decorated with red hearts or sweet-looking animals with innocent smiles and coy eyes or with popular cartoon characters like Spider-Man and Snoopy. Homemade cards were special— reserved only for mothers and fathers. Making them was a yearly ritual in most elementary school classrooms.

Bruce, the most extroverted of Bonnie and Bruce's children, was four years old when his father went missing. He remembered him more than Bryan and Colleen did. Bonnie thought her son a brave young man, never prone to casual tears or extremes of emotions. Bonnie knew that her son longed for his dad but seldom allowed his pain to show. He was nearly nine when his teacher directed her students to make a Valentine card for their fathers.

A Valentine card?

Although the details are sketchy, the story goes like this. Bruce's class returned from lunch. Doilies, red and white construction paper, blunted scissors, and white paper paste had been placed on the art table. The children took out their crayons. The teacher showed them an example of what the card could look like, demonstrating how to fold and cut the paper to make hearts of different sizes. *Make wonderful cards to send to your fathers.*

It was an exciting project, and fun for the children to think of their fathers opening their special Valentines so far away. Each child was determined to make their dad the best card they had ever made. Some children opted to fold and cut doilies to make lacy patterns. Others chose to paste an assortment of hearts. A few students decided to forgo the frills to draw and color their own pictures. The project required much concentration on the part of the children. Each card must be perfect. Several students had to start over because they had made a mess of things, but luckily the teacher dedicated the entire afternoon to their mission.

The students busied themselves with cutting, pasting, coloring, and admiring one another's creations. The teacher strolled around the room, offering encouragement and advice. She noticed Bruce sitting at his desk staring down at half-cut hearts and scattered crayons. His forehead was leaning on his hands, covering part of his face. Bruce's teacher approached him. Tears fell onto his unfinished Valentine. So many, that a small puddle had formed on his desk. A sniffle. *Bruce, what's the matter? Are you having a hard time with your card?* The class hushed. Some of his classmates knew his father was missing, most did not. The teacher again asked what was wrong. The eight-year-old said nothing, choosing to keep his thoughts to himself.

What good will it do? No one knows where my father is and if they did, they won't let him have the card anyway.

Shortly after St. Valentine's Day, on February 27, Walter Cronkite made an unprecedented departure from "objective" journalism by concluding his nightly newscast with a personal commentary. Cronkite, the revered Uncle Walter of the waiting wives, astonished his viewers with his candid observations about the war. His words were a dagger in the hearts of all who believed that America was winning the war, that our leaders knew what they were doing. In a few minutes Cronkite told Americans, not with rash words or accusations for the turmoil in Vietnam but with earnest analysis, that the United States must extricate itself from an honorable mission gone awry. He said, in part:

"For it seems now more certain than ever that the bloody

experience of Vietnam is to end in a stalemate." Cronkite added, ". . . and for every means we have to escalate, the enemy can match us, and that applies to invasion of the North, the use of nuclear weapons, or the mere commitment of one hundred, or two hundred, or three hundred thousand more American troops to the battle. And with each escalation, the world comes closer to the brink of cosmic disaster."

After Cronkite's broadcast, President Lyndon Johnson was quoted as saying, "If I've lost Cronkite, I've lost middle America." Two days after the broadcast, Secretary of Defense Robert McNamara resigned. One month later President Johnson announced that he would not seek reelection.

Bruce never finished making a St. Valentine's Day card for his father that year. In May, while Bonnie's children began to look forward to summer in Harbor Beach and the cherry blossoms bloomed in Washington, the United States and North Vietnam agreed to begin formal negotiations in Paris. The talks were at a stalemate by the end of the month.

The Committee

———

TRUNKMAN

The fashion show committee held their second meeting in the living room of the colonel's wife. Everyone was in a good mood. The weather, though not yet warm, was pleasant. None of their kids were sick. Each had received at least one letter from her husband since their last meeting. The lieutenant's wife was particularly happy as she announced that she had lost three pounds when she weighed in the night before at her SMAC (Schilling Manor Against Calories) meeting. Six weeks remained until she met her husband for R&R in Hawaii. She was determined to SMAC-off ten more pounds by then.

When the meeting finally came to order the women found they had accomplished a great deal. The colonel's wife had enlisted Bonnie and Judi, two of Schilling's MIA wives; Major McKain's wife, Mary Ellen; and a couple of other young and pretty NCO wives to volunteer to be runway models. "One of them is Negro," she continued, "and will look stunning in yellows and oranges."

Commander Miller had agreed to be the master of ceremonies for the event. The committee's oldest member reminded
everyone that they had not decided on a date for the show at their
last meeting, but had found out that the community center's
main room was available every Monday and Thursday evening
for the next couple of months. They quickly decided on a date,
Thursday five weeks away.

The sergeant major's wife told the group that Lois, one of the
girls in the commander's office, had agreed to type up and
mimeograph the programs. She was sure Lois would also agree to
copy several hundred leaflets advertising the show.

The colonel's wife interrupted, "What about special guests,
like the wives of Senator Dole and Fort Riley's commander, or
the wives of the Salina City Commission members? We can't
hand them a leaflet."

"Well," answered the sergeant major's wife, "if we can come
up with a list of special guests I can make individual invitations
for them." The committee members nodded their heads, agree-
ing that the idea was a great solution to the problem.

As far as decorations and refreshments were concerned, the
captain's wife said that she had secured flowers from Cunningham Florists and thought it would be best to ask all the members
of the Waiting Wives Club to make snacks for the event. She
added, "Colonel Miller," which came out sounding like *kerno
mirrer*, "promise to donate stuff for punch."

The women drank coffee, winding down the business of the
fashion show. The colonel's wife invited her guests to stay with a
coffee ring fresh from the oven. While the hostess cut three-inch
pieces of the warm treat for each member the warrant officer's
wife could hardly wait to share some news. "Did you gals hear
what happened a couple of nights ago?"

"No," exclaimed one of the women sipping steaming, freshly
perked coffee. "What happened?"

"Well," the warrant officer's wife continued, "you know the woman who lives two blocks over in the cul-de-sac?"

Most of the women had puzzled looks on their faces.

"You know," she continued, "the French girl, I think her name is Georgette or Gigi or something that starts with a *G*. You know, the one who leaves her kids alone all the time to go to the Pink Pussycat. The one who had a little too much to drink at one of the luncheons and answered her door naked as a newborn when Al delivered her mail."

A chorus of "Oh, yes, her." "Sure, I've heard about her." "Isn't she the one who will only drink wine if it has a cork in it?" and "You mean the one whose kids are always wandering the streets? I think her name is Giselle."

"Well," the warrant officer's wife began in her thickest Southern drawl, "I just happened to be driving around in my car that night, you know, trying to put the baby to sleep. Rocking her in her cradle wasn't working, so I plopped her in the backseat with a blanket and drove around until she fell asleep. It always works and the other kids were asleep so, well anyway, I'm driving from one block to another when I notice her car and decide to follow, at a distance of course. After all, it was so late and what about her kids? I think she has three or four. Anyway, when she turned down her street I went straight ahead so she wouldn't get suspicious. But then I made a U-turn and drove back to her street. By then she's parked in the driveway and you will never believe what I saw."

The women spoke all at once. "Tell us." "Tell us, now." "What did you see?" "Hold on, I need another cup of coffee."

"You gals will never guess in a million years."

"Well, what did you see?" The lieutenant's wife was on the edge of her chair.

"So I turn off my headlights and inch up to the edge of the

road to get a good look." She continued, "I thought maybe I'd see her staggering or something and might need help putting her key in the door, you know, then I could go over and help her. But I will tell you ladies right now, that is *not* what happened."

Her audience nearly collapsed with all the suspense. The colonel's wife blurted out, "Will you tell us for God's sake?"

"Okay, okay. Well, she climbs out of her car, closes the door very gently, then goes to the trunk and I thought, well, it's a little late to be doing the shopping, then she opened the trunk, and let me tell you, I didn't see any packages inside, at least not the brown paper bag kind with bread and milk inside. Anyway, I could hardly believe my eyes when I saw a man get out of her trunk. I could tell it was a man even in the dark because he was big and wore pants. He crawled out, stretched, then closed the trunk, quietly for sure, and then put his arm around her while they sashayed toward the front door. I can tell you right now: that man was not her brother."

The wives were beside themselves; the room ricocheted from one end to the other with "Oh, mys" and "I can't believe its," so tickled were they to hear the juiciest bit of gossip some of them had ever heard in their lives.

"Maybe it was her husband," the youngest member of the committee piped in.

The warrant officer's wife said, "Oh sure, he flies all the way from Vietnam to arrive home in the trunk of his car at one in the morning. Sweetheart, you are so naive."

The captain's wife laughed so hard she got the hiccups and had to get a glass of water from the kitchen.

The colonel's wife could not believe a wife would do that to her husband, especially when he was at war. She announced, "That woman will destroy his career."

"Well, what did you do next?" asked the sergeant major's wife.

"What do you think I did?" she asked in a slightly superior tone. "I did the only thing I could do. I rode around until I found the deputy and demanded he get over to her house before she did something she would regret in the morning." She continued, "We can't have that kind of behavior on this post. If word gets around that women are having night visits from the opposite sex it won't be long before all the horny townsmen and every other Tom, Dick, and Harry from wherever will think they can come on post and have a good old time."

Her coffee ring partners agreed.

"You're so right." "Can't have roose"—meaning loose—"women on post. It bad for rest of us." The captain's wife asked, "What deputy do?"

"He said he'd inform the commander. Let him decide what to do. And," she added, "I told him that he better get on over to the colonel's house right away and remind him that this is the home for waiting wives, *not* the home for willing wives, and that he had better do something before some of these less moral women get us all in a heap of trouble."

"What happened next?" one of the women asked.

"Well, I don't know. I was going to go to the commander's house myself, but the baby woke up so I had to start driving around again. I was going to follow the deputy, but I didn't want him to think I didn't trust him or anything. But when I was about out of gas and on my way home, I saw the deputy's car leave the base with a passenger inside. I'll wager it was Mr. Trunkman getting an escort home."

The women giggled or clicked their tongues while eating the last bites of their cake. Only the sergeant major's wife worried what might happen to Giselle. Surely the commander would bring her husband home. She asked the other wives what they thought. "What makes a woman betray her husband and neglect her children?"

The question was sincere. The answer required thought.

LIVING

The boy and girl, about six and a little bored sat on the steps of their house.

"What will we play now?" asked the little girl.

"Let's play war," said the boy.

"OK, let's play war," said the little girl. "You go off and be a soldier and I'll stay home and worry."

—SALINA JOURNAL, AUGUST 2, 1970

Beverly

PRUDENCE

(1971)

G ail and my mother were always creating projects to pass the
time. They were a restless couple. Neither knew how to sit
still and do nothing. One day they must have been bored or in
between projects or waiting for some craft to dry because when
Lynn and I got home from school during midwinter, when the
temperatures held at freezing and the snow had turned to
mounds of crusty dirt, we were greeted by a silver-colored puppy.
Somehow, Gail had convinced my mother that we needed a dog.
The two of them never told Lynn or me anything during the
weeks they had plotted to add the new addition to the family.

I never thought my mother even liked animals. We had had a
butterscotch tabby when we lived at Fort Devens in Massachusetts.
Puddin'. I can't remember what happened to Puddin' when we left
for Fort Leavenworth. In Japan we had a black-and-white spotted
pointer that my mother continuously complained about. "Keep
him off the furniture." "Someone better feed him." "Don't let

him in the house, he's filthy." She would repeat her complaints, occasionally throwing in a new one like, "Someone better go after the dog, he's loose again and probably shitting all over everyone's yard." We couldn't bring the dog back to the States, so we came home from school one day to find the dog was gone—given to a Japanese farmer from the village outside the post. At least, that's what they told us.

My family's reactions were predictable. In fifteen years I had learned what my mother would say no to. What my father would say yes to. How far to push them to say yes to get me off their backs. And the best: What I could get away with even if they both had said no.

I barely had to lift a finger to send Gail flying into a rage, bellyaching to our parents about what an idiot I was. She hated me in her room, which I often entered when she was not looking, an act that, when she found out, made her so furious she would go after me with claws extended and to which she would emerge, red-faced and holding fistfuls of my hair after my mother stepped in to break us up.

Lynn was an easy target and I had mastered all the little tricks to make her cry. Mostly, I only had to look at her to provoke her into tattling on me for something she anticipated I might do or say. My mother's eyes would narrow whenever Lynn whined, "Mom, Donna's looking at me again." Through clenched teeth she would warn me to leave Lynn alone. I would say, "But I didn't do anything to her," as predictably as anything else that happened in our house.

Monkey faces and eye rolls were so common they had little effect, except for the strain they put on my mother, something we did not realize, especially when my dad was away. I was used to a household that held few surprises. So when I walked in the house that dreary winter afternoon I was caught off guard by everybody smiling, even my mother, who so rarely smiled that when she did the air in the room became easier to breathe. My defenses were dissolved that afternoon by a four-legged bundle of energy that seemed to love us all equally as she leaped from one set of arms to the next without favor.

Lynn and I fell to our knees to pet the puppy. She accepted our rubs and coos with little yips, then jumped up on my mother who was sitting on the hassock, jumped down before my mother could say anything, and then ran down the hall and back wanting more. We were glad to give her so much attention. She paid us back by wagging her tail so fast the entire back end of her body vibrated with joy.

For the first time in months everyone in our house was happy.

While we got to know one another Gail explained that the puppy was a miniature schnauzer. She had found her in a classified ad that had run in the *Salina Journal* a few weeks before. My sister and my mother had driven fifty miles to Manhattan to buy the dog from a farmer. By the time they got there only the runt was left. They decided to take her anyway because she was so cute and only cost $50. The puppy had a cropped tail but her breeders, Gail told us, "chose not to crop her ears because she would never be a show dog." So, although her ears were perky, the tips drooped softly, making her look much more adorable than her high-class sisters and brother, whose ears where cut into sinewy arrows. We agreed. Our puppy was the most adorable thing we had ever seen in our lives.

After an hour or so of fussing, someone mentioned that the dog needed a name and some doggy stuff. Gail volunteered to drive us to town. My mother stayed home with the dog. Lynn and I grabbed our coats and ran for the car. I was always faster than Lynn and she usually complained that I always got to the front seat first, but she only made a little *humph* and got in the back without making a scene. We buckled up, a habit of ours since our dad installed seat belts in all of our cars before they came factory installed, and off we went, three sisters separated by years and personalities, on a cheerful mission without even so much as an argument.

On the way to and from the store we mulled around names: "Toto," Lynn offered. Gail and I tried not to roll our eyes. Gail suggested "Silver" because of the color of her coat. We decided that was an okay name, but not great. She was cuter than silver. Nothing we came up with seemed to fit.

We arrived home with puppy food, two dog bowls, colorful dog treats, a brush and comb, a bottle of canine shampoo, a rubber hot dog that squeaked when pressure was applied to the bun, a royal blue collar with rhinestones that cost a little more than we should have spent, and a tartan-print winter jacket with rubber boots to match—we knew our mother would not tolerate muddy paw prints in the house. The dog greeted us at the door. We went through a lengthy welcome home ritual that was only interrupted when my mother told us that the dog had peed on the kitchen floor.

"Somebody had better get in there to clean it up."

We all went, puppy at our heels, into the kitchen. Gail grabbed the paper towels, I grabbed the cleanser from under the sink, and Lynn ran around chasing the dog so she could pick her up and cuddle her like a baby, which the dog didn't seem to mind although she wiggled around so much that Lynn dropped her. We gasped. Gail and I simultaneously called Lynn a jerk, yelling at her not to pick up the dog again because she was nothing but a klutz. Lynn stomped into her bedroom, wailing about how we always picked on her. *I hate the stupid dog anyway.* The puppy followed Lynn down the hall until she came sliding back into the kitchen after Lynn slammed her door shut.

My mother finished the dinner she had started while we were shopping. Gail organized the dog's stuff. Washed her bowls. Put the collar on her neck, and then helped my mother with dinner. I went into my bedroom, whispering to the dog to come along. She did. I put on *The White Album*, then played with the puppy on my bed. She liked playing tug-of-war with a dirty, knotted sock, and couldn't have cared less about the squeaky hot dog. Once, my mother yelled, "That dog better not be on your bed." How does she know these things? I ignored her.

Gail took the dog to the kitchen. *Here's your food. Here's your water. Wanna go outside? Outside. That's where you're supposed to pee, little puppy.*

I kept my music low so that I could leave my door open in case the dog decided to come back. That winter *The White Album* was my favorite music, even more than the Doors. Most nights I put the album on automatic replay, listening to the songs over and over again until I fell asleep. I had met Lauren, a girl my age who lived across the street, and we were becoming friends, but had not yet made the leap to "best" friend status, so I was alone much of the time. The songs on *The White Album* reminded me of my friends in Japan and all the fun we used to have hanging out at the snack bar or at each other's houses. In the months since we had left Japan the only thing that had remained constant was my family, who were around for better or worse, and the Beatles' music that reminded me of long-gone friends who were slowly evaporating into nothing more than another memory.

The puppy ran back in my room. She was so little she needed help jumping onto the bed. We continued our game of tug-of-war until she pooped out and lay down on the bedspread. Together we listened to John Lennon sing "Dear Prudence," my favorite song of the week.

During the song, I looked at the puppy and whispered, "Prudence. Prudence, won't you come out and play." To my delight the schnauzer got a second wind, jumped up, wagged her tail, and began to lick my face.

I knew what to name the dog. It was now a matter of convincing everyone else—well, Gail and my mother, because Lynn didn't count, although it would be helpful if she agreed. At dinner Lynn seemed to have forgotten that I had called her a jerk and a klutz, which was a good sign. I waited for the right moment. Our conversation was all about the dog, so when the subject of a name came up I said in one breath, "Prudence. We should name her Prudence."

"Prudence?" Gail said with a little too much edge.

"Prudence?" my mother added. "That's not a dog name."

"It's better than a dog name. It's a cool, people name. She likes it." At that point I called, "Here Prudence. Here Prudence." The dog left her water bowl to come to me.

"Wow," Lynn said and called the dog. "Here Prudence." The dog went to Lynn.

"Prudence," Gail said with less of an attitude than the first time and the dog wagged her tail all the way to the other side of the table to Gail. She added, "Okay. Maybe it's a good name. We can call her Prudey for short."

That night we made a tape to send to my father. We were excited to tell him about the dog. It started with my mother saying, "Well, Donald, you'll never guess what we have."

All of us started talking at the same time. "We have a dog." "It's a schnauzer." "She's so little and cute. Wait until you see her." "Mom and Gail went and got it without us knowing." "Yeah, it was a surprise." "She pees all over the floor." "We went shopping and bought her a coat and boots for the winter." "Yeah, but she didn't like the boots so she danced all around the backyard until she kicked them off." "It was hilarious." "Hey, we're a family of five again. Well, five until you come home, then we'll be six." "Of course, she won't eat at the table or anything." "You're going to really like her. Do you like dogs? Mom, does Dad like dogs?"

And on we went until my mother suggested that we tell our father the dog's name. Lynn tried to blurt out, "Prud . . ."

But I shoved her and told her that I would tell him since I thought of it. "Her name is Prudence, Dad. Like the Beatles song. It's a great name and she already comes when she's called. Doesn't she?"

My mother, Gail, and Lynn agreed. My sisters and I said good-bye to my father, knowing that my mother usually finished the tape when she was alone.

Later, after Prudence had been walked two or three more times, we all went to bed, said good night to one another, leaving our doors open so the dog could visit us whenever she wanted. For the next hour we whispered for Prudence. She came to each of us, every time she heard her name, until we fell asleep to the quiet murmur of my mother talking to my father in her room.

Lorrayne

THE WAITING WIVES CLUB
(1965–1966)

By the end of the 1965, another three hundred American soldiers had been killed in Vietnam. Senator Ernest Gruening, a democrat from Arkansas, stated that the conflict in Vietnam was a civil war that posed no threat to U.S. interests.

No one listened.

In the weeks following Thanksgiving Robbie had not spoken a word. Lorrayne could barely get him up off the couch. He stared at the television set, watching everything from cartoons to the news. More than once he had witnessed the gruesome effect mortars and bullets had on human bodies while he was eating dinner or playing games in front of the TV. Were the day-to-day reminders that his father was at war part of Robbie's problem?

Chores were completed without complaint, but Lorrayne's son remained isolated. She tried to reassure him. His father would come home. He had a duty to perform, but that did not mean his father did not love his family. Lorrayne began to think that the boy did not understand what she was saying, or that he may have lost his hearing again.

Lorrayne took Robbie to the dispensary to see Dr. David Nelson, her neighbor and the only doctor on post. Tests revealed that nothing was organically wrong. Dr. Nelson referred Lorrayne to a mental health center in Salina. The diagnosis there indicated that Robbie had internalized an emotional trauma, probably the fear that his father would not return from Vietnam. The only way he could control a situation over which he had no control was to withdraw and cut off communication.

David Nelson was a gentle man with a young family that had been stationed at Schilling Air Force Base. Less than a year remained on his commission when he heard that the government planned to shut down the base. He worried that he would have to pack up his family and move for only a few months before being discharged. When Scanlan opened quarters to the wives, Nelson requested that he be allowed to stay as the interim doctor until the Department of Defense decided how to handle the medical needs of the incoming families. His request was approved.

Dr. Nelson and his wife, Ann, lived a couple of houses down from Lorrayne. One day after school he knocked on her door. *Would Robbie like to come over to my workshop and help me with a project that's giving me a little trouble?* Lorrayne encouraged Robbie to go, feeling that male companionship might do her son some good.

A couple of hours later Dr. Nelson brought Robbie home. He did not tell his mother if he had had a good time, or what kind of project it was that the doctor needed help with. She did not pry. The next day Dr. Nelson picked up Robbie and off they went. Robbie and Dr. Nelson retreated to his workshop a couple of times a week. The doctor told Lorrayne that Robbie never spoke while they were together, but her son followed directions, listening carefully to advice on how to handle wood, glue, nails, and screws. Lorrayne thought Robbie looked forward to the time he spent with Dr. Nelson, but his silence remained disconcerting. The Christmas season came and went.

Lorrayne never stopped organizing, moving from one project to the next, attending get-together after get-together. She had thought about finding a job in real estate, but the needs of the growing community and seeing to the welfare of her sons left her no time to pursue a career.

In January, the experimental community of waiting wives finally became a permanent subpost of Fort Riley. The base was renamed Schilling Manor: The Home of the Waiting Wives of the United States Armed Forces; the Home for Waiting Wives for short. By then over a hundred families had moved onto Schilling. More were moving in daily. Lorrayne often wrote or visited the deputy post commander at Fort Riley, requesting the services she felt were essential to the families. Nothing fancy, she told him. Just a little more than the basics. She had been a military wife for nearly twenty years and knew from experience that the administrative arm of the Army was bound up in red tape. It took forever to accomplish anything, but it seemed like the command at Fort Riley was uncertain as to how to handle the fatherless families on a subpost where the primary spokeswoman's uniform was a hat with a garland of netting, a pair of gloves, and a little lipstick. What do the women need? How much should we give them? Never before had the government taken on the role of what a few of the brass thought of as either a massive babysitting job or, in the more perverse military minds, a government-sponsored brothel.

Fortunately for the wives at Schilling, the majority of the men wanted the experiment to succeed. Many of them had families that, at one time or another in their careers, were left alone during hardship tours. Knowing that the protective arm of the government was wrapped around their wives and children might have made being away less stressful. But the concept of taking care of families was new. The Department of Defense needed time to find its way around the emotional and financial expenditures involved in running an untested community of women and children. The men were warriors accustomed to giving commands that would lead to victory during war, not divining the needs of the women and children.

When Schilling Manor received national publicity, seeing to its success became a priority for the government. But in the first months of its existence, the wives were virtually alone, homesteaders of a sort, responsible for figuring out how to make the community work. And Lorrayne, by way of personality and because she was the first waiting wife, was their leader.

In the early part of 1966, a small coterie of wives, which included Lorrayne and Pat, their neighbors Glenda and Madonna, Mary Lou, and several other women, decided to make their ad hoc group official. The group was the first to arrive at Schilling and had gathered casually on occasion to discuss the needs of the community. Families were moving in by the dozens and the women felt they needed formal recognition as an organization if they were going to be taken seriously by the government, the town, and the women moving onto the base. Toward the end of one of the meetings, after they had discussed for the umpteenth time how to go about creating a wives club, Lorrayne announced, "I'll find out what we have to go through from Fort Riley and from the folks at the Salvation Army. You gals come up with some suggestions for a motto and a name."

Lorrayne said a quick good-bye, put on her coat, and flew out the door so fast that everyone thought she was late for another appointment. The meeting had gone on longer than expected—

they almost always did. Lorrayne was always in a rush to get from one place to the next, but Pat thought her best friend was moving with particular urgency. Pat was in a hurry, too. She did not like leaving Cricket with a babysitter for more than an hour or so at a time. Using her new-mother nervousness as an excuse, Pat left so she could follow Lorrayne. When she caught up with her she asked, "What in the world is the matter?"

Without flinching Lorrayne said, "It's Robbie, he's stopped eating."

After Christmas, Robbie had refused to eat anything except for one half of an orange a day. She was lucky if he went to school twice a week, although he still visited with Dr. Nelson. The doctor had revealed that he had received his discharge orders. He and his family would be leaving Schilling in the spring. Dr. Nelson had been Robbie's lifeline. *What will happen to him after the doctor leaves?* But that was still a few months away. Robbie would be better by then. She had never written Bob about their son, not wanting to burden him with family problems while he was away. What could he have done about it anyway? You can't hug a child from the other side of the world.

Lorrayne returned home from the meeting to find Robbie in the same position in front of the television as she had left him hours before: lying on the sofa staring at the screen. He had not moved. The only thing that had changed was the program on the TV, now airing the nightly news, and one half of the orange she had left out for him was gone. The rest of his lunch—a sandwich, chips, milk, and the other half of the orange—lay dried out on the coffee table.

Lorrayne took off her hat, gloves, and coat. Time to fix dinner. Sloppy Joes. She would make Sloppy Joes for dinner. Both boys loved the juicy, ground beef and spicy barbecue sauce sandwiches. Robbie especially liked them. Next to dumplings, the messy sandwiches were his favorite. Most of time he could gobble up two heaping buns with a big glass of milk. She was sure he would not turn away as she began preparing supper.

Terry walked into the kitchen first after Lorrayne called the boys to the table for dinner. On the way he poked Robbie. "Come on, Mom said supper's ready." Despite Lorrayne's pleas for him to come and eat, Robbie never moved.

Later that evening, after the boys went to bed, Lorrayne sat at the kitchen table writing a letter to Bob. Everything was fine at home. Schilling was growing. The thrift shop would open soon. Her next project was to open the pool. She put her pen down. *Should I tell him about Robbie? No, I can handle it.* She wrote that the boys were doing well. Lorrayne finished the letter, folded it, stuffed it in airmail envelope, and stamped it. She sat motionless, more afraid than she had ever been in her entire life.

A week or so later Lorrayne returned home feeling extremely tired—more tired than she had been in a long time. The day had been filled with meetings and had ended with a visit to the beauty parlor. Before her hair appointment she had met with the couple who ran Salina's Salvation Army to discuss the Waiting Wives Club. The husband and wife team had embraced the women at Schilling. Lorrayne had come to depend on them for organizational advice and they had already helped her lay the groundwork for the thrift shop.

The day was spent filling out paperwork, going over what steps to take to make the wives club a recognized nonprofit organization. By the time she got home she had bylaws, budgets, and mission statements scrolling in her head.

She walked into the house. Robbie was lying on the couch watching the news. She called for Terry, but he must have finished his homework and gone out to practice with his buddies in the Drum and Bugle Corps. She was exhausted, but had to fix dinner. What else could she do to get her son to eat something more than an orange? She had cooked and baked everything he liked. Still, the boy refused food. In a blink she rationalized her tiredness to busy days of running nonstop and worrying about Robbie, whose baby fat was melting from his body faster than the snowman in the backyard.

Before bed, Lorrayne finished the organizational chart, drafted a mission statement, scribbled down some bylaws, and came up with a budget. She looked in on the boys. Terry was still awake reading. "Turn off the light and go to sleep," she told her eldest. "It's late."

In Robbie's room she had to dodge the model airplanes scattered all over the place. He loved to build models. *Maybe,* she leaned over his bed to make sure he was still breathing, *I'll surprise him with a new model tomorrow.*

The next day Lorrayne convinced Robbie to go to school, telling him his teacher missed him in class. Robbie liked his teacher, so he dressed, took the orange out of his lunch bag, and got on the bus without eating breakfast. Lorrayne had already dressed, but had to scramble if she was to accomplish anything before the meeting with the Waiting Wives Club.

Five new families had moved into her neighborhood and, if she had the time, she wanted to welcome them to Schilling. She never stayed long at their homes, maybe half a cup of coffee per visit, but it gave her a chance to tell the women about the Waiting Wives Club, which she hoped they would join. "The more the merrier." And the more likely the group could get things done.

Sometimes she asked Pat or one of the other girls to go with her to meet the new families. If they could not go for the initial visit, they always volunteered to drop off some part of a dinner later on. One of the first things the women agreed upon doing when new families moved in was to bring over dinner. Members of the Waiting Wives Club would make one thing: the meat or a casserole, potatoes or rice, the vegetables, and someone would bring a dessert. But the community was growing so fast the existing members could not keep up with all the families.

By the time she arrived at the meeting the wives were debating the club's motto. The conversation went something like this: "Oh, learn to labor and wait." Or "Those who wait, also serve." Coming up with the two slogans, the first a line from Longfellow's poem "The Psalm of Life" and the second coming from off the top of one of the women's heads, had not been terribly difficult; deciding between the two posed more of a problem.

"One seems like all we do is work and wait around for something to happen," one woman offered.

"Well, that's what we do, isn't it?" ventured another. "Hell, we wait for our husbands to come home, and we work our butts off making sure our lives are as normal as can be considering we never stay in one place long enough to grow roots. Two of my kids were born in Africa where we barely had running water. I couldn't wait to move away from there. So, yeah, we *do* labor and we *do* wait."

"Yes, but labor and wait doesn't seem as honorable as wait and serve," said another wife, obviously on the side of the first wife to speak up. "Using the word *serve* makes it seem more like we have a purpose," she added. "You know, like we serve our country, too."

"Sure," another said, "we wait for our husbands, then we serve our husbands, then we serve our kids, why not say we serve our country? We're serving everyone else for crying out loud."

The women reached a compromise. When the sign at the front gate was installed in the first week of February 1966, the motto published by the *Salina Journal* read, "Those Who Wait, Also Serve." When the first official Waiting Wives Club meeting was held later in the month, the motto used by the press was "Oh, Learn to Labor and Wait."

The meeting, which was held at the elementary school, was a smashing success. A delegation of local figures from the Salina City Commission and the mayor's office, a USO representative from Junction City, and the deputy commander of Fort Riley attended the tea that preceded the meeting. Mrs. Margaret Scanlan returned to the base to pour for the members of the club and their guests, which included many of the new wives. A CBS television crew filmed the festivities. The reporter interviewed several of the women, adding an air of importance to the club's first meeting. Over fifty women joined the club that evening. With the increase in membership, the Waiting Wives Club of Schilling Manor grew from a small clique of women to an impressive organization with concrete objectives.

The primary goal of the Waiting Wives Club, as written out by Lorrayne and approved by the membership, was to provide fellowship and activities for the women. The club was a meeting ground to share friendships, activities such as bridge, ceramics, dressmaking, interior decorating, or anything else they could come up with to pass the long days of waiting.

The most essential program of the Waiting Wives Club was that of mutual assistance. Members of the club agreed to lend a helping hand to any wife and her family in the case of illness, accident, or other emergencies—including in the event of the death of her husband. The women offered babysitting, food, comfort, sympathy, and assistance in making any kind of arrangements that had to be made. No wife in crisis need feel alone.

Other goals of the club included volunteering in the Salina community and planning fund-raisers to help offset the needs of Schilling Manor families.

Lorrayne returned home feeling that the meeting had gone

well, but she forgot all about all the wives club business when she saw Robbie on the couch watching television. The next morning she removed the TV from the living room, putting it in her bedroom. No longer would she allow the boys free access. The days of droning war reports, the drumbeat of death tolls, and silly commercials were over.

Bonnie

ANOTHER TELEGRAM

(1969)

Bonnie and the children returned to Schilling Manor from Harbor Beach when summer ended. Another commander, Colonel Miller, had replaced the old one and Major McKain, the community services officer and psychiatrist, had arrived. Another Christmas came and went. So did Easter and one more summer in Michigan. Two years of birthdays went by, celebrated with lots of little friends—different ones every year. The couch was no longer new. Bonnie helped organized fundraisers. She taught Sunday school and attended meetings of the Protestant Women's Group. She was present at the boys' sports events and went to dance lessons with Colleen. Bonnie kept in close touch with her casualty officer in Washington. The children grew and everyone looked older. Men had landed on the moon. Styles had changed. America had changed. But Bonnie's life had remained at a standstill, shot down, lost somewhere on the perimeter of a rubber plantation on a summer day four years earlier.

* * *

To the side that faces the world, Bonnie was a busy mom engaged in the care of her children. But inside her calm exterior she ached to hear from her husband. No new information about him had surfaced. Her casualty officer told her that our government was doing what it could to find out news about Bruce. She believed him. But more than thirteen hundred men were missing somewhere in Indochina. Didn't anyone know what had happened to them?

Our government advised the families of the POWs and MIAs to wait it out, lay low. Do not talk to the press while negotiations were taking place. In the early days of the conflict, officials suggested that to mention the men's names might increase their torment, putting them in worse harm's way than they already were. So Bonnie waited, making life as normal as she could for their children, living for the day Bruce would come home.

In early November, President Nixon appeared on prime-time TV. America would continue its "commitment in Vietnam until the Communists agreed to negotiate a fair and honorable peace or until the South Vietnamese were able to defend themselves." He had a plan for peace. It would not succeed unless he had the support of "the great silent majority of my fellow Americans." He ended the speech with an appeal to the American people. "Let us be united for peace. Let us also be united against defeat. Because let us understand: North Vietnam cannot defeat or humiliate the United States. Only Americans can do that."

Nixon failed to include the plight of the American POWs/MIAs in his talk to the nation. The silence reverberated throughout Schilling Manor and the extended community of American families and advocates of POWs and MIAs. What was the silence doing to help the men? Aside from a smattering of reports about the treatment of prisoners published in local newspapers, little was known about the men North Vietnam held captive. Nothing about the American men captured or missing in South Vietnam. A column from the *New Haven Register,* written by Jack Anderson, suggested, based on insider information, that "actually the North Vietnamese are sensitive to world opinion and probably take better care of the publicized prisoners. The great Pentagon hush-up seems to be aimed less to protect the prisoners than to protect the authorities from criticism."

After Nixon's telecast, some family members of prisoners and missing men began writing to the president, asking him to make public the dire situation of the soldiers. Bonnie, too, began to wonder how silence protected the men. But she trusted the reassurances from the Department of Defense Casualty Office. She was not one of the many to write a letter following Nixon's speech even though there had been no news of Bruce since the report of "a big American who spoke Vietnamese" was put in his file the year after he went missing. The report allowed for Bruce's scheduled promotions and Bonnie's receipt of his monthly pay.

And it was this document that gave Bonnie hope. She knew in her heart that Bruce was alive. At the same time, she feared for him. What condition was he in? The North Vietnamese, the Viet Cong, and the National Liberation Front (NLF) had persisted in their refusal to release a list of prisoners. They claimed that they need not be held to the Geneva Convention because America, in its persistent aggression against the people of Vietnam, was the one to blame for the condition of U.S. soldiers.

But where was Bruce? Somewhere in the south, maybe only a few miles from where his helicopter went down? Sometimes, when her mind wandered through the possibilities, she even thought he might be in Russia. He had knowledge of a then secret, nuclear weapon—the Davy Crockett—and had even been in Nevada at the test sight, standing next to Maxwell Taylor and Robert Kennedy in the summer of 1962. If the Russians had somehow found out that Bruce knew about the weapon, then found out that the Viet Cong had captured him, then maybe he was part of some kind of trade between America's enemies.

Was Bonnie thinking of all the possibilities when a knock at the door on December 8 interrupted her routine? The afternoon had turned cold and cloudy. A chill was in the air; snow seemed imminent. Perhaps it was one of the neighbors needing a shoulder and a cup of hot coffee. Bonnie answered the door: Western Union. Another telegram. Another urgent message. It, too, looked as if it came from Washington. The last time she read a telegram her future had changed, unexpectedly changed from that of a military wife married to an exceptional man off on a mission to save a country and a people that, to some, needed saving, to that of a waiting wife married to an exceptional man lost somewhere in the country he was sent to save. Might this telegram be the one to set her life in motion again, the one to restore her to the life of a military wife, a hero's wife? Or would it launch her future as the widow of a brave man whom she and her children would never see again, except in old black-and-white photos that would gently yellow with time. The images of an eternally youthful Bruce would eventually be put away in a box and stored away, retrieved every so often over the years by her and the children as they grew older than their father, their superhero. As Bonnie looked at the telegram her heart beat a familiar rhythm—*I know Bruce is alive.*

Bonnie opened the telegram—1600 Pennsylvania Avenue ... The White House. The message was from the offices of Richard M. Nixon, President of the United States of America. It was addressed to Mrs. Bruce Johnson, 138 Denver, Schilling Manor, Salina, Kansas. Inside was an invitation for her to meet with President Nixon on December 12 at the White House. A liaison from the Department of the Army would be in touch with her to give her the details and help her make travel arrangements.

The phone rang almost immediately; it was a representative from the Department of the Army in Washington telling her that she and a few other wives and families of prisoners of war and lost men were invited to meet the president on Friday afternoon, the twelfth of December. Accommodations would be made for her. A military sedan would pick her up at Andrews Air Force Base.

Could she attend?

Bonnie hesitated. *The twelfth. When was that? Friday. How can I be ready by Friday? That means I'd have to fly out on Thursday. What about the children? It is impossible to get away. The president of the United States. What would I say? What would I do?*

Bonnie, caught off guard by the immediacy of the invitation told the young man on the phone, "Well, you know, I really don't know if I'll be able to do that."

Beverly

_____

THE NEWS

(1971)

At Schilling Manor the wives waited for Walter Cronkite to explain the larger context of war during the evening news. Most days they gathered in someone's living room soon after five o'clock. The woman felt better when they were together, waiting for their daily debriefing on events that had unfolded in Vietnam during the previous twenty-four hours. Along with the arrival of the mail, the half hour starting at five-thirty was the most important time of the day. The reporter always arrived on time.

The women trusted Cronkite to tell them the truth about Vietnam. He spoke in tones suggesting care and concern for them and their husbands. Even when the news was peppered with death tolls and failed peace talks, he seemed to single out each wife in a voice only she could hear—*Yes, Beverly, bombs exploded close to Saigon, but don't worry, Donald is safe,* or *It's okay, Lori,*

Jack wasn't in that firefight. He was like an uncle with kindly eyes, a gentle smile, a reassuring voice, and with arms that stretched through the glass to embrace those on the waiting side of war.

One night in March the wives gathered in my mother's living room. Though they had known one another only a short time, had diverse backgrounds and educations, were of various ages, and had husbands of different ranks, they had forged a sisterhood with one thing in common. Each was alone and desperate for information about her husband. Any kids that tagged along stayed outside to play with friends, depleting their day's allotment of energy in the lingering moments of dusk.

The ladies talked about letters they received from their husbands, teachers at school, new classes offered at the community center, and the number of days left until R&R or the final return of their men. They moved easily from the kitchen to the living room where my mother had deliberately clustered chairs in full view of the television set. Younger children needing the security of their mother's touch rested on their laps.

If I was around I sometimes leaned on my favorite spot at the corner of the wall where the L shape of the dining room and living room connected. Once in position I could shift back and forth on my feet and tie and untie knots in my long, black hair until the news was over.

Sitting comfortably in the living room, the women sipped their drinks while waiting for the news to begin. Nancy, the wife of a major, drank scotch and always sat in the burnt-orange rocker. She told everybody that her doctor ordered her to have at least one drink a day as a remedy for the hole in her heart.

Bobby Jo, who almost always wore a kaftan, and probably had a beer, was joined on the beige and brown hide-a-bed sofa by Lori, who drank cup after cup of coffee. Their husbands were captains.

A ginger ale with ice rested on the *zabuton* table next to Marie, another major's wife, who sat on the overstuffed, olive hassock. She was a prim woman who wore out-of-style, below-the-knee dresses and resembled the woman in the painting *American Gothic*. Her son, Anthony, a small, pale toddler, lounged on her lap. My mother may have had a beer or coffee and sat in the chair that matched the rocker but did not rock.

Eventually the familiar music of the evening news quieted the women. Their attention was pulled from one another to the dramas unfolding in the world. Our golden drapes shimmered as the early spring sun slipped from the sky, casting the women in an unrehearsed tableau. They waited for Uncle Walter's introduction to the lead story, listening carefully for the names of the battalions and companies participating in the day's campaigns. Did he say First Brigade, Fifth Infantry? Silence.

The camera cut to a live report from Vietnam and the quiet front of 133 Phoenix Street, Schilling Manor, Kansas, in the heart of America, entered the thick jungle of a noisy war waged thousands of miles away. A reporter was in the middle of his introduction when the whump-whump-whump of a Huey descended on the scene. It was an unexpected interruption in his story and its roar could not be ignored. Along with the music of the Doors and Jimi Hendrix, the sound of helicopters was the Vietnam War's underscore. The wind from the rotors seemed to shatter the television glass as tropical winds gushed forth. For a moment the wives breathed the same air as their husbands.

Nancy placed her scotch on the table, moving to the edge of the chair. The women leaned closer to the action. Noise drowned out the voice of the reporter. Rotor-wash kicked up hurricanes of dust. The newsman ducked for cover against the tempest and the wives' skin crawled with goose bumps. Necks strained to see what was happening. What was going on? Bobby

Jo wondered if it was her husband's company. Wait, did they say Special Forces? Little Anthony's mother shushed his sudden demand for food.

The camera focused on the drama. Soldiers carrying machine guns ran toward the chopper. Other soldiers with red crosses on their arms entered the frame. Medics. Wounded.

The Vietnam War had infiltrated our living room.

The reporter attempted an interview with a lieutenant rushing toward the scene. He was shunned as the officer ran toward the action. The helicopter hovered above the ground before finally touching down. Soldiers on the ground pulled the wounded out of the black hole. Bandages dripped with blood.

The women watched as mouths gasped for breath.

Clenched fists and jaws belied agonizing pain. Arms clutched heads or held together exploded stomachs. Devastated bodies were unloaded from the belly and the side baskets of the aircraft. Less than one minute had passed since the chopper flew into the scene when it took off again, its rotors casting off dead men's souls on the way to another rescue mission.

Movement slowed and the scene became silent. The reporter turned to the camera and told the women that he could not tell them where exactly the injured came from. He promised to investigate further and report back when more information became available. Anthony, as if to release the tension in the living room, cried again for food.

Walter Cronkite returned to the screen. The wrinkles on his brow seemed deeper, his eyes more intense. The one-minute drama had aged him. His duty to report to the women had turned into an unpleasant, even painful task. My sister went into the kitchen, returning with crackers for the crying child. The women watched the rest of the news.

In a one-hour battle in the Quang Tin Province, Communist forces overran a U.S. artillery base leaving thirty-three Americans dead and seventy-six wounded.

In Los Angeles a jury decreed the death penalty for Charles Manson in the Tate-LaBianca murders.

President Nixon's approval rating falls to the lowest point thus far in his term.

A court-martial jury convicts Lieutenant William Calley, Jr., of the premeditated murder of twenty-two South Vietnamese in the village of My Lai.

The U.S. military death toll is approaching the 55,000 mark.

Cronkite closed the half hour. *And that's the way it is!*
The sun had set. The drapes, no longer translucent, shielded the women from the darkening night. Someone switched on the lamps. Lori called the children in from outdoors. The news was replaced by a commercial. A line of young people dressed in tie-dyed shirts, hip-huggers, wraparound skirts, and peasant blouses held hands. They were a human chain across a verdant field.

I'd like to teach the world to sing in perfect harmony

The wives lingered over their drinks.

Grow apple trees and honeybees and snow-white turtledoves

Fears about husbands were buried beneath requests for food from hungry children.

I'd like to build the world a home and furnish it with love

My mother invited everyone for dinner. A couple of boxes of Chef Boyardee make-your-own-pizza, a can of B&B mushrooms, and some pepperoni provided a make-do meal. Gail and I volunteered as chefs. The women refilled their drinks as the children took over the TV in search of cartoons. That evening, the women stayed later than usual, reluctant to face the night alone.

Lorrayne

———

DRIED SQUID AND JELL-O
(1966)

There are weeks in Kansas that are so cold nothing moves but the wind, the only sound its wail advancing on city streets from deep within the plains. It was during such a week that Al, the community's mailman, backtracked to Lorrayne's house after completing his deliveries. Lorrayne vaguely recalls the details. The mailman explained to her that a few days earlier a Korean wife, whose name might have been Kimmie, had decided to walk from her quarters into Salina with her four-year-old son and infant daughter. He told Lorrayne that he had passed Kimmie on the sidewalk outside of her home. He had suggested that it was too cold for the children to be outside. But Kimmie, who did not understand or speak English very well, nodded and continued on her way.

When Al handed Kimmie her mail the next day the baby was lying on the couch while her brother ran around playing cowboys and Indians. The little boy had pointed his plastic pistol at anything—the chair, a stool, his mother—and yelled, "Bang, bang. You're dead." When the boy moved toward his sister, Kimmie rushed to grab him, steering him away from the baby. Her son would cry for a moment, then return to his play.

Al said he suspected something was wrong when Kimmie did not come to the door holding the baby like she usually did when collecting the mail. A day later he glanced into the house. The child was still on the couch. Unusual, but the little boy was hopping around on a stick horse with a cowboy hat on, yelling, "Hi Ho, Silver!" and Kimmie had presented him with the same generous smile she always did when given her letters. Al continued on his route.

On the next day the baby was in the same position on the couch, wearing the same clothes, looking paler than the day before. The boy, still running around pretending to chase bad guys, crashed into the couch. When the baby did not move, Al was certain something was wrong. He gave Kimmie her mail. "Is everything all right?" She shook her head, shrugged her shoulders, unable to understand his question. Al positioned his arms in a cradle and rocked an imaginary baby repeating the words *Baby okay? Baby okay?*

The young mother glanced furtively behind her to the prone infant, bobbed her head up and down, answered the mailman's question with a torrent of okays, smiled, and then closed the door.

Al knew that Lorrayne had been the driving force behind anything that happened at Schilling, so he said, "I think you ought to look in on the Korean lady," adding that he was "fairly sure that her baby might have passed on."

The mailman left Lorrayne alone to figure out what to do. She called Pat. She might be better able to comfort the mother since she had also lost a child. Bundled in wool against the midmorning chill, with kerchiefs protecting their hair from the winter wind, the friends made their way to Kimmie's quarters looking like Welcome Wagon ladies.

Kimmie answered the door to her smiling neighbors. She returned their friendly gesture, inviting them into her home. Sit. Sit. The women sat in the living room on spindly, Army-issue chairs.

The pale, gray body lay motionless on the couch.

Lorrayne and Pat were immediately flanked by the unfamiliar odor of foreign food. Kimmie's son, wearing underpants, his cowboy hat, and a Roy Rogers gun belt, stood behind his mother. He glared at the strangers. One hand clenched his mother's leg, the other held the handle of his gun. She shooed the child away with several clicks of her tongue and a short burst of discordant vowels and consonants that Lorrayne thought sounded more like a record playing backward than any language she had heard. The boy ran down the hall toward the back of the house.

Kimmie turned to her guests, smiled, and backed into the kitchen, leaving them alone with her daughter.

Lorrayne and Pat watched the body for some sign of life. In the background they heard Kimmie muttering softly in the kitchen, the sound of a spoon scraping glass, the rip of a cellophane bag. They looked at each other. Nodded. The child was dead.

Lorrayne took a deep breath and approached the couch. Kimmie came into the living room as Lorrayne bent down to study the baby. The mother shouted, "No. No. No. No touch babee. Sit. Sit." She tightened her fist into her stomach and then jerked it forward as if throwing something toward the sky, shaking her head and repeating, "Bad. Bad." Lorrayne, bewildered, retreated to her chair.

The smile returned to Kimmie's face as she presented her guests with a snack of dried squid and Jell-O.

The three women sat in a semicircle facing the dead child.

Kimmie continued to smile, occasionally pointing to the food. "Eat. Eat." Lorrayne stared at the shriveled squid. Pat closed her eyes as if in doing so she might escape from the withered infant. In the back of the house they could hear the bang-bangs of the little boy's gun as he hunted down his enemies.

Minutes ticked by like hours. Lorrayne and Pat wanted desperately to put a blanket over the baby. They used monosyllables and gestures to explain. Kimmie was oblivious to their appeal, shaking her head in confusion. Her smile was lost in the effort to communicate. Whenever one of her guests approached the infant, Kimmie thrashed her arms in fear, pleading, "No touch. No touch."

The boy rode in and out of the scene grabbing hunks of the dried-up squid before his mother chased him back into his room. Lorrayne and Pat decided that they needed to find someone who spoke Korean. Lorrayne stayed with Kimmie while Pat went home to telephone the local universities. After a while she located a Korean professor who agreed to be Kimmie's interpreter. It was he who finally convinced the distraught and frightened mother that the baby had to be taken away and prepared for burial.

He explained, "It is the way they do things in the United States," and that "everything will be all right."

Only a *Naerim Mudang*, a Korean shaman, can touch the dead and not be swept into the white light of eternity. The holy person must perform the rite of Chinogwe-Kut to guide the deceased spirit safely to the other world. Until then, evil swirls around the body looking for other souls to take. That was what Kimmie believed. It was what her mother believed, and her father, and everyone else in her village back in Korea.

At least that was the rumor that flew around Schilling Manor after the community found out about Kimmie's dead child. The young mother was quickly swept up in American customs she did not understand, her own traditions surrendered to an alien culture. The Red Cross arranged for her husband to return from Vietnam. By the time he arrived a few days later, Lorrayne had organized a group of wives to clean Kimmie's house, take care of her young cowboy, and provide breakfast, lunch, and dinner to the family until they sorted out their plans.

On a snowy February morning eight or ten wives stood outside Kimmie's home, huddled together against the freezing wind, reliving the tragedy of the week's events. The women were waiting for Kimmie and her husband to lead the caravan that would take them to Fort Riley, where their daughter was to be buried.

One or two of the women had agreed to go because they did not feel right not going. Others went because they wanted to participate in the drama and provide their friends on the bowling league or the pinochle club with a blow-by-blow account of the funeral. Most went because they felt compassion for the family and sorrow for the lost child.

As the convoy filed out of the neighborhood, Al the mailman stood on the corner, watching as the Vietnam War's first casualty at Schilling Manor drove by with her family and the small troupe of women.

Bonnie

INVITATIONS

(1969)

It was Christmastime. The children's church recital was in a week and Colleen still needed practice singing "Away in the Manger." Bonnie had not bought a tree yet, and though she had many presents, none were wrapped. Cards needed writing and addressing and stamping. Pies needed baking. The weather was miserable. And now, in the middle of everything, she had to think about taking an unplanned trip to Washington.

Who would watch the children? It was too late to ask their grandparents to fly down from Michigan, but how could she not go? In his telegram President Nixon said there would not be advance publicity, that her invitation came at the last moment "because of the personal nature of this visit with you and the other wives and mothers."

Surely it meant that he had something important to tell them.

What does one wear to meet the president of the United States?

She and Mary Lou Miller had modeled some lovely suit-dresses at the Waiting Wives Club Fashion Show. The last time she passed Robert's she noticed that two or three of them were displayed in the window. She could run downtown and pick one up on her way home from her appointment at her hairdresser the next day.

Bonnie decided to go to Washington to meet the president. The invitation hinted at something—a change in policy, perhaps, or strategy. She needed to be there to hear the news.

On the morning Bonnie flew to meet the president, she could not help but wonder if the North Vietnamese had released more names of POWs; maybe Nixon intended to tell her the good news in person—that Bruce had made the list and was alive in a prison camp. If his name was published, if the world knew that he was alive, the enemy might treat him better. Besides having Bruce home, knowing that he was in a camp somewhere, no matter how deplorable the conditions, would be the greatest gift she and the children could ever receive.

Bonnie left Schilling Manor unaware that other families of prisoners and the missing, some led by POW wife Sybil Stockdale, had begun speaking out, writing letters, and generally demanding that the American government do something publicly about the condition of their men. The families were tired of waiting and keeping quiet, especially since no one had proved that the men were benefiting from their silence. In a letter to Nixon, Mrs. Stockdale addressed their concerns: "Many of the families were deeply disappointed that you did not mention the plight of the prisoners in your message to the nation on November 3, 1969. We are at the point where we feel that we must meet with you personally so that we may be reassured about your own personal interest and thoughts pertaining to the most desperate straits in which our husbands and sons find themselves. If you can find time to see a representative group from our number, we would be deeply grateful. We have been and remain your loyal supporters." The pressure was on the Nixon administration. Not only were the antiwar activists calling for answers but now the families were speaking out.

Thirteen days after her letter arrived on the president's desk, Mrs. Stockdale, Bonnie, and twenty-four other relatives handpicked by the U.S. Casualty Office were invited to Washington.

Accommodations had been made for the families at the visiting officer's quarters at Bolling Air Force Base. Bonnie had opted to stay with her aunt Pauline, who had retired to Washington after serving in the diplomatic corps for years. Late in the afternoon on the day she arrived a military sedan picked her up at her aunt's home, whisking her off to a reception and dinner at the Officer's Club.

Bonnie entered an elegant room the size of a small banquet hall. She was immediately greeted by the women who had arrived before her. The group spoke of the excellent treatment they had received and wondered what it would be like to meet the president. Sybil took the lead. She had been advocating for information on the lost and captured soldiers for a long time. Most of the other wives and mothers had followed the advice of their military liaisons: stay quiet, the government is doing what it can to find your husband or son or father.

Bonnie was impressed with Sybil. The older woman was gracious, articulate, and completely at ease in the company of men that included Admiral Josiah McKain of the Navy, and General Lewis Walt of the Marines. General William Westmoreland of the Army attended the reception, as did Secretary of State William Rogers, Secretary of Defense Melvin Laird, an assortment of undersecretaries, and even more aides and assistants.

The atmosphere in the room was charged with a kind of heady energy. The men shuffled every which way, dancing around women who had lost a significant part of their lives because of the war, women who were eager to know what Washington was doing about their men. Wives and mothers who had no idea if their loved ones were alive, let alone what condition they might be in, chatted with the politicians like pros. At one point Sybil noticed Secretary of State Rogers standing alone, looking very shy. She introduced herself and said, "Come on, Mr. Secretary. Don't be nervous. I'll introduce you to the wives."

Conversations between the guests always came back to one topic: What was the government doing to secure the release of their loved ones?

During the evening Bonnie was briefed by an Army liaison. At ten o'clock on the following morning, President Nixon would speak about his stand on the POW/MIA situation. A press conference would commence directly after their meeting.

If Bonnie was disappointed to learn that the meeting did not include an announcement of a list of names released by the VC, or that no one had new information on Bruce, she did not show it. After the dinner and the speeches by the different departments of government offering reassurances to the families that all efforts were being made on behalf of American prisoners and the missing men, Bonnie traveled back to her aunt's house wondering exactly what kind of efforts were being made on behalf of Bruce and the other men, especially those missing in South Vietnam.

The next morning Bonnie joined the other women at the White House. The group was escorted into the Roosevelt Room. The room was windowless, warmed by a crackling fire, with lovely pieces of American frontier art displayed on dark-paneled walls. It was not a large room, more formal than intimate, the kind of place where people meet to discuss grave subjects such as the lost men of war. Mrs. Nixon entered the room first, shaking hands and greeting each wife to her home with an earnest concern for her well-being.

Moments later a voice announced the arrival of the president. Everyone hushed as Nixon, dressed in a dark suit with a steel-gray tie, approached the podium, hands clasped together, shoulders tensed, choosing not to mingle with his guests before addressing them with his formal comments. Only the occasional snap and crackle from the burning fire punctuated his phrases.

> *Insofar as the treatment of prisoners is concerned, it would probably not be inaccurate to say that the record in this war is one of the most unconscionable in the history of warfare.*
>
> *I assure you, in reaching a settlement of the war, first, that an integral part of any settlement that is agreed to must be a settlement which is satisfactory on the prisoner issue and, second, that clearly apart from reaching an overall settlement of the war that this Government will do everything that it possibly can to separate out the prisoner issue and have it handled as it should be, as a separate issue on a humane basis.*
>
> *While we all know that there is disagreement in this country about the war in Vietnam and while there is dissent about it on several points, that on this issue, the treatment of prisoners of war, that there can be and there should be no disagreement.*

The president concluded his official statement, then took a few questions from the women. He was noticeably uncomfortable, appearing as if he would have rather been anywhere else in the world than in the Roosevelt Room with twenty-six wives and mothers looking to him for answers.

He had no answers.

At the end of his comments Nixon announced that a press

conference with five of the women would immediately take place in the pressroom. Bonnie did not attend the press conference. She remained behind with the other women to discuss what the president's words meant. Despite their respect for their host, he had done nothing to reassure them that everything would be okay for their men. Yet, thanks to the president's invitation, the women had an opportunity to meet, share their stories, console one another, and promise to stay in touch.

Bonnie never doubted Bruce was alive, but now, after meeting the other wives in Washington, she was no longer alone in her belief. It was reassuring for Bonnie to know that there were other women like her who believed with every breath they took that their men would return home. They were women of a kindred heart.

Living at Schilling was wonderful because few of the children had fathers, at least for a time. But even though all of the women were waiting wives, differences remained between Bonnie's family and the other families. The distinctions were sometimes as subtle as the quiet observations of a mother who felt every tremble in her children's hearts, or experienced the trickle of tears down their cheeks as if they were her own. Unlike their friends, her children did not know when their father would come home. Ordinary childhood activities like baking or writing letters affected their lives. Colleen's Brownie troop had made cookies at their last meeting to send to their fathers for Christmas. Colleen brought hers home, proud of her work and with a warning to her brothers: Don't eat them, they're for Daddy. The gift remained in the refrigerator.

Bonnie and the children had sent stacks of letters to Vietnam in the years since Bruce went missing. Every one of them disappeared—never delivered, never returned. Packages were different. For four years Bonnie had sent a Christmas package to Bruce. Five or six months after she posted them, when the holidays were a memory, the packages were returned marked "refused." She stored the packages in a closet, like a hidden altar of faith. But now that the president had made a stand, maybe a fifth package would not be added to the grim collection of travel-worn, brown-paper-wrapped boxes that had traveled to Algiers, and then to an address in Cambodia, and then back to Kansas.

Bonnie was eager to return home to the children so she could tell them about her visit to the White House. She appreciated being invited. It meant a great deal to her to know that the people running the government cared enough about the fate of the men—the fate of Bruce—to come out personally to meet the families. If they were willing to speak out, maybe she would find out where her husband was taken after his helicopter went down. Colleen did not remember her father. Bryan never said much about him. Bruce clearly remembered, perhaps missing his father the most because he knew what he had lost.

It would mean so much to the children if Bruce came home.

Bonnie arrived home on Saturday morning. She told the children that no, no one knew where their daddy was, but now more people than ever before were trying to find him, and that no matter where he was, he loved them and missed them as much as they loved and missed him.

A few days after returning to Schilling, during the week of December 15, Bonnie's telephone rang. On the other end of the line a gentleman identified himself as a representative of H. Ross Perot. He told Bonnie that Mr. Perot was organizing a flight to Paris for the women and children of men missing in Vietnam. Would she and her children like to go? The flight leaves from Kennedy Airport in New York City on December 24 and would return the following afternoon. Our hope, he told her, is to have a group of women meet with the North Vietnamese delegation on

Christmas Day. Telegrams had already been sent. The Braniff was chartered. Mr. Perot would pay for everything.

Bonnie had heard of Perot and his efforts to communicate with the North Vietnamese regarding the treatment of the prisoners of war. He was very wealthy, yet appeared to have honorable intentions regarding the prisoners in Vietnam. Bonnie did not think long before she agreed to go on the trip.

"Good," said the gentleman. "One of your neighbors, Margaret Clark, has also agreed to go. We'll make arrangements for you to fly to New York City together where you'll join over one hundred other families who hope to find out information about their loved ones. The flight is named the 'Spirit of Christmas.'"

Welcome aboard!

A trip to Paris with the children? Perhaps it would be a memorable Christmas after all!

The Committee

THE NEIGHBOR

Two weeks had passed since the last committee meeting. The women had postponed their last session because former president Dwight Eisenhower had died. All of the journalists, dignitaries, and statesmen had flown into Schilling Manor's airport. The Waiting Wives Club had volunteered to host a "freshening-up center" in the ballroom of the Army Community Services building for the family members of the press who would not be accompanying the reporters to the funeral in Abilene.

The women had baked over one hundred breakfast treats and snacks with barely a day's notice.

On the morning of the funeral they were up before dawn and ready to serve their guests when the first plane landed on the tarmac. The hostesses brewed over five hundred cups of coffee for the adults watching the funeral on the television and served enough Kool-Aid to the children to fill the swimming pool. At the end of the day the fashion show committee was so tired that they decided to wait until the next week to meet.

* * *

Four weeks remained until the show when the group met at the captain's wife's house a little after lunchtime. The former Japanese citizen had made snacks for the members in case they hadn't had a chance to grab a bite before the meeting. She had discovered that most Americans loved *gyoza*, little rice dough pockets stuffed with pork and vegetables dipped in tamari, and maki rolls as long as they were made without raw fish. Cookies, hard candy, coffee, and soda pop accompanied the Japanese food. She had even placed several Viceroy cigarettes in the cigarette caddy on the coffee table. The holder came with a matching lighter that she had recently filled with butane. The chapter entitled "The Social Side of Army Life" in *The Officer's Guide* had advised that

> *The wife of an officer exerts a powerful influence upon the success of his career. In many assignments her personality, grace, character, and capacities are a strong and necessary complement to her husband. She can be an asset or a burden; an inspiration and help, or a stone around his neck. Not all women are cut out to be good Army wives. The majority succeed because they see that which is fine and rewarding beyond the hardships and inconveniences of their military life. They are the ones who help make the history of our country through her help and inspiration they give their husbands.*

The captain's wife took everything in the book seriously and worked hard to become the perfect American officer's wife.

Everyone was on time for the meeting except for the sergeant major's wife. While waiting for her to arrive the women gratefully accepted their hostess's invitation to eat and talked casually about how to set up the community center. When the sergeant major's wife finally arrived she was all aflutter. She said, "I am so sorry for being late, but, girls, you are not going to believe what I just heard from one of my neighbors. I spent hours with her, listening to her talk, and drinking so much coffee I'm about ready to float away. I am so heartbroken for her."

The rest of the women were a little surprised to hear their friend talk about her neighbor since none of them had ever heard her initiate any conversations about anyone. Every one of them, almost at once, responded "What happened?" "Did her husband get killed?" Even if they had not asked what happened, the sergeant major's wife would have had to talk, so upset was she by her friend's situation. She began to tell the story.

"Well, she said the problems began when she hadn't received a letter from her husband in so long she wondered if he remembered that she was still alive. It had been nearly two months since she had heard from him when she decided to drive downtown to the Red Cross to see if they could help her find out where he was and if he was okay."

"I didn't know the Red Cross could do things like that," the lieutenant's wife interrupted.

"Oh sure, they can track 'em down anywhere whether they want to be tracked down or not," the warrant officer's wife said.

"But only in an emergency, and even then it takes a while, sometimes a couple of days," the colonel's wife added.

The sergeant major's wife continued, "That's what happened. After a couple of days she went back and they said they couldn't help her. They explained that they could do many things to help families, but what they could not do was make a soldier write home. They said they were certain he was alive because her monthly allotment checks had not stopped and that if anything had happened to him the unit commander would have sent a wire."

The warrant officer's wife piped in, "Maybe her husband is in a situation where he can't write letters. Lots of soldiers have a hard time writing home. I hope you told her she's not alone."

"Wait," said the sergeant major's wife, "that's not the whole story." She continued, "My neighbor told me that after she left the offices she felt so sick and her head pounded so bad that on her way back to Schilling she had to pull the car into a parking lot because she couldn't see the road. She kept thinking, if he were alive why hadn't he written? Was he missing or dead and they forgot to tell her? Did he have amnesia? She was going crazy thinking that her only option was to wait for him to walk through the front door one day and say, 'Hi honey, I'm home from the war, gee, sorry I didn't write. What's for dinner?'" The statement drew a few chuckles from some of the girls until one of them asked, "What did she do?"

"Well," she said, "she knew she couldn't very well sit in the parking lot until she heard from her husband. At the rate things were going she might be there for a very long time, so she got herself together and went home." She continued, "And you know, I think I remember that day because it was so nice out and a bunch of us girls were on lawn chairs when she pulled into her driveway. We invited her over for a drink, but she said no because she had an impossible headache and needed to lie down for a while. We all liked her. Some of us thought she was pretty lucky because she didn't have a bunch of kids to run around after. She always looked so nice. I don't think I ever saw her in curlers, not even to hang out the laundry. And I have never seen her in pants or flats."

"Maybe she's one of those old-fashioned women who's not into women's lib," said the lieutenant's young wife.

"Women's lib schmib," offered the colonel's wife. "Sounds like she simply wants to be a good military wife."

The sergeant major's wife continued, "I thought something was wrong because it seemed like whenever we asked her to do anything, she almost always had an excuse. Heck, thinking back now, all we girls ever talked about was our children and our husbands. She probably got tired of us chattering on and on about stuffy noses and love letters."

The warrant officer's wife said, "Love letters? Well, I'd about fall down dead if I got a love letter from my husband. Unless you consider one I love you, one I miss you, current weather conditions in Vietnam, and a few x's and o's a love letter." A couple of the women smiled, shaking their heads in agreement.

The colonel's wife told the sergeant major's wife, "You know, you're probably right, she might have stayed away for a reason. It's one thing to go a few weeks without a letter, we all have, but to go months without news probably made her feel like everyone pitied her. Or worse, felt relief. As long as someone else hasn't heard from her husband longer than you, then your situation doesn't seem so bad."

"Maybe so," said the sergeant major's wife. "I could tell she was crazy about her husband. Pictures of him were on practically every table. He's a good-looker. One evening she came over to my house for a glass of wine and confided that on the night before he left for Vietnam he promised he would write to her every day. And he did write every day—for the first few months. Then less in the next months, then a trickle, until finally the letters stopped altogether. She couldn't figure out what had happened, which is why she went to the Red Cross in the first place. Oh, I don't know, the story gets so complicated." The committee members encouraged her to go on, fearing that she would stop midstory because she was so overwrought. The sergeant major's wife said, "It is simply the strangest thing I've ever heard in my whole life."

"Tell us the best you can," said the warrant officer's wife.

"I'll try." The wife continued: "One morning Al finally delivered a letter from her husband. When she opened the letter she couldn't believe what he wrote."

"What did he say? Was he all right?" asked the lieutenant's wife.

"Oh, he was more than all right," the wife told the group. "In fact, her husband asked her if they could adopt a war orphan."

"A war orphan? Are you kidding?" asked the colonel's wife.

"I swear that's what he wrote. She even showed me the letter. He said that his company found her wandering around a village they had attacked. They had taken her in and he had grown to care a great deal for her. Then he begged her to forgive him for not writing sooner, but between his duties, trying to make sure the little girl was protected, and then all the work he had to do to find out about bringing her home with him, left him no time to write. Besides, he told her, he wanted to make sure he had all the facts so she wouldn't get her hopes up in case they weren't allowed to adopt a Vietnamese orphan with the war going on and everything. He said he was sorry for not sending a photograph and that he hoped to hear from her soon because he only had a couple of months left on his tour to get through all of the crazy red tape."

"What did she tell him?" asked the warrant officer's wife.

"She was stunned," the sergeant major's wife said. "He had told her he never wanted kids, explaining that he was a career officer, in for life, and that worrying about a family might hurt his chances for promotion. The letter puzzled her and she didn't know what to think. The only thing she cared about was that she wanted her husband to be happy when he came home, so she wrote him, telling him to send the paperwork and that she would sign whatever he wanted her to sign."

"I can't believe anyone would agree to something so strange and from out of the blue. You know it all sounds a little peculiar. There's something else to this, isn't there?" suggested the colonel's wife.

"You won't believe what happened." The sergeant major's wife continued: "They exchanged paperwork and short notes for a while until he wrote and told her he would be home in a couple of weeks with the girl, but that the adoption would not be final until they signed the paperwork in the States."

By now almost all of the cookies were gone and a second pot of coffee was percolating on the stove.

The sergeant major's wife continued: "She had written him to find out the little girl's size so she could make her some dresses, but he had never responded. And you know what I can't believe? I can't believe she never told any of us what was going on. She kept it all to herself for weeks."

The warrant officer's wife was beside herself. "My goodness, well, what happened. I never heard about any little Vietnamese girl coming home with a soldier. It seems to me I would have heard something about that. I can't believe no one told me about this. It's so . . . so . . . big."

"There is a reason why you never heard about it, because when my neighbor met her husband at the airport she nearly passed out when he got off the airplane holding hands with someone that was not the little helpless orphan she had envisioned, but a young woman wearing a skintight minidress, heels, and makeup." This information sent the committee into a tailspin.

"You kidding me," said the captain's wife.

"You mean to tell us that he brought home a Vietnamese woman?" The lieutenant's wife was distraught.

"Are you saying that her husband came home from Vietnam and presented his wife with an adult who was suppose to be their child but was really his girlfriend? Unbelievable. What kind of a jerk would do that?" asked the warrant officer's wife.

"His career is over," exclaimed the colonel's wife.

"No wonder he didn't send her dress size," commented the warrant officer's wife.

"What an asshore," offered the captain's wife, replacing the *l* with an *r*. The sergeant major's wife went on with the story.

"It gets worse. When she met him at the gate, still uncertain as to what was going on, he warded off her kiss by handing her a piece of paper. He wanted a divorce."

"Holy cow," said the group's gossip.

"He told her he would appreciate it if she would sign the papers right away and—get this—he apologized to her, saying that he felt awful about misleading her."

The lieutenant's wife said, "This is too terrible for words."

"But," she continued, "her husband admitted that he had fallen in love and that the adoption was a ruse so he could bring the girl into the country. He had to marry or adopt her as soon as possible or she would be sent back to Vietnam. His plan was to marry her and that she had better not try to stop him."

Some of the women were speechless, but the warrant officer's wife asked, "Oh Lord. What happened next? What did she do? What did they do?"

The sergeant major's wife continued telling the story of her neighbor. "Well, all of them got in the car. He dropped her off at home with the papers and then drove to a local hotel with their so-called daughter. After a few days of pressuring her, she finally gave the papers back to him, signed. The next morning he went to their quarters to pack up his things while she stood by saying nothing, as if she were frozen. After he processed out of Schilling Manor he slipped a note with a twenty-dollar bill attached to it under the door. The note said that she had to be out of the house within the week and not to expect any more allotment checks. He even took their car. And what I still can't believe is that she never said anything to anyone and that none of us knew that this was going on right in front of our noses."

"Oh, that poor girl," offered the colonel's wife. "He ought to be hung upside down from his—and excuse me for saying this girls—upside down from his balls. We have to do something to help her. Where is she now?"

"All this happened a couple of weeks ago. When I talked to her this morning she said that after he left she didn't eat or drink. She was a mess for days. You know what I think? That bastard"—the members were a little shocked to hear her use a cuss word—"cut out her heart."

The lieutenant's wife had tears running down her cheeks. "And no one knew what she was going through?"

"I don't think it was because people hadn't tried to stay in touch with her," said the sergeant major's wife. "I think I even called once. She never answered the telephone until one day when it rang on and off for the entire afternoon. The next day someone knocked on her door. Later on, when the phone rang again, she snapped out of her daze and answered it. The housing officer called wanting to know when she planned to clear quarters. She told the officer she would get back to him. Later that afternoon, around dusk, when she knew we would be indoors tending to the children, she washed her face, tied a kerchief around her head, and walked across the tracks to the commander's office."

The colonel's wife, appalled by what she was hearing, thought out loud, "I wonder if her husband can be brought up on some kind of charges."

No one knew the answer.

The captain's wife said "Ah, smartu girr. Go to Commander Mirrer."

The sergeant major's wife went on, "She said the commander was heading toward his car when she came around the corner. When he saw her he invited her back into his office and asked how he could be of service."

The colonel's wife told the group, "I think he's an excellent commander. Can you imagine what it's like to be the commander of a bunch of women?"

"My neighbor told him the story, then asked if she could stay in her house until she sorted things out. He told her to take all the time she needed, that he would find a way to keep her at Schilling, and as long as she didn't tell anyone, including her neighbors, about the situation no one would be the wiser."

The warrant officer's wife, awed by the fantastic nature of the story said, "I still can't believe I didn't know anything about this."

The colonel's wife added, "When my husband found out who was commanding Schilling Manor he told me that he was well-connected and respected with a lot of friends in high places. I'll bet he took care of everything for her."

The sergeant major's wife said, "Yeah, he did, including arranging for her to receive emergency funds from a local charity. And to top it off, one morning she woke up to discover a car parked in her driveway. The commander had arranged for her to use it until she got on her feet."

The lieutenant's wife asked how the wife was doing.

"It's going to take her some time to recover, but she told me she'll find a job in town to make some money, then she'll decide what to do.

"If I were her," offered the warrant officer's wife, "I'd put out a contract on that . . . that . . . thing that was her husband. In all my born days I have never, ever, heard of anything so disgusting. If my husband ever did something like that to me, I'd castrate him with the dullest catfish knife I could find."

The lieutenant's wife said if something like that ever happened to her she'd "have to kill" herself.

The colonel's wife, noticing the time, said, "Ladies, I think we need to get to work, but how about we take turns making her a covered dish every night. She might appreciate not having to cook while she tries to get her life in order."

The women unanimously agreed, then spent the next half hour deciding on the logistics of the fashion show before they went home to their children.

Beverly

_____

ONE MINUTE

(1971)

My mother and her friends once figured out that they would have to wait over half a million minutes at Schilling Manor before their husbands would return from war. They said that some days lasted an eternity, that hours passed as slowly as winter. Sometimes they would bemoan that even one minute took a lifetime. I did not understand their lament until a day I stayed home from school.

It was midday in spring when the sun shone its brightest, unobstructed by clouds. Front and back doors were open to let in fresh air. Young flowers preened in the sun. Birds sang, bees buzzed, flying around one another like miniature rockets carried on warm breezes. A weatherman might have designated it a perfect spring day.

I was lying on the couch suffering from some sort of now-forgotten ailment when my mother stopped in the middle of making lunch. She went to the front door. No one had knocked, no doorbell had rung. She simply quit stirring the soup as if some-one had whispered a command in her ear, walked to the door, and stared out into the street. When I asked what was wrong she qui-etly said, "There's a sedan in the neighborhood."

I peeked through the blinds on the front window. I did not see a sedan. The street was empty and, except for the gentle trills of the birds, quiet. I was about to ask my mother what she was talk-ing about when I noticed that Lauren's mom had opened her door and stood in the door frame. Then my mother's friend from across the street appeared at her door. She, too, stood in silence. Within moments a woman waited in the threshold of nearly every door. I am not sure if the women ever acknowledged one another. They were experiencing something beyond my under-standing. I knew to stay quiet. Whatever was happening was theirs alone to bear.

The sedan appeared on the corner.

How did they know? Perhaps they had felt that strange tingle in their necks when someone's watching without them knowing. Women had left their ironing and had put down their crafts. Idle chatter and laughter surrendered to the quiet moan of a hundred *oh, nos*. They hung up telephones and shushed young children, ordering them to go to their rooms and play. Prayers were mur-mured sotto voce, lips trembling after each *please God* and *not me*.

The sedan turned, casting our street in eerie twilight and the ominous darkness of my mother's childhood entered our house. I thought about how she relied on her father when she was afraid as a child, but now, this time, she had no one to call to for help. I sat helpless while my mother stood alone, waiting for the shadow to pass.

The car drove as if in slow motion. My heart pounded. The air stilled. It seemed as if the birds ceased chirping, animals scur-ried for a place to hide. The only movement was the shift of a dozen pair of eyes as they followed the sedan.

When it passed the O'Learys' house, Mrs. O'Leary came out on her porch. Mrs. Chandler and Mrs. Miller did the same after it passed their homes. The women remained alert, arms at their sides, making sure the car did not turn around.

I watched my mother in the doorway. She stood straight, afraid, but determined to face the sedan as it advanced toward our house. I joined her. Together we watched as it slowly moved up the street. The men in the car faced forward, avoiding eye contact with the women waiting behind their doors. My mother held her breath but did not waver even as the sedan seemed to slow in front of our house before continuing forward. After it had passed, she stepped out onto the porch, joining the other women as they watched it progress toward its final destination.

In the next few seconds we learned that it was a young lieutenant's wife whose future had been determined by an explosion that had lit up the sky twelve thousand miles away. The only sound in the neighborhood was the echo of car doors reverberating throughout the base as the men continued their mission. When the women felt it was safe to breathe, after the soldiers had entered their neighbor's home, it was like a wail of silent voices responding to the devastation of another lost life.

The wives returned to their chores, all of them mindful of the thousands of minutes they had left to wait before they could return to regular life, families intact. If one of the lucky ones, the minutes would pass slowly, but they would pass. If not one of the lucky ones, like the young wife whose life was eclipsed in the spring of 1971, one of those minutes became an eternity.

Lorrayne

MODEL AIRPLANES

(1966)

Robbie was alone in the house. Lorrayne had gone out after supper, knowing that Pat was next door should her son need anything. The ten-year-old was in his bedroom surveying his model airplane collection. He loved all of his aircraft, spent hours gluing the plastic parts together. Some of the pieces were so small he had to use tweezers to set them in the right place. With his face close to his work, his fingers gently maneuvering the parts into their proper slots, it seemed as if he and the model were one.

Robbie studied each step of the directions, making sure every piece was attached perfectly, otherwise the propellers might not turn or the landing gear would not retract properly. Working slowly, he carefully applied the airplane's decals. They had to be straight and the exact distance from the cockpit or the wing. His concentration was so complete that hours sometimes went by without him ever emerging from his bedroom.

Robbie chose one of his models, probably a MiG-19 or a P-40 Warhawk Flying Tiger. He took the replica out to the backyard and grabbed some wire, Terry's BB gun, and some lighter fluid. *Don't forget the matches.* The sun was setting, but the weather was nice enough to go outside. He looked around for a place to hang the airplane, finally settling on the clothesline. Robbie tied the wire around the center of the airplane, positioning it to balance in the middle. It took a while to get the plane perfect. He kept at it until the model looked like a fighter in the sky when he held it up by the wire. *Now, douse it with lighter fluid.* Most of the fluid rolled off onto the patio, but some good puddles got inside the model's air pockets.

Robbie fastened the wire on the clothesline with a clothespin, grabbed the BB gun, and began a ground offensive on the airborne enemy. Papapow. Whack! Papapow-papapow. And another whack! BBs struck. The model spun—an aerial top wobbling in the sky. Tethered, the toy could not escape the surface-to-air attack. Once the enemy was rendered harmless, Robbie put down the gun. *Use the matches. Set it on fire.*

The fire was slow to take, but once the lighter fluid ignited, the model incinerated from the intense heat. The sky had turned to dusk, with only a few neighbors' porch lights illuminating nightfall. Robbie kept the lights off and sat on the stoop watching the parts of his model, once carefully assembled, bleed into one another until the airplane melted into an unrecognizable glop of plastic. Fiery appendages began to drip off the aircraft. Comets crashing to earth. After a while nothing was left but a gooey residue and the notion that a spectacular ending was worth its destruction.

Terry had come home at some point during Robbie's solitary war. He had watched the obliteration through to its final moments when nothing remained but a dangling wire and a mess of quickly hardening plastic droplets all over the grass. Terry looked at his younger brother—what a waste of time and money. But instead of telling him so, he turned to his brother and said, "That looked really cool, but you better clean up this mess before Mom comes home." With that he grabbed his BB gun and went into the house, leaving Robbie alone in the backyard. The little boy cleaned up as best he could, throwing all evidence of the battle into the garbage can.

Lorrayne arrived home a little while later. Robbie was in almost the exact some position he was in when she left. She was at a loss. What would it take to make her son move from the couch. The boys went to bed. Lorrayne retired to her room, turning on the ten o'clock news while preparing for sleep.

What was that? Something grabbed her lower stomach. It would not let go. The pain lasted for what seemed like minutes before it finally ebbed, but never completely went away. When she arose the next morning to wake the boys for school an ache remained. Then grew. It became so severe that she had to bend over until the pain subsided before she was able to move on with her day.

Bonnie

WHAT DO WE SAY TO OUR CHILDREN?

(1969)

The children raced down the hall. They could not wait to tell Bonnie who they thought had ridden up in the elevator with them. Bruce, Bryan, and Colleen charged into their room at the hotel in New York City, excited to tell their mother the news of their encounter with someone famous. No one remembers who told her first and more than likely they talked over one another, telling her at the same time. They were sure, they exclaimed with childhood certainty, that Mike Douglas had been in the elevator with them. You know, they said, that man who's on TV in the afternoons when we come home from school.

Bonnie was not surprised that the talk show host was in the hotel. The press had been informed that fifty-eight wives and ninety-four children of military men captured or lost in Vietnam were staying in one of the city's finest hotels on the first leg of their journey to Paris, thanks to the beneficence of H. Ross Perot. Perot had arranged for the women to leave from John F. Kennedy Airport on December 24. He intended for them to land in Paris on Christmas Day to meet with members of the North Vietnamese delegation, asking them for news of their husbands.

The women and children began arriving in New York on the twenty-third. The billionaire had reserved a wing of the hotel for the families, giving free rein to the children and their mothers to roam the hallways and ride the elevators at their convenience. The round-trip journey to Europe would take twenty-one hours. Seven hours to Paris. Seven hours in Paris. Seven hours or more to return from Paris.

Bonnie had accepted Perot's invitation without reservation. She and her children, along with Margaret Clark, a British woman married to an American MIA living at Schilling, left Salina with hope that they would find out the status of their husbands. It was an exhilaration that became harder to come by as the years passed without news—a feeling both women held on to as tightly as they held on to their dreams for a happy end to their long wait.

Perot had sent cables to the delegation representing the Republic of North Vietnam at the Paris Peace Talks, telling them of the arrival of the women and their request for a meeting with a representative.

"Hopefully," he said at a press conference as the families were about to depart on their evening flight to Orly International in Paris, "we have good luck."

At the same time the women and children boarded the Braniff plane, two cargo planes chartered by Perot called "United We Stand" were being loaded with flats of Bibles and Brach's candies, food and medicines, blankets and air mattresses, along with several pouches of letters addressed to the soldiers from their families. The North Vietnamese had warned Perot that he should use "regular postal channels," usually via Moscow, to send things to the American prisoners. Perot had his own ideas. He insisted that the best thing the North Vietnamese could do to enhance the public's perception was to accept and deliver the goods he was sending on the special flight. *Let us in. Show the world you have a heart.* He was an early believer that international public opinion played an important role in the way the North Vietnamese conducted the business of war and the treatment of their prisoners.

During the flight to Paris one of Perot's associates asked Bonnie if she would be a representative for the women during press conferences and when they met with the North Vietnamese delegation. "Yes, of course," she told him.

Perot's aides were kind and helpful. They had suggested that perhaps they should coach her about what to say in case the international press asked hard questions. Bonnie, confident in her ability to field whatever questions were asked of her, said, "It's better for me to answer spontaneously. Not rehearsed."

Bonnie learned from Perot's associates that he had three goals for the mission. The first was to secure the release of all American prisoners. Second, if a full release was not possible, he wanted a complete list of the names of all the prisoners. The final goal was to receive permission for the two cargo charters to fly in the supplies for the estimated fourteen hundred men thought held by North Vietnam. To the women on the flight the goals seemed not only attainable but also reasonable.

Why not, they thought. What could it hurt?

Some women tried to nap during the journey, but adrenaline was too high—and restless children too distracting—so they stayed awake for most of the trip. The crew had empathy for their passengers, doing everything possible to make the Christmas Eve journey comfortable. The stewardesses gave the children coloring books and crayons, keeping most of them busy for long stretches at a time. A sense of anticipation, mixed with occasional rushes of anxiety, kept the flight quiet, the women pensive, and the children in check. Women rarely spoke above whispers as they shared their histories, their hopes, and their expectations for the trip. The children, perhaps sensing that they were involved in something important, stayed with their mothers, sometimes giggling quietly with new friends made across the slender aisle that separated them.

The carol-less Christmas Eve flight flew through the night. The plane landed at around eight on a gray Christmas morning in Paris. The sun stayed hidden behind winter clouds, an ominous forecast for the city that day.

The wives gathered themselves, their children, and their belongings; departed the aircraft; and boarded one of three buses waiting for them on the tarmac. The women had no luggage to collect, having brought only what they wore when they left New York and whatever they could bring in their purses and small carry-on bags. Bonnie, Bruce, Bryan, and Colleen, who carried a new Raggedy Ann doll that was nearly half her size—an early Christmas gift from her grandparents—went from wings to wheels without commotion. Bonnie was the last to board the bus that would transport her to the door of the enemy, the North Vietnamese consulate on the rue Le Verrier.

They traveled through Paris. A contingent of the international press corps followed the women from the airport to their destination. The reporters had been alerted to the arrival of the American families in Paris by Perot's public relations team. *We're bringing one hundred and fifty women and children to Paris. They're going to find out what has happened to their husbands and fathers. Let the world know.*

As the buses turned down the rue Le Verrier the women checked their makeup in small vanity mirrors and brushed the wrinkles out of the clothes. They were one hundred yards from the consulate.

S'arrêter! S'arrêter!

A patrol of French gendarmes blocked them from proceeding farther down the street. Perot's aides exited the buses, as did some of the women. An official told the American emissaries that it was Christmas Day; the mission was locked and barred. Return to the hotel. Told that the women had not planned to stay longer than a few hours in Paris, the police apologized, but said that nothing else could be done—they had their orders.

Keep the women away.

The group lingered on the sidewalk. *Now what'll we do?* The press seized their opportunity. A reporter asked what was the purpose of their trip to Paris.

Bonnie answered, "We are here merely to ask about the status of our husbands and ask about the status of the husbands of the fourteen hundred ladies in the States who couldn't come." She got personal. "When your husband has been missing for four years and your children haven't had a Christmas with their father in five years, there's just a yearning to know about him, just an utter concern about him that dominates everything. If even one daddy comes home as a result of this trip . . . it will be worthwhile."

What should we do now?

A light rain forced the women back onto the buses. They were in Paris. At another time it would have been an occasion to celebrate. Disappointment overcame the travelers. Some quietly wept. Children began to fuss. What were they going to do until it was time for their plane to leave for home? Margaret Clark, the MIA wife who had traveled with Bonnie from Schilling, spoke up: "Well, here we are in Paris on the holiest day of the year. We could all at least go to church and pray."

Margaret, what a wonderful idea.

After a little research, the aides chose to take their charges to the Île de la Cité in the heart of Paris, to the Cathedral Notre-

Dame; it was the only church large enough to hold one hundred and fifty-two women and children.

The Catholic women searched their purses for scarves or anything else they could use, even an unused tissue held fast by a bobby pin, to cover their heads before entering the church. They had not thought to bring their religious veils to Paris.

The press followed in the wake of the women. They asked no questions as the mothers and their children, transparent in their disillusionment, yet awed by the cathedral's greatness, walked silently, gazing up at the majestic archways, ribbed vaults, and flying buttresses. Gargoyles loomed from lofty parapets—home to Hugo's Quasimodo—and kaleidoscopes of stained-glass windows depicting wondrous images of piety and Christian lore greeted the travelers as they passed under the Gallery of Kings and into the holy house to pray. François Cardinal Marty, archbishop of Paris, was saying mass in the nearly filled cathedral. The women entered quietly, and knelt in the back pews. They prayed for a Christmas miracle.

Not long after she and the children settled down to pray Bonnie felt a tap on her shoulder. A Perot aide asked her to join him and two other women outside.

The North Vietnamese had a change of heart. A member of the delegation would see three women. Only three. No children. Come quickly. And alone.

The news spread swiftly to the women inside the church. They left silently in twos, so as not to disrupt the Mass, and joined the three women chosen to represent them. Bonnie; Margaret Fisher, wife of an Air Force pilot shot down over North Vietnam in 1967; and Andrea Rander, wife of an Army sergeant captured in early 1968, huddled together as they rode back through Paris to meet with the delegate.

The gendarmes ordered the buses to stop several blocks away

from the North Vietnamese stronghold. *From here, the ladies must proceed to the embassy alone.*

Dressed in a sleek, knee-length, blue suit-dress, Bonnie refreshed her makeup and smoothed the curls gracefully woven into her updo. The women were revitalized; their prayers had been answered. Bonnie and the two other mothers kissed their children, promising to return soon. They began their journey to meet the enemy. But as the wives walked arm and arm down Paris's streets, holding letters to their husbands, surrounded by press and police, they realized they had one problem. Quietly, so as not to alert the press to their predicament, the women asked one another, "Do you have any idea where we are going?"

"No, do you?"

"I haven't the slightest idea where the embassy is."

"Well, what'll we do?"

"The press is walking backward, in front of us. Let's follow them. They must know were it is."

"Okay, we'll stop when they stop and look around for a sign."

The plan worked. Reporters and cameramen leading the way stopped slightly beyond a set of steps so they could film the women arriving at their destination. The sign on the brick wall beside the door read,

TONG DA DIEM
CHINH PHO NHUC VIET-NAM DAN-CHO CONG—HOA
DÉLÉGATION GÉNÉRALE
DU GOUVERNEMENT DE LA RÉPUBLIQUE DÉMOCRATIQUE
DU VIET-NAM
RUE LE VERRIER

They had made it.

With arms interlocked, creating a wall of strength, the women walked up the few steps to the embassy and rang the bell. They were led into a living room setting with European decor where they met with Tran Viet Dung, a North Vietnamese political counselor and delegate to the Peace Talks. An interpreter was present, as was a man to take notes. A fourth man served tea.

For twenty minutes the counselor told the women the history and politics of Vietnam. He referred to North Vietnam as "nonaggressors" and as a "peace loving" nation. The delegate mentioned that it was the aggressions of the Japanese, French, and American governments that had put his nation in its most unfortunate circumstance. After his monologue the women presented their request for the return of their husbands and for a list of all American soldiers held captive in all of Vietnam. Tran Viet Dung answered, "We have no jurisdiction over captives held in South Vietnam."

The tea turned cold in the women's cups. Again they asked for information and a list of captives.

Their host responded, "The release of prisoners is inconsistent with North Vietnamese policy and will be part of an overall settlement of the war. Continuing information about the status of all prisoners held by Hanoi will be gradually released." He added, "Go ask Nixon when you will see your husbands again."

The delegate asked for a list of the husbands whose families had made the trip to Paris. Bonnie turned over the names, ranks, serial numbers, and the dates when their husbands and the fifty-five other men whose wives and children waited for news a few blocks away, became missing or were taken captive. Tran Viet Dung told the wives that he would forward the list of names to Hanoi but indicated no specific time for reply. One hour and fifteen minutes after the women arrived the meeting ended with one final question and one final answer.

Bonnie stood to leave. She had not learned anything about the condition or whereabouts of Bruce or any of the other American captives. Bonnie made eye contact with her host, "What do we say to our children?"

The official looked at his guest. "Return home and tell your children that their fathers are murderers of North Vietnamese children."

He turned and left the room, leaving the women emotionally stunned and having to face reporters eager for details about the meeting. The journalists saw the tears flow from two of the women's eyes. There would be no statement. The wives and children waiting at the buses saw the three women. Such sadness. Their miracle had not happened.

Back in New York Santa Claus greeted the children when they arrived at their hotel at about three o'clock on Christmas Day. Each of the ninety-four exhausted, fatherless children was handed a gift from Santa or his elves. Bruce opened a cardboard city. Bryan's present was a picture-making machine. Colleen Joy received a toy vacuum sweeper that she pushed around the lobby until she was too pooped out to play with it or anything else. All the wives received a bottle of Fabergé's popular Woodhue cologne and a Desert Flower sachet. The hotel had also made arrangements for Catholic and Protestant services so the families would not have to search the city's streets to celebrate the birth of Christ.

The long day finally ended for the women and their children. While they slept a final night in New York City before returning home, Hanoi refused permission to admit the "United We Stand" cargo. The North Vietnamese delegation also released a communiqué regarding the wives' visit to Paris. It said that the trip ". . . was a dark scheme of the Nixon administration." It continued: "Besides seeking every means to distort the humanitarian policy of the democratic republic of Vietnam, the U.S. authorities have blatantly used the sentiments of the U.S. soldiers' relatives as an instrument to serve the scheme of aggression of the Nixon administration."

Bonnie and the children flew to Harbor Beach the next morning for a belated Christmas celebration with the family. Reporters from the *Salina Journal, The Kansas City Star*, and *The Wichita Eagle* telephoned her, asking for a comment. The children were out snowmobiling with their uncle David, Bruce's brother. Bonnie, though weary from travel, told the reporters that she "was grateful they were granted a meeting, but could not bear to tell her children the news from the North Vietnamese official." She added, "It was good to share the trip with each other and in a particular way, to share it with our husbands. It's been an unusual Christmas, but it's been one that, no matter how long we live, will be one to remember. But there was great disappointment. I'm sure you can understand we had so hoped this would be a truly meaningful Christmas."

By the end of 1969, nearly 48,000 U.S. servicemen had lost their lives fighting in Vietnam and 1,406 were listed as missing in action. The "Spirit of Christmas" flight had opened the door to public opinion regarding the North Vietnamese, but the National Liberation Front—the Viet Cong—refused to acknowledge that Americans were being held captive in South Vietnam. For two years the Peace Talks had been stalled because no one knew exactly how to acknowledge the political organization said to represent Vietnamese citizens living south of the DMZ. As early as 1968, Bonnie had written letters to Madame Nguyen Thi Binh, the head of the negotiating team for the NLF, appealing to her for information about Bruce. What harm, Bonnie asked, could come from letting her children know so important and basic a matter as whether their father is alive or not? What harm might come from allowing letters between loved ones? "We're feeling a desperation for our husbands and for ourselves. Hanoi and the National Liberation Front must act. They must release the names."

Bonnie's meeting with the president and her trip to Paris helped her to realize that she could do more than wait for someone to tell her about Bruce. When she and the children returned to Schilling Manor after Christmas, she began making plans for another trip to Paris, but this time she would go alone to meet Madame Binh, the petite, trim woman whose name meant peace in Vietnamese and who had become known as the flower and the fire of the revolution.

Beverly

SUMMER DREAMS

(1971)

Summer on the prairie, so hot it scorches the sidewalks, siz-zling the bottoms of shoeless feet. Intemperate wind snarls hair and ruins skin. It is an edgy wind, the kind that can stir up a whirlpool of debris at the slightest change in the air.

At Schilling we were all fairly careless about the weather. We took it for granted that someone from the commander's office would drive around with a bullhorn warning us of a cataclysmic forecast. Sometimes Gail and I stood on the porch, watching the sky turn colors. The clouds swept by as if running from a bad dream. *Please let there be a tornado.* We wished one would land somewhere close so we could watch it rouse whatever life existed on the boring horizon. Waiting for funnel clouds, even at the slightest threat, was about the only thing my sister and I had in common. We spent hours sitting in the sun in the front yard until the hope of living through a dangerous meteorological event turned into just another sultry day.

My mother liked to have her friends come to our house with their kids on Saturdays in summertime after the Little League games and after the shopping excursions to the commissary and PX, or to the beauty parlor in Salina. One-piece bathing suits or colorful culottes with a matching tank top, or the occasional pair of hot pants were as ritzy as anyone got during those late afternoon get-togethers.

A few of the children had crinkly, pink noses and blossoming freckles from too much time spent in the sun. The littlest ones swam in a twelve-inch-high blow-up pool to keep cool. My mother always kept a plastic basin filled with water beside the pool. She hated seeing dirt and grass on the bottom of the portable pond.

Conversations about their day mingled with mild reprimands directing the kids to dip their feet before jumping into the water. But the water got cruddy anyway—kamikaze bugs, twigs, candy wrappers delivered by the wind, and bits and pieces of lawn from the bottom of undunked feet ended up in the pool—so every hour or two, the mothers took turns dumping the skuzzy liquid, and refreshing the pool with a good dousing from the hose.

Most of the time, while the women and the kids were outside, I stayed in my room listening to music, not doing much of anything. One Saturday Gail had started me on a decoupage project for my friend Lauren's birthday present. It was an easy art. Cut out a picture from a magazine, spray mount it on a precarved hunk of wood, then apply layer upon layer of thick goo that resembled Elmer's glue. Even the least gifted could make something look good.

That afternoon I alternated between listening to music in my bedroom, eavesdropping on adult conversations in the backyard, and applying more goo in the living room. Anything to ease the tedium of the day.

In between their afternoon sunbathing sessions, when my mother basted her body with baby oil until her skin cracked, she and Gail spent time in the kitchen. They liked preparing for the parties together. Gail was a perfect hostess, offering drinks and at the same time preparing freezer-to-oven hors d'oeuvres. Hungry kids volunteered to pass around minipizzas and bite-sized egg rolls. Occasionally, one of the wives concocted an exotic dip, like hot crab or clam, from the Waiting Wives Club Cookbook. Gail had arranged the celery sticks stuffed with Velveeta and the cream cheese–filled olives on one side of a bowl of chips and dip. A couple of the wives who were members of the SMAC club opted for the unfilled celery and carrot sticks placed on the other side.

Tom Jones or Englebert Humperdink sang in the background. These middle-aged versions of the British invasion of the 1960s were the women's favorite singers. After a drink or two the ladies would giggle and say things like, "He can eat potato chips in my bed anytime" or "Wouldn't you like to be Delilah for a day?" Gail rolled her eyes, but went along with their fun. I think she secretly liked listening to Tom Jones but would never admit it.

By the time I came out of my room to eat something, the citronella candles were lit, the burgers were on the grill, and dusk gave way to moonlight and stars. Kids ran around playing red light/green light until their bodies turned to shadows on the grass. The wives settled in lawn chairs and chaise longues with drinks, occasionally poking at their food. They spoke of small things: the tornado that landed in the next county last week; the problem of dogs running loose on post; the next craft class; and who had volunteered for the POW/MIA committee at the last Waiting Wives Club meeting. Someone wondered when the next space flight was taking off. Nancy mentioned something about Pentagon Papers and thought it too bad that Louis Armstrong had died.

Two of the wives received letters that afternoon. One received a tape the day before. My mother mentioned that we had not heard from my father in a long time. Weeks, it seemed. The talk of letters turned to a conversation about dreams. One of the wives, a newcomer to the group, sipped her beer and listened to the dreams of her new friends. When they finished she told them about her recurring dream:

"I get in the car to drive the kids to school or to run errands."

The kids chased the fireflies that speckled the night.

"It can be any time of the day, or any time of the year."

I loaded sticks with marshmallows.

"It's business as usual, as if nothing is wrong, but for the whole time I'm driving."

Crickets began their nightly chant.

"My husband lays on the backseat of the car."

A marshmallow fell into the fire.

"Dead."

Her friends understood and tried to reassure her. *Don't worry. It's just one of those dreams that come with the territory. Everyone has them at one point or another.*

Tired children with marshmallow-filled bellies drifted toward their mothers' laps.

I went into the living room to apply another layer of glue to Lauren's present. Lynn turned on the TV to watch *My Three Sons*. Tired kids piled on the floor, their bodies wrapped in warm towels. The women helped my mother and Gail clean up the mess.

After a final cup of coffee they collected their sleepy children, returning home to give baths and read bedtime stories. Exhausted little eyes closed.

One woman slipped in between the cold sheets of her double bed unable to sleep.

Another stayed awake nursing her scotch in the dark, looking out onto the deserted street.

And another sat under a solitary light, pulled out her stationery, and wrote a letter to her husband.

Lorrayne

PAIN
(1966)

By March 1966, two hundred families had moved into Schilling Manor homes. The streets were active with cars. Snowmen had popped up on lawns after the last of the season's snowfall, and coffee klatches formed with little effort after the kids were off to school. Al's part-time job quickly turned full-time. His route increased by a few houses nearly every day. The community was alive with women getting to know one another by telling stories of their children, over tears of worry for their husbands, and by sharing hopes for a dream assignment in Hawaii after their tour at Schilling had ended.

Many women joined the Waiting Wives Club. They formed committees, relieving Lorrayne of a few of the tasks she had started. Too many women had moved on post for her to meet them personally, especially if they had not joined the Waiting Wives Club. Still, most of the women knew of Lorrayne. She was the godmother of Schilling Manor.

During the cold winter months, Robbie had maintained his silence.

The snow eventually melted. Temperatures began to climb. Lorrayne's youngest still showed no sign of wanting to talk. She continued to set aside a large chunk of every day for writing letters, visiting local businesses, calling Fort Riley, and meeting with her neighbors. Her efforts to make life at the base more comfortable for herself and the other families were tireless.

As a result of Kimmie and her baby, Lorrayne had started an emergency call system for the wives to use if they were in trouble and needed help. Or if an emergency arose. Or if they received bad news from Vietnam. If a wife became incapacitated for any reason, especially in the case of illness—a bad flu could put a mother down for weeks—most of the other wives rallied around her by caring for her children, making meals, driving to the doctor, cleaning, and anything else that had to be done to maintain a household.

The town's ambulance had Lorrayne's name and phone number on the inside. If something happened on base, she would be the first person the ambulance attendants would call. That way she could organize the women to action.

Bob had been gone about six months when fatigue began to overwhelm Lorrayne. She had a constant pain in her belly. Sometimes it wasn't so bad, but it never went away. Robbie's refusal to talk had put a strain on her. She knew it, and could do nothing about it. Bob was working in an increasingly dangerous situation. Did she worry? *No. Well, maybe.* Lorrayne monitored the TV in her bedroom. Soldiers were being deployed to Vietnam by the thousands—over three thousand had been killed since she had moved to Schilling. Did she worry? *Yes, sometimes.* Battles fought, agreements broken, bombings halted or resumed, demands made and ignored, and death tolls had begun to dominate the national news reports. Vietnam had turned into a hot zone and it was getting hotter by the minute. Whenever she thought about the escalating war, she immersed herself in her work. Lorrayne was confident Bob could take care of himself. But she could not help being thankful that his tour was half over.

Lorrayne had a long list of things to accomplish, including working with the Chamber to organize sports leagues for the growing number of children. One day she even went unannounced to the new Westinghouse factory. *Help me fix up the swimming pool by summer as a community service.* To her surprise, the management agreed.

On an afternoon in March, Lorrayne was in the living room going through her list when she looked out of the window. Al was walking to her door carrying a large box with holes in it. He appeared a little overwhelmed. The box was not only unwieldy as he tried to carry it along with his postal bag, but he looked as if he was struggling to keep from dropping it on the sidewalk.

Lorrayne opened the door. The box was making noise. Hundreds of little peeps emanated from inside. Al told her that it looked like someone from back East had sent an early Easter present. He handed the lively box to Lorrayne. She peeked inside one of the round air holes, "Oh my goodness," she said, "they're alive." She put it on top of her portable dishwasher and ran over to tell Pat what had come in the mail.

Pat scooped up Cricket and ran back to Lorrayne's kitchen. The peeping seemed louder. "Oh no. Tuffy. You bad dog." The boys' Boston terrier had climbed up onto the kitchen table, over to the dishwasher, knocking down the box while investigating its content.

A hundred little chicks were running this way and that. They were all over the house. Lorrayne, Pat, and even the dog sidestepped, tiptoeing to avoid crushing any of the yellow babies running between their legs. Every single one of them peeped as loudly and as aggressively as all babies do when they are hungry or scared, and separated from their mothers.

Ouch! Lorrayne doubled over. *That pain again.* Pat did not notice.

Cricket oohed and aahed at the furry critters. The women scrambled to gather up the chicks, crawling on their hands and knees to grab the feistiest of the flock. The dog occasionally howled out of frustration, somehow knowing not to hurt the moving fur balls. The chicks responded to Tuffy with equal fervor. The sound was so deafening the women could not hear each other speak.

Forty-five minutes later they had captured the last of the escaped fledglings. Lorrayne and Pat sat down to a cup of coffee, their captives chirping safely out of the way on the back porch with Tuffy standing guard.

Lorrayne was exhausted. She mentioned to Pat while she was hunting the chicks that she had some kind of pain in her lower stomach—a stabbing pain that she had been having for a while. Pat suggested she go to Fort Riley for a checkup, especially if the pain didn't go away. Something might be seriously wrong. Lorrayne dismissed the pain as nothing to worry about. *I'll just get some pain pills.*

Lorrayne had to figure out what to do with the chicks before the boys got home. She knew they would want to keep every single one of them. The note taped to the inside of the box came from a farmer in Pennsylvania. He wrote that he and his kids had heard about Schilling Manor on the news. *Chicks might help the children pass the time while their fathers were away.*

The gesture was thoughtful, but Lorrayne knew that chicks turned to chickens and imagined what the neighborhood would look like in a few months with a hundred full-grown birds pecking at and running around the lawns with children chasing them all over their and everyone else's yards. The post had enough trouble with women arguing over unleashed dogs roaming around, pooping on everyone's grass but their own.

The transient lifestyle of Schilling kids did not lend itself to the care of chickens. Families abandoned dogs and cats all the time when they moved from a post. As cute as the chicks were, they would be nothing more than a big headache if distributed among the juvenile ranks of Schilling. Lorrayne would not condemn them to an uncertain future. Better they were raised properly for eggs or meat in a coop on a farm. She and Pat figured the chicks would have a better chance in the civilian world than in the backyards of military housing units.

Pat and Cricket left. Lorrayne went to check on the chicks. They were still peeping away. She went back in the house, got out her phonebook. Someone in Salina might have an idea on what to do with a hundred furry babies. She picked up the phone. Another sudden, fierce pain shot through her body. It was bad, worse than before. She double over in agony. It took minutes before it subsided enough for her to stand straight. Even then she had to sit down. Time passed. The pain eased, but her body still smarted.

I had better call the doctor and get some kind of pills for this pain.

Lorrayne made a few calls to her acquaintances in Salina. After conferring with Pat, they decided to give the chicks away to a boy in town who was looking for a 4-H project. The boy and his father would come over that afternoon to pick up the babies. The chicks were dealt with.

Lorrayne called Fort Riley's dispensary. They asked her what was the problem. *A fierce pain in my belly. It never goes away for long.* The nurse assigned her to a doctor in the ob-gyn clinic. She did not care who saw her as long as he gave her something for the pain.

A few days later Lorrayne sat in the dispensary listening to her doctor—a former neighbor when she and Bob were stationed at the base—diagnose her condition. Endometrial cancer. He was still waiting for lab results, but he was positive of his diagnosis. Positive. He looked at his patient. "Lorrayne, you need surgery."

"What? When?" she asked.

"Right away. It can't wait."

Lorrayne turned to her doctor. "Well, I just can't do that. I can't leave the kids. Give me some pills for the pain that will last me until Bob comes home."

Her doctor was firm. "We can't wait, Lorrayne. The pain will get worse. You'll bleed all of the time. And what if the cancer spreads in the next months? You have no choice."

She continued her argument. "There's no one to watch the boys. My mother can't come. It's planting time. Robbie hasn't been well. And I can't ask any of the other women to watch my kids while I'm laid up in the hospital. They have their own problems and their own kids to tend to."

"I'm sorry, Lorrayne. We'll call Bob home. He'll help you through this."

"Well, you just can't do that." She persisted.

Her former neighbor was adamant. "Yes we can, and we will."

Her attempts to postpone the operation failed and Lorrayne's surgery was scheduled for a week later. The pain was truly awful for her, almost unbearable at times, but still she did not want the doctor to call Bob home. She reminded him, "You know if my husband comes home it might hurt his chances for promotion."

Her physician assured her, "Lorrayne, we will call him home on emergency leave. You need him more than Vietnam needs him. And it will not hurt his chances for promotion, if anything, they'll extend his duty to make up for the time spent at home."

Lorrayne knew better, but her pleas for him not to bring Bob home were futile. She thought of the timing. The Red Cross would call his commander. The doctor probably already had the call in the works. Bob would be home within a few days. She would not have time to write him, or even call him. Hopefully he would get in touch with her as soon as he landed stateside so she could fill him in before he got home.

She had never told him about Robbie.

Bonnie

BRYAN'S DREAM

(1970)

The Christmas trip to Paris and the unsettling meeting that Bonnie and the two other wives had had with the North Vietnamese delegate had opened her eyes, turning her into a natural and willing advocate for her husband. She had answered reporter's questions with grace and honesty. Bonnie had told a *Salina Journal* reporter that the North Vietnamese seemed particularly sensitive to the public's perception of their treatment of prisoners—Americans must speak out against the enemy's treatment of U.S. soldiers.

The town answered her call. Barely two months after Bonnie returned to Schilling, messages of support popped up on billboards and business marquees all over Salina. Vernon Jewelers sponsored a billboard along US81, depicting a photograph of an American soldier sitting numbly on a cot in a bare cell. Written across the image were the words *Don't Let Them Be Forgotten*. The same message was inscribed on Cunningham Florists's business envelopes. The Holiday Inn's sign on South Broadway displayed a message in bold, capital letters:

LEST THEY BE FORGOTTEN
THE MISSING IN ACTION
PRISONERS IN VIETNAM

The Travelodge had a similar message on its marquee, as did the First National Bank. The *Salina Journal* began publishing a weekly missing-in-action/prisoner-of-war address for people wishing to express their concern for POWs/MIAs and to ask the enemy to adhere to the Geneva Convention provisions concerning the treatment of captives and the release of prisoners' names. The first address given was that of the Soviet ambassador to the United States, Anatoly F. Dobrynin. The weather scan on Salina's cable TV station occasionally flashed a message that read, "Express your concern for missing in action and prisoners of war. Write H. Ross Perot, Box 100,000, Dallas, TX 75235."

Bonnie's life had changed. She was no longer a woman passively waiting for the return of her lost husband. After Christmas, Sybil Stockdale had telephoned, asking her to become involved with the newly organized National League of Families of POW/MIA in Southeast Asia.

"Be on the board," Sybil had said. "You can represent the Army families."

Bonnie had agreed, her only trepidations having to do with leaving the children for days at a time to travel to Washington. Besides her trips east, she often traveled to cities in Kansas to speak to the Rotary and women's clubs, business gatherings and

Chambers of Commerce, colleges and church groups, on behalf of the movement and its message—speak up for our men, write letters, and whatever else, don't let them be forgotten.

In the beginning her friends at Schilling helped her by watching Bruce, Bryan, and Colleen when she was away. Later, as the travel demands increased, Bonnie hired two women from Salina to care for them. Whenever she started to feel guilty about her time away from home, she thought: *But I'm doing it for the children.*

Finding their father became Bonnie's calling.

One morning before school, Bryan came to Bonnie and said, "Mama, I had a dream about Daddy last night."

Bonnie turned her attention to Bryan. "Did you, Bryan? What was Daddy doing?"

"Bad people were beating him up," he told her, "but I saved him and we ran away."

"Well," said Bonnie to her quiet middle child, "what did Daddy look like, Bryan?"

Bryan replied, "I don't know. I didn't see his face."

"Why didn't you see his face?" asked Bonnie. Her son looked at her, intent on answering her question, yet confused. Why didn't he see his father's face? He finally answered.

"Because I don't remember what Daddy looks like."

Bonnie had tried to soothe her son, she may even have brought out a picture of Bruce, one of her favorites, the one where he was squatting down, surrounded by five or six Vietnamese children, handing them rations and smiling broadly when the photographer snapped the picture.

The memory of young Bruce's Valentine's Day sadness and now Bryan's unsettling dream gave Bonnie the courage to make her next journey to Paris. She did not want to leave her children, but to finally be able to come home and answer them when they asked "When is Daddy coming home?" would mean more to her than just about anything else. With God's help she would find a way out of the limbo her family was in. If she had to, she would perch on Madame Binh's doorstep.

Where is my children's father?

The Committee

THE FARMER

The next meeting of the committee was held in the community center's ballroom. The captain's wife brought a batch of Toll House cookies. The lieutenant's wife saw the sugary treat and exclaimed, "Keep those away from me or I'll be too fat to model anything in the show but a muumuu. My husband will never recognize me when I meet him in Hawaii."

The sergeant major's wife comforted her friend. "You'll look great on the runway. Stop worrying."

"Why, thank you. That is so sweet of you to say," replied the lieutenant's wife.

"What are we using for the runway, by the way?" The sergeant major's wife directed the question to no one in particular.

The colonel's wife had the answer: "When the commander agreed to MC the show, he asked if we needed anything and I told him, yes, we needed a runway. He suggested we use the platforms from the Schilling Little Theater. He'll arrange for one of the maintenance men to set them up for us a couple of days before the show as long as we tell him where we want them."

"Oh, that's wonderful. That way we'll have plenty of time to decorate," offered the warrant officer's wife.

"And," added the colonel's wife, "he said the Chapel Annex has plenty of chairs we can borrow. I've already called Mr. K. One of his guys will deliver them. Now, what colors do we want to use to decorate?"

In her choppy accent, the captain's wife suggested, "I thinku redu, whitu, and brue is good corrors for show. Very American."

"That's a great idea," said the enthusiastic sergeant major's wife. "We can use crepe paper to make streamers and bows and we can even cut out little stars to decorate programs. Maybe," she added, "I can ask the Girl Scouts to help with the decoration."

"Good idea. Let's talk to Judi and see if her troop will help. They might even be able to count it toward one of their badges," added the colonel's wife.

"I'll ask the shops for red, white, and blue outfits for the show," said the warrant officer's wife.

"That should make finding matching shoes and accessories easy," the colonel's wife stated.

The lieutenant's wife blanched when the colonel's wife mentioned accessories. The warrant officer's wife asked if she had gone to or called the stores she had suggested.

The young committee member admitted, "No, not yet," then ate another cookie. She offered her excuses, "I simply have not had a chance, you know, with everything else going on, and the children, you know my daughter had the sniffles, and I'm so worried about my husband, then we had that whole funeral thing last week, and then there're those car lights that shine in my window at night that make me so nervous I can't sleep, and well, frankly, I have never in my life asked to borrow something from a stranger and I'm not sure what to do or say. Gee, I have tried to call, but every time someone picks up the phone I panic and hang up. I'm sorry, I don't know if I can do it."

The colonel's wife reprimanded, "Well, it's a fine time to tell us. You should have said something before, or not volunteered in the first place."

"I know, I know, I mean, I thought I could do it and I'll still try if someone can help me or show me or something. I really want to help."

The warrant officer's wife allayed the lieutenant's wife's fears. "Don't worry about it. I have a lot of experience in the beg, borrow, and steal department for these sorts of things. Come along with me when I go to the stores I have to visit. We'll do the accessories together. That way we can match things up perfectly. And don't forget, some of the girls will have shoes and bags to match the outfits."

The group thought the lieutenant's wife was going to cry, so pent up was she with anxiety and, now, gratitude. In the meantime, the sergeant major's wife thought about what the lieutenant's wife had said about car lights. "What do you mean, car lights shine in your windows at night."

"Every couple of nights a car rides around the cul-de-sac and shines the lights in my bedroom window. All my neighbors have noticed it, but we don't know who it is so every night we triple check our locks," explained the lieutenant's wife.

"Now that shouldn't be," the colonel's wife announced. "No one is allowed on this post unless they have a sticker or prior approval from the commander's office. You had better call over to him, or better, go to his office right after the meeting, so he can tell the deputy to make sure he's patrolling your street."

"She's right, you know," said the warrant officer's wife, "you never know who's out there waiting to take advantage of women without a husband in the house. Did any of you read about Sharon Tate in the papers the other day?"

"Who's Sharon Tate?" asked the lieutenant's wife.

"She's that Playboy Bunny turned actress who married a

director named Roland . . . Roman or something like that, anyway she played the drug addict in *Valley of the Dolls*. She was also an Army brat. I think I heard that her father was an officer. Well, a bunch of hippies and a guy named Charles Manson . . ."

"I don't think we need to know anything more about Sharon Tate right now," interrupted the colonel's wife. "Let's get on with business."

"Oh, you are so right," conceded the warrant officer's wife, and then addressed the lieutenant's wife: "Promise to go over to the commander's office right away."

"I will. I will," promised the lieutenant's wife.

"I'm sure whoever it is, is harmless," offered the warrant officer's wife. "Probably some old coot whose wife kicked him out for being drunk or stupid or both."

"You know, one of the women in my ceramics class told me the funniest thing the other day about a stranger who visited Schilling Manor when it first opened," said the sergeant major's wife.

The lieutenant's wife asked her, "How would she know about what happened in the early days?

"She had a friend who was one of the first women to live at Schilling, before they opened the PX, even before the government contracted the sheriff's department to patrol the post."

"What she terr you?" asked the captain's wife, trying hard to pronounce her *l*'s.

"Well," the sergeant major's wife continued, "there was this farmer who came around one day. He had on a pair of those old rumpled overalls you see in old movies, or like what Grandpa wears on *The Real McCoys*."

"Oh, sure, I know what you mean. My father wears those when he's working in the garden or tinkering around with his car," declared the lieutenant's wife.

The colonel's wife made a request. "Can we finish up our meeting first, ladies?"

"Of course. What else is there to report?" asked the sergeant major's wife. No one had any other information to offer, so the colonel's wife suggested they set a time for their next meeting. After they agreed to meet at the lieutenant's wife's house the sergeant major's wife went on with her story.

"So this farmer wanders onto the post and knocks on one of the women's doors. I think only a hundred or so families, maybe even less, lived at Schilling back then. I guess he looked fairly scruffy, with a beard and all, although he didn't appear dangerous or anything. When the woman answered the door he was polite enough to take off his hat, probably a John Deere wouldn't you think, and that he was real nervous?"

The warrant officer's wife piped in, "I think I've heard this story before. Lois or one of the other civilians working in the commander's office told me about this fella. He was from somewhere in Pennsylvania and had taken a Greyhound Bus all the way to Kansas after he read an article in the local paper about Schilling Manor."

"I don't know if he was from Pennsylvania. My girlfriend told me he was from Hutchinson, Kansas, no, maybe she said somewhere in Nebraska," replied the sergeant major's wife.

"I thought he was a Mennonite or something. No, maybe a Quaker," thought the warrant officer's wife aloud.

The colonel's wife attempted to keep the story on track, "Does it really matter where he was from, ladies?"

The women said, "Of course not."

The sergeant major's wife continued the story. "When she asked if she could help him he told her that he was looking for the home of the waiting wives. When she told him he had found it he said well good enough then, because he was in dire need of a new wife and where could he go to arrange to take one back home with him."

"You're joking?" said the colonel's wife.

"Hory, mory," proclaimed the captain's wife, making an attempt at American slang. The warrant officer's wife contributed by saying, "It's true. This is the same story I heard. The man came all the way from wherever to find a wife. Can you believe that can happen in this day and age?"

"What did the woman do then?" inquired the lieutenant's wife.

"She didn't have much of a chance to talk 'cause he went on and on about how he had a good farm back home, wherever that was, and that it was a nice place to raise kids and that planting season—"

The warrant officer's wife interrupted her. "I heard it was harvest season," then let the sergeant major's wife continue.

"—was about to start and he sure could use the help of a fine woman."

"No kidding? I can*not* believe this," admitted the lieutenant's wife as she chewed on a cookie.

"It's true. I swear it. Well, as much as the story was told to me anyhow. Luckily the wife on whose door he knocked was not easily rattled. She had been a military wife for over twenty years. She let him go on while she sized him up, you know, to see if he was sincere or another jerk fooling around on post."

"Did she send him up to the commander's office? I think I heard that's what she did, so she wouldn't have to deal with him," offered the warrant officer's wife.

"No, that's not the way I heard it. In fact, my friend said that the wife believed the farmer was earnest enough. Though I don't think she invited him in for lemonade or anything."

"I hope she sent him on his way with a boot in the pants. He had no right to come on the post, let alone knock on a stranger's door. He could have scared some poor wife to death," stated the colonel's wife.

"I think she felt bad for him," said the sergeant major's wife.

"Me too. I ferr badu for him, too. He ronery man," offered the captain's wife.

The lieutenant's wife agreed, but said, "Just the same, I'm glad he didn't knock on my door."

"What did she do to set him straight?" asked the colonel's wife.

"I guess she tried to be as kind as she could be under the circumstances. Goodness, can you imagine how strange the whole thing must have been?" said the sergeant major's wife.

The colonel's wife turned to the group. "She probably had supper burning on the stove to boot and there she was being nice to a stray farmer from wherever, east hopscotch probably, who got his information all wrong. I tell you, there is no end to what we military wives have to deal with on a daily basis."

"What happened?" asked the lieutenant's wife.

The sergeant major's wife repeated what she had heard: "She told him that he had indeed found his way to the home for waiting wives, but that the wives were waiting for husbands they already had. She explained to the poor dear that this was Schilling Manor, the Home of the Waiting Wives of the United States Armed Forces, and that the women were the patriotic and dedicated wives of soldiers fighting the war in Vietnam and were performing their duty to our country by taking care of the family until their husbands returned home."

"Goodness, I bet that shocked him. I'd have been so embarrassed I would have run out of there with my tail between my legs," admitted the lieutenant's wife.

The warrant officer's wife put in her two cents. "I heard that he turned as red as an overripe tomato and apologized like crazy before leaving. Is that the way you heard it?" deferring to the sergeant major's wife.

"Yes, that's about it. He said he was real sorry, turned and practically ran down the sidewalk to a waiting taxicab I think, no, maybe she said he walked back to town, oh I don't remember what the heck she said. Either way, he hightailed it out of there as fast as possible I'll bet."

"But," the warrant officer's wife was dying to add something to the story, "you know the important thing that happened after that?"

"No, I didn't hear about that part of the story," confessed the sergeant major's wife.

"Well, after the visit from the farmer, those first women decided that Schilling needed protection. As it was, anyone could come and go as they pleased. It took a while and practically an act of Congress, but eventually the government contracted out the post's security to the Salina sheriff's office. That's why we have civilian deputies that patrol the post and not military police."

"I wondered about that," said the colonel's wife.

The lieutenant's wife said, "Gee, I never even thought about it," as she nibbled another cookie and got ready to go to the commander's office to file a complaint.

Beverly

———

THE CURSE OF THE FRENCH
(1971)

On the way home from school on a Friday afternoon during the final days of one of the most unsettled springs on record, the sky opened up with the worst storm Saline County had seen in decades. The bus had no sooner pulled out of Salina High South's parking lot when black clouds covered the sun, letting no light through the thick billows. The effect was not like the inky darkness that replaces the light when the sun sets and the moon has yet to rise; it was more like the eerie blackening cast by a giant shadow created from something hovering above. When the shadow took position, angry torrents of rain, then hail, pelted the bus with a fervor that I thought would surely break the windows. Fierce thunderheads kept us on the edge of our seats, the cracking booms penetrating the yellow armor until the sound seemed to come from within.

While we were throwing out "wow" and "groovy" and "cool man," lightning struck so close at one point that we involuntarily ducked behind the seats in front of us. The wind whipped the bus. I was sure it would lift up off the ground at any moment and fly us to Oz.

Lauren, who lived across the street and had become my best friend, and I wondered how we were going to make it home from Schilling Road without being bombarded by hail balls as big as grapes. The bus driver must have picked up on our concern because he decided to drive everyone to his or her front door. Phoenix Street was the next to the last road on the officer's side of Schilling Manor, so Lauren and I were among the last ones to get dropped off. Before making a run for it Lauren said, "Call me as soon as you find out if she'll let you go."

Then me, "Okay, I'll ask her as soon as I walk in the door," and off we went.

Ten yards separated me from my house. In the few seconds it took to run from door to door, I was pummeled by hail. My mother opened the door. In I flew followed by a dozen of the icy rocks. Prudence growled at the hailstones that rolled around like marbles. I was soaking wet, and my skin broke out in goose bumps.

I dripped down the hallway to my room. My mother warned me, "Hurry. Get changed before you catch pneumonia." It was a warning she repeated whenever we were caught off guard by foul weather. Prudence, frustrated by her melting prey, followed me into my room, tail waging, and looking for attention. After a quick pat on the head she went back to tend to her new toys, leaving me to James Taylor and the decision of what to wear that night to the movies.

Dry and changed, I went back into the living room to ask my mother about the movies. Gail was wiping up the water from the melted pellets. Prudence, no longer in battle, lay on the couch beside my mother. The hail had subsided, the shadow had passed, but it was still raining and the thunder and lightning were raging somewhere in the distance.

I was about to ask my mother about going out when I noticed that she was studying her tongue in her couch-side mirror. She always kept a mirror in the end table drawer, along with a pair of tweezers that she used daily for the plucking of what she called "pain-in-the-ass facial hair." Otherwise known as the curse of French blood. I do not know why she blamed excessive facial hair on our Canadian French heritage, except that every woman in her family had had to deal with it for as long as she could remember and they were all Canucks.

Coming home from school to see my mother with her face an inch away from the magnified side of a mirror, cigarette smoke wafting from the ashtray, plucking away at newly sprouted hairs was a common sight, as much a part of her beauty ritual as the net she put on every night to protect her hair. But seeing her with her tongue hanging out was alarming.

"What are you looking at?" I asked.

"There's something the matter with my tongue," she answered.

"What do you mean there's something the matter with your tongue?" I said, trying not to sound annoyed because I couldn't immediately ask her if it was okay to go to the movies to see *Billy Jack.* How could I ask her about my plans without her thinking that I did not care about her tongue problem? I pondered my predicament as Gail came into the room.

My mother turned to her. "You have to take me to the dispensary."

Gail did not sound sympathetic. "Are you sure there's something wrong? I've never heard of anyone having tongue problems. The doctor will think you're nuts."

"I don't care what he thinks," said my mother. "It's getting worse."

I was curious. "What's the matter with your tongue?"

She said, "It feels prickly, like there's sand all over it, and the back hurts like hell." I saw Gail roll her eyes. My mother also saw Gail roll her eyes.

"Don't roll your eyes at me. It's swollen and starting to throb and I can't smoke or eat without having stabbing pains." She added, "You're gonna have to take me whether you like it or not."

"Let me see," I said.

Gail and I moved in on my mother. Prudence sat up, looked at us, then at my mother, cocking her head as we searched for anything suspicious in my mother's mouth. She stuck her tongue out as far as she could without gagging.

I do not recall seeing anything strange on her tongue; what I do remember is that my mother looked vulnerable—a rare weakness—and that I felt so bad for her that I forgot about asking her if I could go to the movies.

The last time I had seen my mother in pain was after she had had a biopsy for uterine cancer when I was in the fourth grade and we were living at Fort Devens. My father brought her home from the hospital, put her to bed, and went back to work. I came home from school, and when I couldn't find her in the kitchen, I went to her bedroom door. It was closed. I heard her quietly moaning from the pain. I didn't dare knock.

Gail wasn't around to figure out what to do, and Lynn was too young to be helpful, so I went outside, crept behind a hedge next to her window, stood on a rock, and looked inside. My mother was curled up in her bed. Tears streamed down her face. She held her body for comfort.

I was so scared that I practically fell from the window.

I ran as fast I could across the street to Mrs. Shakarian, my mother's best friend, and told her my mother was in trouble. She took one look at her, called my father, then called an ambulance. It came. Red lights flashing. Siren screaming. It took her back to the hospital. I never forgot the anguish on my mother's face, and I never wanted to see it again.

* * *

Researchers have proven that strange things happen to a person's body when under pressure. Glands go crazy, spilling all kinds of chemicals into organs, nerves, veins, and muscle tissue when a person is under duress. Blood pressure can rise, hypertension is common, and all kinds of unusual symptoms—weird things a regular person has never heard of before—result from the body's struggle to maintain balance when emotions are heightened by fear and uncertainty, especially when that fear and uncertainty is suppressed.

I am sure my mother did not think living at Schilling was stressful. I am also certain that it never occurred to her that everything happening outside our insulated world had taken a toll on her. She had grown a tough skin during her years in the military and had learned to free herself from excess emotion, remaining unconcerned about anything happening beyond her view.

At Schilling Manor she was a waiting wife biding her time until the return of her husband. She was not an activist or a politician, a hawk or a dove. She did not even have to have an opinion. What she knew was that not to hear from my father for several days or weeks was not unusual. To go to the mailbox and find it empty was common. To turn on the television and see the world upside down was routine.

During the wet, stormy spring of 1971, reports from the war were rarely good. The Paris Peace Talks had entered the fourth year and were deadlocked—again. In the final weeks of April thousands of antiwar demonstrators had converged on Washington and San Francisco, filling the streets with placards of hate for the American government and its policy in Vietnam. Almost thirteen thousand protestors were arrested during the weeks-long demonstrations. And why, my mother and her friends wondered, were Vietnam vets demonstrating in Washington?

In Saigon, not far from where my father was, a bomb went off leaving dead and wounded scattered all over the streets. And every day the news announced the death tolls. My mother and her friends watched the news day after day like addicts. I heard them say more than once, "I don't understand what's going on." Or "When will it end?" I am not sure any of us realized how we were affected by what was going on in the world, in America, and in our own homes. We simply led our lives.

Gail told my mother that she didn't want to go out in the middle of the storm. She asked, "Can't you wait until it's over?"

My mother responded, "I don't care what it is doing outside." She said her tongue hurt like the dickens, she could hardly stand the pain. Gail had better take her to the dispensary. "Now," she added.

Gail, exasperated, had no choice but to take my mother to the dispensary, leaving me to wonder if she had cancer again. I called Lauren to tell her of the latest development. We decided to forgo the movie, but she could still spend the night.

Gail and my mother returned an hour or two later. My sister went into her room and closed the door. The doctor had not laughed at my mother's pain. He gave her a diagnosis—neuralgia of the tongue, also known as tic douloureux, French for painful tic. It was a rare condition, he told her, maybe a few cases in a million, and is caused by a problem with nerves. My mother described the diagnosis to Lynn and me, and then to her friends on the phone that night, as the weirdest thing she had ever heard of and how she had to tell the doctor over and over that she was not the nervous type.

Lauren came over and we spent the night pin curling our hair while my mother watched, giving us advice on proper techniques. She tried to eat. She tried to smoke. Frustrated, she went to bed.

* * *

My dad had sent us a tape around the time of my mother's tongue problem. He told us that everything was good.

He'd had a near miss during a helicopter ride to an area outside of Saigon. Ammo flew every which way around the chopper. It was so bad that the pilot had to nosedive to escape the barrage of bullets. Pretty scary, he admitted. He nonchalantly mentioned that the guys had given him a nickname, "Bad luck Moreau," because four out of every five flights he flew on resulted in some sort of mishap, usually ending in an emergency landing. Isn't that funny? We did not laugh.

We recorded a tape to send to him, filling him in on some of the details of our lives. Prudence was really big. I had joined the chorus. Lynn fell off the monkey bars and broke her front tooth. Gail couldn't wait to go to school in Chicago at the end of summer. The Waiting Wives Club was sponsoring a petition drive for the POWs/MIAs. We told him about the ordeal with my mother's tongue, making light of the problem that had caused her so much pain. My mother added a final comment: "Can you believe that the doctor told me that this tic doula-whatchamacallit is caused by nerves?"

Lorrayne

_____

THE EASTER BUNNY

(1966)

On the ride home from Fort Riley, Lorrayne blocked out any thoughts about the seriousness of her cancer. She'd had breast cancer and survived. No doubt she would come through this bout without too much trouble.

Dealing with sickness was inconvenient at any time, but to have cancer when Bob was at war and with so much to accomplish on post was downright unfair. It was bad enough that a hysterectomy would slow her down for a few weeks, but now Bob had to come home, and no matter what the Army touted about taking care of their own, she had been around the military long enough to know that it was a terrible thing for a career soldier to leave his post in the middle of a tour of duty because of family matters. But nothing could be done, so as she drove back to Schilling she thought about what to tell the boys.

As soon as Terry and Robbie returned from school they went to their rooms to change into play clothes. Lorrayne gave them their snacks, then sat down to tell them what was going to happen in the next couple of weeks. She worried how Robbie might react, but with Bob home maybe he would be okay. Their child was so thin from eating nothing more than an occasional orange that when Bob saw him he might think Robbie was the one who was sick. Lorrayne could do nothing for her youngest son except reassure him that everything would be fine and that she'd be home in no time. No sense in dragging it out.

The boys sat on either side of her on the couch. Lorrayne had searched her bookshelves, looking for a dictionary or an encyclopedia or something that might help them understand. The first thing Lorrayne explained was that she was sick. She was not one to beat around the bush. The conversation went something like this: "Boys, the doctor told me I need to have surgery to remove something from my stomach."

Terry spoke for both boys. "What's the matter with you? Are you going to be all right?"

Lorrayne reassured them, "Oh Lord, of course I'm going to be all right. I have to have an operation, a hysterectomy, which will probably lay me up for a while, but I'll be fine. It's nothing for you boys to worry about." Lorrayne saw the concern on their faces.

Robbie held her hand. Terry thought for a moment then asked, "What is a hysterectomy?"

Lorrayne turned to a page in the book that had a diagram of female organs. She pointed to the picture and said, "First, the doctor will take out things that don't work anymore. Here, see this picture"—Lorrayne pointed to the uterus, fallopian tubes, and ovaries in the picture—"these are the parts the doctor will remove, then I'll be fine. Besides, I don't need them anymore. They're not doing me one bit of good."

Terry still needed some answers. "Is it dangerous?"

Lorrayne never lied to her children. "All operations can be

dangerous but I'll be fine. The doctor said I'll be good as new after the surgery."

Terry responded, "Oh. Okay." Robbie never let go of her hand.

"Do you believe me?" Lorrayne asked her children. Both boys nodded yes, looking at Lorrayne, then back to the diagram.

She was about to close the book when Terry stopped her. "You know what that picture looks like? It looks like a cow's head. You have a cow's head in your stomach, Mom."

Lorrayne looked closely at the female organs, turned to her son and said, "Well, I'll be darned, Terry, but I think you're right. I hope I don't start mooing with that cow inside me." She broke into a big smile as the boys laughed.

She had one more thing to tell them before they went outside to play.

"And I have a big surprise for you. Since it's Easter time I asked a special Easter bunny to take care of you while I'm in the hospital."

Robbie turned to her with big, saucer eyes. Terry, dubious of his mother's announcement said, "I bet Grandma and Grandpa are coming to stay with us."

Lorrayne looked at him and said, "You'll see in a few days." Then she told them they could go out and play until it was time for supper.

Friends were waiting on the front stoop when the boys went outside to play. Lorrayne watched through the window as Terry mounted his skateboard, tearing down the street with a couple of kids from the block. Tuffy and a neighbor's Dalmatian, along with a bunch of littler kids ran alongside trying to keep up, hoping to have a turn on one of the skateboards. Lorrayne saw Robbie plop down on the curb after running half a block.

She feared for her young son. What little nourishment he nibbled on barely sustained him through the day. He could only play in spurts before he had to sit down and rest. And if he didn't start doing better in school, she was certain his teacher would recommend holding him back.

She looked out the window; the boys were having a blast. They had tied a rope around the collar of the Dalmatian and the friends were taking turns having the dog pull them on their skateboards. The dog seemed to be having as much fun as the boys so she didn't worry. The kids were giggling, saying "mush" to the dog as he worked with all of his might to tow his passenger. Kids running beside the skateboarder screamed "me next, me next" and Tuffy added to the hullabaloo by barking and running around the runners and riders in circles. Every once in a while one or two of the kids would take a break from the action and join Robbie on the curb. Lorrayne could see them talk to him. He answered his playmates with shrugs and nods. They had learned to ask him yes or no questions.

Lorrayne contemplated how she was going to tell Bob about Robbie, then got distracted. Pat came over with Cricket to see how she had made out at the doctor's. Lorrayne told her. Pat reinforced that it was better she take care of the problem before it got worse. She offered to help Bob with Robbie and Terry while she was in the hospital and so would, she thought, some of the other girls on the block. Before Pat left the Red Cross telephoned. Bob would be home in two days. He would fly in to the Schilling Airfield.

Lorrayne turned to Pat. "Now don't tell the boys Bob's coming home. I want it to be a surprise." Then added, "What do you suppose it's like for a man to leave a war and in less than twenty-four hours be with his family in the middle of a post with nothing but a bunch of women and kids?"

"I'd say that man was pretty lucky."

Two days later Lorrayne took the boys out of school early so they could meet the Easter bunny at the airport. Terry was pos-

itive the surprise visitors were his grandmother and grand-
father. If it wasn't them, then maybe he'd see their uncle
Dwayne, Lorrayne's brother, walk off the plane. Robbie did not
say who he thought was coming. The boys washed up and put
on their Sunday clothes. Lorrayne, dressed in her two-piece suit
with matching accessories, drove to the airport. It was a chilly
April, so they wore overcoats, but the sun was out and the sky
free of clouds.

On the way she thought about everything that had happened
since the last time they were at the airport. Schilling had
changed significantly. Cars and kids were everywhere. The
women had rescued the air base from a sure death; no longer did
it look like a ghost town with tumbleweeds and critters waiting
on the borders to take over. Schilling had been transformed into
a community, a neighborhood, and a home for families who had
no place to go. It had a long way to go before it would resemble a
regular post with all the amenities, but Lorrayne was determined to do whatever she could before she left.

Lately the pain had kept Lorrayne from doing much of
what needed to be done. Everything would have to wait until
she was back on her feet. Hopefully, some of the other women
might pick up the ball and accomplish a few things while she
was laid up.

Lorrayne parked the car. "Are you ready to meet the special
Easter bunny?"

Terry said, "Ah, come on, Mom, tell us who it is."

Lorrayne did not budge. They walked inside the terminal and
over to the area set aside for passengers and families waiting for
the Frontier turboprop to land. Several soldiers, with their wives
and children, stood at the window waiting for the airplane to
take them away. The building was quiet except for the occasional
click of heels on the hard floor and the whispers of children in

their mother's ears. Lorrayne prayed that the sharp pains would stay away until they returned home. Robbie and Terry were caught up in the mystery.

Anticipation permeated the air. No one who goes through the doors of an airport comes out the same way they went in. They are either flying to or returning from somewhere or someone. Or they are reuniting with one who has flown above the clouds, and landed beyond their own borders to different experiences, seeing things that will affect their lives forever. When they return, the lives they touch will never be the same. Coming, going, staying, waiting—an airport is the crossroad where new experiences begin or end and where there is always an expectation that something is about to change.

Terry heard an engine. The boys ran to the window; Lorrayne followed. She took a quick glance at her reflection in the glass, making sure that her hat was straight, that her lipstick had not faded. They went outside to wait for the plane to land.

Other families joined them on the walkway outside of the building. The group watched the aircraft gently glide onto the tarmac and taxi to within a few hundred yards from where they stood. The door of the plane faced the terminal.

Terry fidgeted, each hand held tight to a link of the fence.

Robbie stayed next to his mother, his hands in his pockets, barely moving, staring at the plane.

Lorrayne stroked her son's head, waiting to see the man she married, the man she hadn't seen for seven months, walk off the plane.

The pilot cut the engines. Propellers stopped spinning. An airport employee rolled the staircase to the body of the plane, abutting it below the doorway. He locked the wheels in place, gave a thumbs-up to a member of the flight crew, and then unlocked the gate on the fence that separated the terminal from the tarmac, allowing people to step outside so they could greet the passengers on the runway.

Terry bounded through the gate.

Robbie stayed behind until Lorrayne coaxed him to stand on the other side of the fence with her.

The small group waited for the hatch to open and for the passengers to disembark. The door opened. The crowd breathed a sigh of relief. Finally. For some, the long flight had ended. The longest minutes had passed, the waiting over. For others, it was all about to begin. For Lorrayne's family, it was a thirty-day reprieve from worrying about Bob's safety exchanged for weeks of concern for her well-being.

The aircraft was small, holding no more that fifty people when full. The passengers exited quickly, eager for a reunion with their families. Civilians outnumbered the military personnel on the flight. Anyone in uniform stood out a little bit brighter.

In the middle of all the passengers Bob appeared in the doorway.

As soon as Lorrayne saw him she waved, watching him scan the crowd, looking for her and the boys.

Terry saw him at the same time, turned to his mother and said, "It's Dad! It's Dad! The Easter bunny isn't Grandma and Grandpa. It's Dad." He ran to meet his father.

Robbie stayed behind, walking forward only when Lorrayne moved closer to the plane.

Terry met his dad at the bottom of the staircase, hugged him quickly, then grabbed a bag before the father and son walked back toward Lorrayne and Robbie. As Bob approached, Lorrayne left Robbie to meet her husband. What was she thinking in the few seconds it took for her to kiss and hug him for the first time in months? *It's so wonderful to see him. I hope he's not disappointed he had to leave Vietnam. He's so thin. What's he going to say about Robbie? Has he changed? Will things be the same between us? I hope he likes what I've fixed for dinner.*

Lorrayne knew things between her and Bob would be fine. They were old hands at dealing with separations. He had been on hardship tours to Korea and Lebanon. When the duty was over, he came home and everything returned to normal.

Lorrayne watched Robbie. She could not figure out if he was happy or sad or scared. Her little boy simply stood with his hands digging deeper in his pockets, his forehead as furrowed as an old man's brow. It did not look as if he was breathing, so rapt was his attention on his father.

Bob walked toward Robbie. Terry and Lorrayne followed at close range. How would Bob react to Robbie's refusal to speak? She wished that she had warned Bob, but she had not wanted her husband to worry, hoping that Robbie was going through a phase that would pass before Bob returned home. Everything had happened so fast as a result of her cancer. Now it was too late.

Lorrayne could do nothing but watch the drama of her son's silence and his father's reaction unfold before her eyes. Even Terry kept quiet while his younger brother was reunited with their father. Nothing outside of what was happening on the tarmac of the Schilling Airfield mattered to Lorrayne at the moment Bob greeted his youngest son. Robbie looked up at his father, fists still buried deep inside his pockets. The boy never took his eyes off his dad.

For the first time in five months Robbie spoke. "Well, I guess you can come home."

Lorrayne nearly fell over with happiness. And relief. She even, for a moment, forgot the incessant pain that now plagued her for nearly every minute of the day. Her only thought while she watched her son smile and hug his father was that something good had come of her illness. If it took her being sick to make her son better, then she would gladly sacrifice every organ in her body to make sure the youngest of her family stayed happy and healthy.

Bonnie

APRIL IN PARIS
(1970)

In March, as winter lingered in Kansas, the National Liberation Front acknowledged that the Viet Cong was holding an American major prisoner in the south. With the aid of a French correspondent, photographs and a letter from the major were given to his wife. It was the first known communication between a VC prisoner and his family.

Bonnie heard the news, feeling renewed hope that if Bruce was still in the south, his captors might let him send her word that he was alive. Maybe her trip to Paris would be successful. At the very least, she might find out where they were holding her husband. A few weeks before she was scheduled to leave, Bonnie composed a telegram informing Madame Binh of the date of her arrival. She kept it simple:

Madame Binh
Provisional Revolutionary Government,

49 Avenue Cambaceres,
Veurievia-le-Buisan, 91 Esome France:

I will arrive in Paris on April 17. Request audience with you
regarding my husband, Army Major Bruce G. Johnson,
missing in South Vietnam since June 10, 1965. Will contact
your residence upon arrival.

Kathleen Johnson
Salina, Kans

Although Bonnie had written several letters to Madame Binh
since the delegate had joined the negotiating team at the Peace
Talks, she had never received a response. In Bonnie, Binh had
met her match. If the NLF representative was known as the
flower and the fire for the revolution, then Bonnie was the
flower and the fire for her family. She remained fearless in her
mission.

Somewhere Bruce was alive, waiting to be found. Waiting to
be rescued. The U.S. government continued telling her they were
doing everything in their power to find him. It was not that she
did not believe them. The Army had done everything to reassure
her. And she knew the military officers she had worked with during the years after Bruce's disappearance wanted to find her husband as much as she did. It was just that, in some cases, the
government's hands were tied. And so she went forward, confident in her goal to find Bruce.

Six weeks before Bonnie's second trip to Paris, Henry Kissinger
and Le Duc Tho, the fifth ranking member of the Hanoi Polit-
buro, held the first of three clandestine meetings in Paris. Several weeks later a second meeting was held and only days before
Bonnie left for Paris, the third and final meeting took place. Le
Duc Tho told Kissinger that the North Vietnamese position con-

tinued to be an unconditional U.S. withdrawal and an abandon-
ment of the South Vietnamese government as a precondition for
progress in the stalled negotiations. Kissinger proposed a mutual
withdrawal of military forces, the neutralization of Cambodia,
and a mixed electoral commission to supervise elections in South
Vietnam. Kissinger refused Tho. Tho refused Kissinger. The
stalemate continued.

Colonel Miller drove Bonnie to the airport, where she caught the
first of three flights that would bring her to Paris. Bonnie
checked into her hotel, secured an interpreter, and telephoned
Madame Binh's residence. A secretary answered the phone. Bonnie made her request, "I would very much like to make an
appointment to speak with Madame Binh." The woman told her
that Madame Binh was very busy.

Bonnie reiterated, "I am here to speak with Madame Binh in
regard to my husband."

Binh's representative responded, "Madame Binh is very busy
and she cannot meet with you."

Bonnie was resolute. "Is there anyone with whom I might
speak in regard to my husband?"

"No," was the reply.

Again Bonnie asked, "There is no one who could tell me the
status of my husband?"

The secretary repeated, "No."

Bonnie refused to give up. "My husband went missing in
South Vietnam on June 10, 1965—nearly five years ago. My children and I have not heard one word from him; not one letter has
been received. Please, isn't there someone who will meet with
me and give me some information on my husband?"

The woman on the other side of the telephone line told Bonnie, "War is a tense time." She added, "We do not know of our
men; why should you know of yours?"

Click.

The secretary had hung up before Bonnie could give her the phone number of the hotel where she was staying.

Bonnie, undaunted, prepared a letter to Madame Binh.

Friday, April 17, 1970

Dear Madame Binh:

I was pleased to have the opportunity to talk with your secretary this morning. I, of course, had so wanted to speak with you in regard to my husband, Major Bruce G. Johnson, who is missing in Vietnam. I can appreciate that you are a busy woman since you occupy so high a position within the National Liberation Front.

I'm sure you know, Madame Binh, how earnestly I have yearned to hear some word of my husband in all these many years and how our children, even now, are anxiously awaiting my return with word of their father.

I hope you will understand the concern I feel for my husband and would be grateful if you were to try to find time to meet with me, even if only very briefly.

It occurs to me that it might be easier for you if I could come to your residence and not further inconvenience your schedule by meeting me at some other place. With that in mind, may I come to your home tomorrow morning, Saturday, April 18, at 10:30 A.M.? I will look forward to meeting with you at this time unless it is too inconvenient for you. If this does not meet with your convenience, would you please call me at my hotel and leave a message for me.

Sincerely,
Kathleen B. Johnson

Bonnie carried the letter to Madame Binh's residence, gave it to a man at the gate, and watched him carry it into her residence. She returned to the hotel to wait.

No one called.

At 10:30 the next morning, Bonnie and her interpreter arrived at the gate of Madame Binh's home. A man, speaking only French, told Bonnie that she "was not in." Bonnie asked for the secretary. She "was not in" either. Bonnie persisted. The man told her to wait while he returned to the house to consult with someone. Bonnie waited. And waited. It seemed as if hours passed before the man returned to tell her to leave her name and a number where she could be reached. He volunteered that "Madame Binh might possibly be in at two P.M."

Bonnie returned to her hotel, waiting patiently until two o'clock when she once again presented herself at the gates of the enemy. She was turned away. "Madame Binh is resting."

The next morning Bonnie went to church services, telephoned the children, and passed the afternoon planning her next move. In the evening, alone in her hotel, without the benefit of her interpreter, she phoned Binh's residence only to be frustrated by a brief conversation with someone who only spoke French. She had nothing left to do but pray that the next day might be the day when she could call her children with good news.

When Bonnie called the next morning, the secretary explained that Madame Binh was very busy and would not be able to meet with her. The woman added, "Here is Madame Binh's reply to you and all the other wives and families of American Army men."

Bonnie requested that the secretary speak slowly and carefully so she could copy the message on paper. The secretary read Binh's statement to Bonnie.

Since the American government has sent American Army men to South Vietnam to wage an aggressive war against the South Vietnamese population, it is responsible about the fate of these men, and on our part, we have always advocated and put into practice a humanitarian policy toward the American Army men who have come to make war against our people and who have been captured by the Liberation People's Party.

Bonnie asked the secretary to repeat the statement once more, then asked, "Why in all of these years, almost five years, if the policy of the National Liberation Front is a humanitarian one, as they say that they are, have I been unable to hear from or receive a letter from my husband? Wouldn't it be part of a humane policy that a man would be allowed to write to his wife and children?"

After some thought the voice suggested, "In war it is difficult to know where anyone is. Ask President Nixon where he is."

Bonnie refused to give in. "President Nixon does not know where my husband is; my husband is not missing in the United States. No one knows where he is except someone from the National Liberation Front." She continued to plead her case. "Is there anyone with whom I might speak? If I went to Vietnam, would there be anyone there who could tell me the answer to my question?"

"No," she was told again. The secretary added, "You have Madame Binh's reply. Now I must go."

Click.

In a final effort to implore Madame Binh for information about Bruce, Bonnie sent via special delivery another letter to the residence. She restated everything she had written or said to the secretary and ended the note with one final plea.

Even if a meeting would not be granted by you, I feel that it would be no more than humane to tell me or to ask your secretary or someone from your delegation to tell me of the exact status of my husband. I came to Paris only for this information and for my children's sake; it would be difficult, indeed, to return to them without word of their father. I await your reply.

No reply.

Bonnie called the following morning. The secretary refused to speak English, so the entire conversation was carried on in French with the interpreter. She was told she had been given Madame Binh's response. They did not know where Bruce was. Her final comment to Bonnie, "We are too busy to continue to take all of these calls."

Click.

During the next week Bonnie appealed to the Bureau of Information of the National Liberation Front and several embassies, including the Egyptian, the Russian, and the Chinese, hoping that someone might be able to tell her something or have enough pull to find out about Bruce. Many representatives merely dismissed Bonnie. Some treated her with respect and without insult to her husband, or to America. A few men she appealed to were kind and understanding of her situation. When asked what she should tell her children, the delegate from the Bureau of Information of the National Liberation Front said, "Give them my deepest sympathy. I am a father and I understand. I have lost many relatives in the war."

Eleven days after arriving in Paris, despite impressive efforts on her part to find Bruce, Bonnie returned to the United States without knowing anything more about her husband than when she left Schilling Manor.

* * *

Around the same time Bonnie began her campaign to find Bruce, somewhere in South Vietnam's jungle, a group of stealth Americans—it is uncertain whether they were military or civilian—raided a Viet Cong stronghold. Piles of enemy papers and films were captured in the raid. The plunder was categorized top secret, then sent to various U.S. government agencies for analysis. It took time for the agents to interpret the thousands of things captured during the war.

One of the films, *The Flames of Dong Xoia*, depicted a major encounter between the VC and American troops at a South Vietnam rubber plantation in June 1965. A scene from the confiscated film showed the downing of a UH-1B helicopter. Later footage panned the aftermath of the combat zone, including images of the aircraft and the area surrounding its torn, bent frame, still smoking from the explosion that caused its ruin. The tail was still intact and the numbers read 63-08557—the Huey that took Bruce into battle before he went missing.

In the pictures, strewn around the twisted metal and debris, were the lifeless bodies of several U.S. soldiers.

Beverly

LAUREN

(1971)

I had a knack for choosing friends who were braver than me. Especially when it came to boys. I'd always go so far, then retreat in fear, my mother's warnings of ruination assaulting my conscience if I was ever tempted to go beyond "first base." I was certain she had a crystal ball hidden somewhere in her bedroom that signaled her if my libido elevated beyond acceptable levels.

Despite my mother's imposing presence, I was once bold enough to sneak out of the house with my best friend, Lauren, one midsummer's night when only the pale glow of nightlights shown through Schilling Manor windows. Earlier in the day, Lauren had revealed that she had met a guy. Since we were together practically all the time, I could not imagine where or how she might have met someone without my knowing it.

Lauren was tall and lean. Her body resembled that of a long-distance runner, although I had never known her to be involved with anything athletic. She had a long neck and a natural slouch, the kind young girls slide into during adolescence when they begin to tower above their peers. Her forehead was high, offset by a narrow jawline, and plump lips that curved into a wide, endearing smile revealing large, pearl-white teeth. We wore our hair alike, long with a part slightly askew of center, though hers fell straight while mine insisted on crimping into waves.

From midwinter through the summer of 1971 we did practically everything together. We shared makeup and endlessly fussed with each other's hair—one day knotting it into pin curls, the next day pressing it with my mother's steam iron. After school let out in May we ventured into Salina to attend driver's education classes every morning, and once a week we attended meetings of the Smokey Hill Junior Law Enforcement Post 219, an evening activity we had picked up earlier in the year.

In July we got our licenses, finally free of the need to ask our older sisters or Lauren's mother to drive us around. We spent hours going in and out of shops, looking for culottes or funky shirts to wear to the roller rink or to the drive-in on the weekend.

With mornings free and still half of the summer to go we decided to take art lessons at the day-care center. Most of our afternoons were spent at Kanopolis Lake slathering oil on our skin or refreshing our hot bodies in the cool water. We sat around a lot at night, peeling layers of skin off of our crisped bodies and talking ceaselessly of boys and what it was like to be in love, as if it were the only thing that could make us happy. If I wasn't at her house, she was at mine, so when Lauren told me she had met a guy I wondered where this interloper in our friendship could have come from. Lauren told me that if I wanted to meet him, she would introduce us that night after everyone else had gone to bed.

She added that he had a friend and that he wanted to meet me.

I was almost sixteen and had yet to discover the pleasures or pitfalls of free love, a romantic notion perpetuated by a slightly older generation of flower children that, in the long run, had nothing to do with love and everything to do with sex, but was supposed to be a lot of fun without the bridle of commitment. The news, TV, magazines, and advertisements reported on and in some cases encouraged free love and I was anxious to experience it, free or otherwise, and looked at Lauren's invitation as a means to that end.

I spent the night at Lauren's because she had already figured how to sneak out without making any noise. We could hardly wait for everyone to go to sleep, even went to bed early hoping her brothers and sister would follow our lead. They didn't. At one in the morning we squeezed ourselves out of the narrow windows in Lauren's bedroom, stifling giggles that came out as snorts that we hoped would be mistaken for the noisy sounds of sleep.

Once certain our escape had not roused the house we made for the bikes we had stashed behind her garage earlier in the day. We mounted our Huffys armored in short-shorts, tank tops, and flip-flops, our faces garnished with rouge, eyeliner, and white frosted lipstick. Off we went, being careful not to be caught in the back-yard spotlights and on constant lookout for the deputy's car. I had no idea where we were going, it was a surprise, but when Lauren rode toward the railroad tracks beyond the housing area I won-dered if we were going to ride all the way into Salina on the back roads.

"Where are we going?" I asked Lauren, who was pedaling faster than the prairie's night breeze.

"Not too far," was her answer.

The only things on the other side of the railroad tracks were the airport, the administration buildings, the commissary and PX, the gym, a day-care center, the pool, the movie theater, and the teen club. We passed all of those buildings; the only ones left were the deserted barracks and some warehouses, the chapel, and the dispensary.

Headlights.

We jumped off of our bikes, laid them and ourselves down on the ground behind a minor knoll, and ducked our heads, hoping whoever it was had not seen us. My heart beat with such force that I could feel it throbbing in my head and, as in the days when I played hide-and-seek with friends, as soon as I hid, I had to pee like crazy. Lauren made faces—I held in my snorts and crossed my legs. Finally, the car passed out of sight. We contained our giggles. My need to pee subsided. We resumed our adventure.

I have always understood mortality, something that most American children don't usually face until well into their twenties. Death was everywhere when I was growing up. Not so much in my immediate family, but the deaths of thousands and thousands of boys were reported daily on the radio, in the newscasts, in the newspapers, and by my friends during recess from when I was a little girl with a conscious memory.

Death was something that happened to fathers and brothers, rarely to grandparents or other old people. Death came in dozens. I was always impressed by the rows of coffins laid out on a runway somewhere, probably in Washington, each one exactly alike, blanketed with an American flag. The display of flags seduced me into feeling that death was okay. Maybe the flags' power over me was like the dreamy spell Dracula casts over his victims before sucking their blood. The enchantment is irresistible, but deep inside lurks a terrible dread.

Or maybe it wasn't like that at all. Maybe I simply did not know any better. As long as I saw fifty stars and thirteen strips, death had a purpose. Sometimes, I imagined that the guys in the coffins were my brothers. I felt like crying. I never did, fearing that someone in my family might make fun of me. Instead, I thought about my death, secretly hoping that since I was going to die anyway, it would be good to die a hero while fighting for my country.

* * *

But I was not thinking about death as I rode beside Lauren that night. She was my best friend. We were alone, traipsing across the base, free to do whatever we wanted; no one would stop us because those who cared about us had no idea that we were not where we were supposed to be.

I could have ridden alongside of her the entire night, relishing our brazenness, feeling superior to everyone else sleeping in their safe beds. We were gloriously selfish, not caring about anyone but ourselves. It did not matter where we ended up; the air was sultry, the wind calm, and the stars in the vast sky surrounded us in the darkness, arousing in me a feeling that I had not felt before.

No one could catch me, or hurt me.

Parents and sisters, nonexistent.

War, history.

I was not in Kansas; I was somewhere else, a safe place free of confusion and frustration and death. Everything seemed clear, as if a door had opened, inviting me in to participate in an exhilarating world I knew nothing about. In this world I was immortal.

Lauren did not experience an epiphany that night. Her goal was to ride to our destination as fast as possible. I complied, following at a breakneck speed and despite my newly discovered invincibility, I was sweating off my carefully made up face wondering where the heck we were going.

Up and down a few ramps and around a couple of old wooden buildings later we ended up at the side door of the dispensary. *What are we doing here?* I had never seen anyone use the side door as most visitors used the front door. But there we were at the narrowish door, standing in the shadow of an awning, away from any available light, smoothing our knotted hair, and wiping ourselves down in an attempt to look as presentable as possible to whoever was inside.

Lauren had had the foresight to bring the tube of lipstick, which we reapplied before she knocked three times on the door. The handle turned and the door eased open so slowly and deliberately that I began to get the willies. I poked Lauren who seemed as nervous as I was, but ready for whatever lay ahead. To me, it was beginning to feel like the opening scene of a scary B-movie—innocent young girls are lured into a lunatic's den, given hallucinogens, raped, and eventually skinned alive, though alert enough (despite effects of the drugs) to wish they had listened to their mothers' warnings and had stayed at home.

Of course, regrets never occur until it is too late to change the course of fate.

The door opened. I followed Lauren. She stopped to give our doorman a peck on the cheek. I was surprised to find that in the darkened hallway he appeared much older than a high school boy. On closer inspection I was astonished to see that he was wearing the kind of white pants, white tunic with a nameplate over the left pocket, and white shoes that I had seen Army corpsmen wear during my visits to Army dispensaries over the years.

What's going on?

Lauren continued down the hall with a confident glide and what looked like a new sway in her hips. We entered a well-lit room where another male dressed in white waited to greet us. I looked to see if anyone else was around—there wasn't—and returned my gaze to the tall, black man who never took his eyes off me.

He was old, maybe twenty-six, had a pleasant enough smile, and an Afro that was bigger than allowed by Army regulation but smaller than Angela's Davis's, whose hair took up half of any photograph I'd seen of her in the newspaper. I tried not to stare, and forced myself instead to take in my surroundings—white walls, stainless-steel carts and trays, plastic chairs with metal arms. The air smelled like rubbing alcohol and cough medicine, and the lights, bright and fluorescent, stretched out in strips across the ceiling. I might have been stunned, or excited, or terrified, but I was not a prude, so I fought the urge to run out of the dispensary like the underaged schoolgirl that I was.

Small talk is better than no talk, though I cannot imagine or remember what two girls and two married men—I knew they were married because all the men assigned to the post had to be—who did not appear to have their wives on their mind might have talked about in the few minutes before Lauren and her guy retreated to one of the examination rooms.

Left face to face with a large black man in a medical uniform I did the only thing I could do. I sat down on one of the plastic-and-chrome waiting room chairs and started talking. Who knows about what? He sat dangerously close to me. At some point during our conversation I began to shake. Not the outside kind of shaking that comes with being cold, but the inside kind of shaking that often signals a seminal moment in one's life.

I avoided eye contact and continued talking throughout the visit. What I was saying had nothing to do with what I was thinking. He heard, "So you're in the Army? That's great, so's my dad." Inside I heard, *My mother is going to kill me.* "Yep, my dad's in Vietnam. Have you been there?" *I wonder if he wants to kiss me?* "Gee, I thought you guys had to be married." *I think he wants a kiss?* "Wow, it's really bright in here." *Should I let him kiss me?* "I bet you don't have too many sick people come in at night." *Maybe I should let him kiss me.* "Bicycles are a great way to get around when you don't drive."

I chattered on until my aged wooer, perhaps out of disappointment, offered me a soda and the decision to kiss or not to kiss was replaced by the fear of my mother freaking out should someone wake up and report us missing. We had been gone for nearly two hours. My immortality dissolved with each tick of the minute hand on the dispensary's clock. Finally, Lauren and the medic emerged from the examining room looking a little rumpled. Her lips were no longer frosted.

I don't know how we made our exit that night. I imagine it was a cordial exchange of good-byes and see you sometimes. We were quiet on the ride home. Lauren's mood was dark. She pedaled slowly, as if each rotation depleted her energy. I was in a hurry to get back to her house, but dying to find out what happened with the guy. When I asked, she said she hoped she was not pregnant.

I nearly fell off my bike.

"You mean you went all the way?"

I could not believe it. As much as we had talked about experiencing sex as soon as possible, I never thought it would happen, let alone against the colorless backdrop of an examining room with a married, enlisted medical corpsman. I'm not sure Lauren expected that either. She asked if anything happened between me and whatever his name was.

My simple no put us in different leagues. She had done it. I had not. We had made different choices. I pondered what I had missed. She wondered what she had lost. We sighed when she finally got her period, although the weeks of worrying had put a damper on our breezy, careless summer.

Lorrayne

DISRUPTION
(1966)

Lorrayne made dozens of phone calls before she checked into the hospital a few days after Bob came home. She told her neighbors and the people she had been working with in Salina—the Chamber, the Salvation Army, one or two businesses—that she would be out of touch for a few weeks and to go ahead and do whatever they could on the projects they were working on.

Robbie was back to his old self, eating up a storm of Sloppy Joes, meatballs, potato dumplings, and anything else Lorrayne put on his plate. In a short time his color went from gray pallor to healthy pink. He and Terry horsed around the way they used to, but because their father was home, their horsing around took place outside of the house. Both sensed that Lorrayne wasn't feeling well, especially when their father reminded them to stay quiet or to go outside and play.

On the morning that Lorrayne went into the hospital she told the boys to behave until she got home. Their father had come home to take care of them and they should do whatever they could to help out—clean their rooms, take out the garbage, wash the dishes, feed and walk Tuffy—without having to be asked.

Do not disturb your father.

Do what you are told.

Bob was a little on edge, probably because the transition from Vietnam to home had happened so fast. No matter how much she reassured him that she would be fine, Lorrayne knew he was worried about her health. She never told him about Robbie, figuring that it could wait until some other time especially since their son was behaving like a normal nine-year-old.

Lorrayne kissed Robbie and Terry good-bye, assuring them again that she would be home in no time, then sent them off to school. Tears ran down Robbie's cheeks as he walked beside his brother to catch a ride to school with one of their friends.

Pat came over with Cricket to wish her friend well. She told her not to worry about a thing, and as soon as she was up for it, she'd find a sitter for the baby and visit her in the hospital.

A few hours later Lorrayne lay in her hospital bed. Bob had left so he could be home when the boys returned from school.

She was not afraid.

What she felt, the thing she hated feeling more than anything else, was helplessness. Her family and the women of Schilling needed her healthy. And where was she? Forty miles away, in a room that smelled like Lysol where she was incapable of doing anything for anyone. All she could do was pace the floor, fretting about how they would manage without her.

Bob drove back to see her in the evening. The boys were fine. They had come home from school, asked how she was, and went outside to play. Lorrayne asked if they had changed out of their school clothes. Yes, it was the first thing they had done after they walked in the door. At five-thirty they ate the casserole she had left in the fridge. When he left the boys were cleaning up the dishes. Afterward they were to do their homework, take their baths, and go to bed by nine if he wasn't home. Lorrayne wondered how Terry and Robbie reacted to their father's time frame. Since Bob had left she had kept up a steady but much more flexible routine with the boys.

Lorrayne's relationship with Bob was never strained or formal. Neither was it overly affectionate. They loved each other in the way people who had been married for nearly twenty years loved each other—with ease, without the need to constantly remind each other of their love, and with the belief that no matter what was happening in the world, she would wait for him. And no matter where he went, he would always come home.

She would follow him to whatever forsaken post he was assigned to, whether it be on the Alaskan tundra or the baked landscape of Texas. It was her duty as much as it was his. Lorrayne made the best of it for her husband and sons, protecting and caring for them with the vast wings of a mother and a wife who with hat, gloves, pearls, and a fearless personality could bear the burden of every challenge that faced her family.

Bob relied on her to hold things together when he was away, and Lorrayne did a stellar job. So when it was time for Bob to take care of her and the boys, their relationship, for those few weeks, went askew with each of them trying to figure out how to handle their new roles. Both were preoccupied with the lives they had learned to lead without each other: Bob at war, Lorrayne alone at Schilling.

Surgery took longer than anticipated. When the doctor came out to the waiting room he told Bob that Lorrayne was fine, but would be under the effects of the anesthesia for some time. *Go home. Come back in the morning.* Bob hesitated, not wanting to leave Lorrayne in case she woke up, but decided to go home to be with Terry and Robbie, who he knew were worried about their mother.

After dinner Bob suggested they go out for a walk before it got too cold. The April air was warm during the day, but still brisk enough at night to require a jacket. The boys jumped at the chance to go for a walk with their father, thinking it was swell that they could show off the only dad in the neighborhood. A couple of their friends were out skateboarding but knew enough to leave the boys alone while they were with their father.

Bob told the boys that when he went back to Vietnam it was up to them to help their mother. He saw that his sons were concerned, especially Robbie, who had turned pensive and quiet. Their father reassured them. *Mom will be fine. It's just going to take some time.* He would stay for about two weeks after she came home. But when he left, he reiterated, it was their responsibility to make sure their mother did not do too much until she regained her strength.

The boys said they understood.

They asked their dad if he wanted to watch them skateboard with the dog. He said no, that it was time to go inside, finish homework, and get ready for bed. The boys knew better than to disobey a direct order, telling their friends they would see them the next day.

On Saturday morning the boys routinely watched *Space Ghost,* one of their favorite cartoons. Robbie especially loved watching the little monkey Blip hop all around, helping Space Ghost catch all kinds of evildoers in the universe. *The Mighty Thor* and *Batman* were two other favorites, along with *Underdog* and his girlfriend, Sweet Polly Purebred.

"Have no fear. Underdog is here."

On cold or rainy Saturday mornings Robbie and Terry could spend hours watching animated characters rescue damsels, save the universe, and laugh as Daffy, Tweety, and Bugs performed their weekly antics, but on the first Saturday after Lorrayne's surgery, as they were settling in to watch the week's animated adventures, their father came into the room and flipped the channel to the news. The boys were about to protest. Instead they went over to one of their friends' houses to watch the shows while their dad looked for any news about what was happening in Vietnam.

Lorrayne spent eleven days in the hospital. Pat visited. She combed her friend's hair, letting her know about the goings-on at the base, which Lorrayne found out did not amount to much. Pat mentioned that the boys were fine, following Bob's routine to the letter. "And don't worry about Easter dinner," Pat reassured. "Me and Madonna will make sure Bob and the boys have plenty to eat." Lorrayne had thought ahead and had made and hid Easter baskets. She asked Pat to remind Bob to put out the baskets in case he forgot.

Bob visited nearly every day, making small talk with Lorrayne, sometimes having to tell her unpleasant things. Like one morning he and the boys woke up to find that the two rabbits they kept in a pen out on the back patio had been attacked, killed by something the night before. *Downright dead.* Bob and Terry had suspected Tuffy. Robbie could not believe that his beloved little dog would do such a thing. Lorrayne told Bob she did not think Tuffy would kill the rabbits, reminding him how gentle their dog was with the chicks.

She asked her husband if any of the neighbors had come over with covered dishes.

"Yes, Pat and Madonna had dropped by with dinner a few times."

Lorrayne was a little taken aback that no one else had made an effort. She was glad she had the foresight to prepare some meals and stick them in the freezer before she left. And she knew Bob did not mind treating the boys to pizza while she was away.

Bob brought Lorrayne magazines and mail, cards from family and friends and well-wishers, which she opened and read, pleased that people had thought about her while she was in the hospital.

She was especially tickled to receive a card from the civilians in Salina she had worked with over the past months. Everyone at the Chamber of Commerce, the folks at the Salvation Army, and several businessmen had all signed and sent her a get-well card. Reading the card nearly made her cry. She thought that whenever she and Bob were ready to retire, that Salina should be high on their list of options. The people were so friendly, most of them going out of their way to help her and the other wives at Schilling.

About a week after her surgery, Lorrayne began feeling better and was ready to go home. She was able to have two or three brief conversations with the boys—they sounded fine, but also eager for her to come home. Her children had never been without her for very long.

Lorrayne arrived home in the middle of the school day. She crept through her house, walking slowly, holding on to her stomach because it felt as if something might fall out if she moved too fast or stood too straight.

Everything was the same. When the boys came home they could hardly stop themselves from jumping on her while she sat on the couch. She hugged them with all her might. After the reunion the boys went out to play. That night, while Bob and Lorrayne slept, Robbie snuck in bed with them. A little later, Terry joined them.

Bob left for Vietnam two weeks later, returning the family to their Schilling routine. Schilling was not a place where men could stay for long periods of time unless they had a purpose, like the commander or the doctors. Bob and any other husbands wandering around without an assignment stood out like ducks in a lake of swans.

The men looked and smelled different. Without wanting to, they called attention to themselves by merely existing. Men were stared at, somewhat idolized, and deferred to in a way they wouldn't be if they had been one among many. Other women's husbands were asked to do mundane chores by neighbors who batted their eyes, looking for attention, and who made them cookies as thanks, sometimes for doing nothing more than screwing in a simple lightbulb.

Bob had been at Schilling for nearly thirty days, a long time for a soldier to live at the base, especially in 1966, when there was nothing for him to do.

No barbershop to cut his hair.

No rathskellar to have a beer with other men.

No range on which to practice shooting.

No formations to follow.

No parades to march in.

No one to salute.

No PX to poke around in.

No chain of command to follow.

No reveille in the morning.

No taps at the end of the day.

And no authority to adhere to except for the rules set down by their wives.

Schilling Manor was the home for waiting wives, not the home for a soldier at war.

The boys were sad to see their father go, but on the Saturday after he left they took up their old positions in front of the TV, watching cartoons. Not long after Bob left, Lorrayne sat at the kitchen table, Tuffy at her heels, and began making a new list of the things to do before Bob returned home in a few months. At the top of the list, open the pool before summer vacation.

Pat and Cricket visited Lorrayne every day, the phone started ringing as much as it had before her surgery, and the Waiting Wives Club members filled their founder in on what they had accomplished during her illness. The Lending Closet was open and "Hello and Good-bye" teas were scheduled for each month. So far, no one had left, but by the end of the summer, the first group of women to arrive at Schilling began rotating out, making room for new waiting wives and their families.

Bonnie

LOVE ALONE IS
NOT ENOUGH

(1970)

Before returning home from Paris, Bonnie stopped in Washington, D.C., at the request of Senator Bob Dole.

The Kansas senator served as chairman on the Senate-House Appeal for International Justice Committee. The committee had proposed and Congress had passed a resolution assigning May 1, 1970, as a day to appeal for international justice on behalf of all the American prisoners of war and servicemen missing in action in Southeast Asia. The resolution also stated that every possible effort would be made to secure the early release of all U.S. prisoners from captivity.

Dole was speaking before the House Foreign Relations Subcommittee on April 29 to encourage members of the committee to attend a rally celebrating the passing of the resolution at Constitution Hall at 8:00 P.M. on May 1. Almost eight hundred wives and parents of prisoners of war and the missing soldiers would be attending the program. Dole wanted to fill the nearly four thousand seats. *Let's show the families that Washington and all of America cared about them and their lost men.*

The senator knew Bonnie planned to attend the rally. When he found out about her trip to Paris he asked her to testify before the committee. "Tell them," he told her, "about your family and the attempts you've made to find out information about your husband."

Bonnie agreed. Despite jet lag and disappointment she walked into committee room number 2255 in the Rayburn House office building with Kansas's senator at ten in the morning after her return from Paris.

For nearly an hour she told the members of the Foreign Relations Subcommittee some of her experiences since June 10, 1965. She began with the children.

"If I could share with you just a few of the difficult moments that children of our missing men face," she continued her comments without benefit of a script, "I think it would help us realize the terrible burden of hardship that is imposed on so many little ones across our nation by the present attitudes and policies of the National Liberation Front in not giving information on whom they hold and in not permitting communication between the men and their children, wives, and parents."

After describing examples of her three children's experiences, Colleen's brownies, Bruce's Valentine's Day card, and Bryan's dream, she provided the committee with details of her efforts to locate Bruce. She read her letters to Madame Binh, spoke of her visits to Binh's residence, of the responses she received, of the time she spent in the Communist embassies, and of the dream she still had of one day reuniting with her husband. Bonnie sat next to

Senator Dole and concluded her impassioned statement, meant not only for the politicians in the room, but for the American people.

"I think that it would not be, perhaps, overly dramatic to say that the problems of our prisoners of war and missing in action could be viewed as a national emergency. I would ask each of you to realize that many of us wives and parents have acted spontaneously as a result of our own love and caring for our husbands and sons and have done all that we can to attempt to change their awful plight and gain some information. Our efforts and love, alone, are not enough. I am deeply convinced that this matter must not only be a matter of top priority in those homes where that loved one is missing, but it must become a matter of top priority within our nation—from each home and heart across our land reaching even to the highest levels of government.

"I know that this problem is a unique one and a terribly difficult one for our country, but I am completely confident that America has the talent, the dedication, and the abilities from within her greatest natural resources—her people—to honorably find the solution to this problem.

"There has never been a difficulty or problem too great for the American people to solve. With all America joining together in prayer and in action, we will not fail these, our men, nor will we fail America."

Before Bonnie left the room, Wisconsin Senator Clement Zablocki, chairman of the subcommittee, thanked Bonnie. "I know my colleagues join me in extending our admiration of your courage, and there is little that we can say at this time that would be comforting. But I can assure you we join you in your hope and prayers that the whereabouts and the fate of your husband, and indeed all prisoners of war, will soon be known and in whatever way we can join in your efforts and the thousands and millions of others, hundreds of thousands, rather, of Americans, who are concerned, we will do the utmost."

Chairman Zablocki announced that the hearings on the prisoner-of-war problem would continue the next morning and that Bonnie was welcome to attend.

Bonnie went back to the Rayburn building the next day. She listened to the testimonies of Sybil Stockdale and several other women with missing or captured husbands. H. Ross Perot also spoke of his efforts to break through the North Vietnamese roadblock.

Later that evening she spoke at the Appeal for International Justice rally along with other wives, politicians, movie stars, Perot, and even Captain James A. Lovell, the *Apollo 13* command pilot who nearly didn't make it home from his excursion in space the year before. Bonnie saw few faces that had been in the Foreign Relations meetings, but was grateful to the ones who did attend.

Early the next morning Bonnie accompanied Sybil Stockdale and other members of the National League of Families to a press conference. Along with Mrs. Stockdale, Bonnie answered questions, eloquently stating the objectives of the League. Their statement always remained the same: They sought news about the men they loved, proper treatment as accorded them by the Geneva Convention, and awareness of the predicament of the nearly fifteen hundred soldiers whose fate was determined by an enemy who was committed to fighting and dying for the freedom of their people and would not hesitate to use U.S. prisoners as pawns in the politics of war.

Bonnie did not realize it, nor did she ever think about it, but her experiences in the years since Bruce had gone missing, and especially in the last months, had given her confidence. She had learned quickly, had become determined to find answers, and had grown into a vigorous advocate, not only for her family but for all the other families of soldiers missing in Vietnam.

Bonnie returned to her children two weeks after she had left them. Colonel Miller picked her up with all three of her off-spring, each of them eager to tell her everything they had done while she was gone. Colleen announced that she had learned how to make cheese crepes. She could not wait for her mother to taste one. Her children seemed to have grown inches since she left. On the ride home Bonnie noticed that one of her neighbors had moved away. It reminded her that so many of her friends and her children's playmates came and went, leaving them behind to wonder who would be the next to arrive, to make friends with, and to inevitably leave.

Her family's life was transient, though they remained in the same house. Bonnie looked at her oldest child and thought, despite her unchanged status as a waiting wife, time had passed and how quickly he was approaching his teens.

She began to mull around the idea that perhaps, before he entered junior high school, she should consider moving into a regular community, a place that offered stability and the promise of making lifelong friends.

The Committee

THE SEDAN

The committee met a week before the fashion show at the lieutenant's wife's house. She had spent the entire morning trying to clean up the place. But at eleven, after she had taken the girls to the day-care center, she had not vacuumed the living room, picked up the toys, emptied the dirty diaper bucket, or cleaned the bathroom toilet. She thought, "Oh, when my mother comes to watch the girls next week she's going to kill me when she sees this house."

The only things she had to serve were coffee, celery sticks, and the Mars Bars she had stashed in the freezer. For a moment she thought about stuffing the celery with peanut butter, but decided not to because the girls needed more than jelly on their sandwiches.

She had run out of money for groceries.

The lieutenant's wife hoped the committee wasn't hungry and didn't mind the mess. She had had too many things to do and to top it off, the warrant officer's wife had her running all over town to find shoes and accessories in the last week. She even

225

dragged her to the Fort Riley PX to see what the women's clothing manager would donate to the show. The outing took almost the entire day, but she managed to buy new makeup and an empire-style dress for her trip to Hawaii. The warrant officer's wife told her that the cut was very slimming, encouraging her to buy it without thinking that the young woman would spend her food money.

The lieutenant's wife's doors and windows were open because it was the first beautiful spring day. A mild breeze blew through the house, refreshing the stale air. The birds in the backyard warbled songs that reminded her of home, making her feel nostalgic for the days when she had nothing to worry about except bringing home good grades and setting the table for dinner.

The doorbell rang. Her daydream ended.

In came the women, every one of them only minutes apart. The lieutenant's wife was relieved to see that the sergeant major's wife had brought homemade doughnuts.

The wives got down to the business of making a list of everything they had to do in the final days before the show. Plenty of people had volunteered to help with the last-minute preparations. Judi's Girl Scouts would arrive two days before the show to help decorate. The girls had been making red, white, and blue crepe-paper flowers during their last two troop meetings.

Sergeant Medina from the housing office had already built the stage and the runway. He had even constructed a trellis for the models to step through before walking into the crowd.

Other members of the Waiting Wives Club were making baked goods for their guests to snack on, and Colonel Miller provided the ingredients for the punch. Miller was supposed to come to their meeting to go over his MC duties, but the colonel's wife told the women he had called her that morning. He couldn't come.

"It seems," she pronounced, "that the commander had an emergency with one of the wives."

"Oh really," said the warrant officer's wife. "What now?"

"A truck driver knocked on his door at about six this morning wanting to know if he was the commander." She continued, "Can you imagine, a truck driver on Schilling Manor?"

"Why not," said the sergeant major's wife. "The commissary has to get stuff from somewhere."

"Come on now, at six o'clock in the morning?" said the warrant officer's wife.

"Well, ladies," said the colonel's wife, trying to go on with her story, "to make a long story short, he's tied up because the woman brought the trucker home last night and when he left this morning he was not five miles down the road before he discovered he had been rolled. The deputy directed him to the commander's house. He wants his money back. The colonel wasn't sure how long it would take him to deal with the situation."

"Rorred?" asked the captain's wife. "What rorred mean?"

The lieutenant's wife wondered, too. "I know what rolled means, like he rolled up his sleeping bag, but I don't think you mean what I think it means. What does it mean?"

"Rolled, I'll be, I haven't heard that word since I was a teenager and overheard my father and my uncle talking about my cousin's big trip to New York City," admitted the warrant officer's wife and then gave her friends the answer. "It means that one of our less than decent ladies brought that man home, gave him a romp in the hay, and while he was asleep—in her husband's bed mind you—she fished his pockets for a payday."

"Sounds like he had it coming. Sleeping with a man's wife is not exactly honorable behavior," commented the colonel's wife.

"Who knows why she did it," offered the sergeant major's wife. "Don't you remember when we passed the hat at one of the wives club meetings to raise money for that poor English girl whose husband sent her about ten dollars a month to feed herself and her kids. One of her neighbors told Major McKain she thought something was up and when he sent someone from his office over to her house pretending to check the electricity or something, all he found in the fridge was a quart of sour milk and stale bologna."

"That's right," remembered the colonel's wife, "that poor family was starving. It's true, some husbands are real jerks to their wives. Still, that's no excuse to have loose morals. It gives the rest of us a bad reputation."

"She not have choice, maybe," offered the captain's wife. "Stear, or starve. What they do to her you thing?"

"Colonel Miller probably got Major McKain and went over to her house to tell her to give the guy his money back. They might even call her husband home if she puts up a squawk. Depends. Anyway," continued the colonel's wife, "the commander will meet with us at the community center one day this week before the show." She was about to continue when the doorbell rang.

The lieutenant's wife left the committee to answer the bell.

It was Colonel Miller.

Wow. He sure knows how to take care of business fast.

After she opened the door to invite him in to join the group she saw the post chaplain standing beside the commander.

Then she saw the sedan: Property of the U.S. Government, for Official Use Only.

"Good Lord," she said as her heart began to race. "What's this all about?"

"Can we come in? I have to tell you—" Colonel Miller started but was cut off.

"Tell me. You have to tell me? No, no. You can't just tell me. The other gals are here. You know that, don't you, Colonel. I'll call them for you. Come in. Come in. Girls," she shouted, unable to control the panic coursing through her body, "come quick,

Colonel Miller's here to tell us something about the fashion show."

The women had already left their seats by the time the soldiers had entered the living room. They saw their friend smiling, but moving randomly between them, the men, and the furniture, stepping carelessly on the toys she had never found time to pick up.

"Look, everyone," the lieutenant's wife said to the committee, "Colonel Miller brought the chaplain along."

"Oh dear God," whispered the colonel's wife when she saw the chaplain, then looked outside and saw the sedan.

The commander turned to the women, "I'm sorry ladies. Perhaps we could talk to——"

"No, no, no," interrupted their hostess, her arms closing in around her. "No. It's okay. They can stay."

The chaplain addressed the lieutenant's wife. "Why don't you sit down?" The warrant officer's wife put her arms around her friend, gently leading her to a chair. The women closed in. They would not leave their fellow wife to face the news alone.

Colonel Miller continued, "I am so sorry, but it is my duty to inform you that your husband was killed in action two days ago while on a mission in South Vietnam." The lieutenant's wife was speechless.

The colonel's wife asked, "Are they sure it's him, Norman?"

The dead soldier's wife looked at Miller, hopeful that there was a mistake.

"They are certain," affirmed the colonel. "He has been identified by his dog tags and his remains are being readied for transport back home."

No one said anything, so the colonel sat beside the young widow. Instead of reading from the Army telegram he spoke from his heart, hoping to ease the woman's grief.

"Your husband died a brave man. Before his helicopter was

shot down he had rescued several soldiers surrounded by VC. They would have died if it weren't for him. I'll bet they'll give him a medal for his courage."

The room was silent except for the murmur of the chaplain's prayer and the birds singing in the background.

The commander added, "All of Schilling Manor is here for you. Let us help you with all of the arrangements. Whatever you need, just say the word."

Minutes passed.

Several of the other wives tried, but could not stop the tears from falling down their cheeks.

The widow finally spoke, struggling for words. "A medal?" she choked, holding in a pain so violent that her face contorted. "What good is a medal if my husband never comes home?"

TROUBLE SEEING

(1971)

I did not know what my mother thought about when my father was in Vietnam.

In fact, I did not know what my mother thought or how she felt about anything, even when my father was around. She seemed on edge most of the time. Eating was secondary to smoking and drinking coffee. I cannot remember her laughing. The only time she relaxed was when she was making crafts, or socializing, or talking with Gail, who had become her pal sometime during the year.

I don't know exactly when my sister crossed over from miserable teen to mother-friendly adult, but I suspect that it was an evolution that took place because Gail was friendless and my mother needed a chauffeur.

They went to ceramics class every week, pouring and painting sets of chessmen, nativity scenes, and half a dozen one-foot Christmas trees that lit up with mini-bulbs. Christmas presents to send to relatives. A box in the hall closest was filled with glazed soap dishes molded to look like frogs with huge open mouths, painted in a variety of colors, including a Jackson Pollock–like multicolored spattering pattern, and a slew of various-sized figurines that I knew my dad would refer to as white elephants—useless whatnots worth nothing. But it gave them something to do to pass the time.

When they weren't making crafts, Gail drove my mother wherever she wanted to go. My mother and my sister probably did a lot of other things during the day when I was in school, and I can't say that I noticed them becoming closer. I am certain that I did not care because my mother left me alone.

A few months before Gail left for school, when she and my mother were fully involved with their routine, around the end of the school year, Lauren's mother consistently put her on restriction or gave her so many chores to do that we had less time to spend together. One day, when Lauren's mother had picked her up from school, I met Penny, the daughter of an enlisted man, who had sat beside me on the bus during the ride home. When we got off the bus we decided to hang out on the footbridge that divided the neighborhoods.

We smoked a pair of Virginia Slims that I had snuck out of my mother's pocketbook. I usually took a pack at a time from the canned goods closet where she kept her cartons, but my mother was still having trouble with her tongue and was not smoking a lot. I was afraid she would notice if a whole pack disappeared. I crossed my fingers that she would not discover three or four cigarettes missing every couple of days. Penny and I leaned against the railing, puffing on our cigarettes until nothing was left but the filters, sharing stories about our past, our parents, places we had lived, and hitting it off so well that by the time we left the bridge we had become friends.

Penny was about five feet four with a small, boxy frame. Almond-shaped eyes, nearly black hair, and pale skin were traits she inherited from her Japanese mother. She was the first person I had ever met who wore braces, causing her to smile more with her eyes than with her mouth. Her dark hair fell tight to her head in a forward flip at the bottom of her earlobes. Her most memorable feature was thick bangs cut at a blunt edge to the middle of her eyes.

I envied her straight hair.

The first time Penny slept over my house she emerged from the bathroom with her bangs held fast with strips of cellophane tape swathed around her head in a weird mummy design. I was in awe. "So that's why your hair is so straight."

"Yep," she admitted. "It's kind of a pain to do every night, but if I don't I'd have a big case of the frizzies in the morning."

"Show me how." Off we went to the bathroom.

Penny had a cosmetic case filled with hair-straightening stuff and plenty of ideas on how to tame unruly hair. After an hour or so of experimenting with different methods my curls were finally controlled under the influence of tape, soup-can-sized rollers, four-inch bobby pins, and half a jar of Dippity-do—a green goopy gel that crusted up when it dried. Penny and I came out of the bathroom, our hair wrapped and stuck to our heads.

Gail came out of her room, looking at us as if we were aliens. "You look like sci-fi queens from one of those stupid B-movies." She walked toward the kitchen shaking her head, calling out to my mother, "Wait till you see what your middle daughter did to her stupid hair."

My mother was watching the *Lawrence Welk Show*, beading a sweater under her craft light. She demanded we appear in the living room so she could see what we had been up to for such a long time in the bathroom. She saw us, smiled, but could not stop from reprimanding me. "I don't know why you want straight hair. You're lucky to have curly hair like me. Some girls would give anything to have a little body in their hair. Look at your sister's hair."

Gail hollered from the kitchen, "Don't include me in this stupid conversation."

My mother finished her comment. "She has to set it or it just hangs there."

I heard Gail's tongue cluck in the background as she opened a can of Tab. Penny and I went to my room. I heard Gail ask my mother, "Do we have to watch this? I think the *Mary Tyler Moore Show* is on."

That night Penny also introduced me to the magic of kohl—"black eyeliner," she explained, "guaranteed to widen narrow eyes." She told me her mother used it to make her eyes look bigger, less Asian. After a half hour of messed-up attempts I finally got my hand steady enough to smear a thick, slightly wavy line across my upper eyelids.

I agreed with Penny when she said, "Wow, you look so much more mature."

The next morning we did our makeup, eyeliner and all, before we undid our hair. I was eager to find out if I had been cured of my unmanageable waves. After the unfurling and a brushing I turned to the mirror to find that I had become a new person. Along with my new eyes, every strand of my hair hung in perfectly straight threads down my back.

It did not matter that my mother said I looked like a floozy when she saw me, because for the first time since the day I graduated from kindergarten, when I had dressed in a gauzy lilac-colored dress with a crinoline lining, lacy white socks, and my first pair of patent leather shoes—the kind that clicked like grown-up shoes when I walked—I felt pretty.

* * *

Summer vacation arrived. June slipped into July. The Pentagon Papers were published in the *New York Times*. My mother's friends never talked about the publication of the biggest indictment against the U.S. government's handling of the Vietnam War. What the reporters of the Papers uncovered did nothing to help their husbands or their families. I remember Lauren's mom talking about it while we were at the lake one afternoon, that she had always known something wasn't right with the war and now it was a proven fact that her husband and our fathers were overseas fighting for nothing but the whims of a bunch of self-serving politicians. Lauren's mother was well informed about the world. Most of the time we listened until we found an opportunity to leave.

During the summer Penny and I had deepened our friendship over my mother's cigarettes, rock and roll, and long walks around the base. In late July she met a guy named George who played keyboard in a band that had performed at one of the teen club's dances. After the dance he invited her to come and listen to the band rehearse in his garage, which, as it turned out, happened to be a block from where I lived.

Penny was at my house on a hot afternoon in August when we heard live music. She was sure it was George's band because she recognized the Sly and the Family Stone song they had played at the club.

"Besides," she said, "who else has a band in the neighborhood? Let's go see what's going on. You'll get a chance to tell me what you think of George."

While we applied our makeup—thick lines over our eyes, blush across our cheeks, and frost on our lips—Penny told me that George was black.

Was that okay?

I confessed my brush with the black medic at the dispensary a few weeks earlier.

"No lie, really?"

I assured her that the story was true.

Penny told me that the lead guitarist in the band was a really cute guy. He was kind of dark, but from Puerto Rico and, she thought, a little older than George because he had graduated from Salina Central the year before. She pondered, "Wouldn't it be groovy if you guys hit it off? We could double-date."

My sixteenth birthday was less than a month away. Except for my near miss at the dispensary, I had not been kissed since I had dated a senior at Narimasu High School in Japan. The relationship ended up as nothing more than a blip because Gail stole him away from me when they went on their senior class trip.

I was obsessed with boys. They had taken up a majority of my thoughts ever since I had developed a huge crush on Mickey Dolenz, the drummer of The Monkees, when I was twelve. Somehow I thought that having a boyfriend would make me cool. Penny was on the verge of a relationship with George. Lauren was still slipping out to meet the medic. Both of my friends were being kissed on a regular basis and I was not. I did not care that the guitarist was from another country. The only criterion I had was that he be a guy.

I admitted, "Yeah, it would be cool if we hit it off." Then asked her, "If he's all that cute, don't you think he might have a girlfriend?"

She didn't know the answer.

I surveyed myself in the full-length mirror. Thanks to the magic of Dippity-do my hair was perfectly straight, despite the Kansas heat. The cotton blouse imported from India with embroidered flowers on the yoke hid my chubby middle well, but I looked fat in my pegged jeans. I wiggled them off of my body, replacing them with copper, hip-hugger bell-bottoms. The pants, a favorite because they made me look thin, had silver studs up the side seams that I had pounded into the fabric with a knife handle. Penny and I looked each other over, making sure nothing was out of place. After a dab of patchouli we rushed toward the door.

My mother yelled from the kitchen where she was having a cup of coffee with a friend. "Where are you going?" she asked.

"Around," I replied, running out of the house.

"Donna Jean, get back here and tell me where you're going."

I thought about not turning back, pretending that I had not heard her, but I figured I had better not make her mad because although my mother's tongue was better, her eyesight was failing. She said she woke up one morning and could not see up close anymore. She was nervous about losing her vision. It did not take much to set her off. I wanted her to let me use the car so I went back.

"We're going around the corner to listen to music."

"You look cheap with all that makeup."

"No, I don't."

"Yes, you do."

"*No. I don't.*"

"March into the bathroom right this minute and wash it off."

I backed out of the kitchen. She turned to her friend who had deflected her attention. "Beverly, why don't you let me make an appointment for you at the eye clinic? I'm happy to drive you there . . ."

I was gone.

Penny and I cut through the backyard of the house across the street to get to George's house. The closer we got, the slower we went, not wanting to seem too excited as we approached the garage. Penny and I rounded the corner. George looked up from his electric piano, gave Penny a wink, his hands moving too fast along the keyboard to wave. We sat in a couple of empty lawn chairs. A bunch of little kids and a puppy were playing on the lawn, the music was loud and full of bass, drowning out most of their giggles and screeches.

I scanned the band, trying not to appear too interested in anyone in particular. All the members were a shade of brown, some bordered on black. Everyone had an Afro except the lead guitarist who restrained his wavy hair under an orange knit toboggan. I thought about what Penny and I went through to keep our hair dead straight, and there we were, sitting among a dozen adults and kids with the liveliest hair I had ever seen. Most of the band looked much older than high school kids and I thought, oh boy, my mother's going to love this. At the same time, I rationalized that she was preoccupied with Gail's move to Chicago, Lynn always needed her attention, she had her POW/MIA petition campaign to attend to, and now she could not see.

It was unlikely she was thinking about her floozy daughter.

The group took a break. George gave Penny a peck on the cheek. "Good to see ya girl. You must be Donna. I know you from school. I know Lauren. Don't you hang out together?" I nodded yes, surprised to learn that he knew Lauren. He added, "Nice to meet you."

I probably did not say much more than hi, nice to meet you, too, before George introduced us to everyone. The lead singers were married. Both wore dashiki shirts from Africa. One other woman sang, too. The band members were too cool to be very friendly, greeting Penny and me with slight nods of their heads. I could not tell if they couldn't have cared less that a couple of white girls with very straight hair had arrived to listen to their music or if they wanted to practice their music without it turning into a social event.

Ricky, the lead guitarist, never looked at me. If he acknowledged George's introduction it was too subtle for me to notice. I ignored him back, focusing on my conversation with George and Penny.

George was hip. His skin was the color of well-roasted coffee beans, he wore a blue beret with a hair pick sticking out of his short-cropped Afro, and had a Cheshire-cat grin framed by a jazzman's mustache and goatee.

The band went back to work, practicing "Shaft" repeatedly until the lead singer, whose voice was like warm gravy, thought they had it right. George was attentive to Penny, and she to him, each one smiling at the other whenever their eyes met. I focused on George and the rest of the band, and only glanced in Ricky's direction when I was sure he wasn't looking.

George's mother came out of the house to gather up her younger children and to shoo their playmates home for dinner. Her coming out must have been a signal for the band to end their session because no sooner had she gone back inside than the lead singer announced, "We're about as good as we're going to get today."

Someone said he wanted to do one more song.

Penny and I were playing with the puppy that was scampering around when I heard the same voice say, "Hey, this one is for you." I picked up the puppy and was petting it until the voice spoke again. Penny poked me in the arm. I looked up to see Ricky staring straight at me.

He repeated, "I said, this one is for you."

I looked around to make sure no one was standing beside me or anywhere near me and to be certain he wasn't talking to someone else.

I looked at Penny.

She looked at me.

I looked at George. He smiled at me.

I looked at Ricky, who was the dreamiest guy I'd ever seen in the whole world, who had begun singing "Your Song" by Elton John with his dark-skinned, dashiki-donning, Afro-haired, funkadelic band as backup. Outside, I was cool as snow. Inside, I was melting into the tar. Our eyes met, but I could not sustain the gaze for fear of giving away how I really felt.

I managed a slight smile in Ricky's direction.

The song ended. Penny, me, and the kids all applauded. The dog barked.

Soon, most of the band members were packing up an old station wagon. George gave Penny a kiss on the lips—serious evidence of their affection for each other. I went on about how much I liked his band until I felt someone standing behind me: "Did you like the song?" I noticed his scent. It was not a safe smell, like the sweet lily of the valley fragrance in my grandmother's bedroom, or the crisp, starchy smell of my father. The tang of wet trees and musk with a hint of mild sweat unsettled me.

I turned to Ricky. "Yes." I did not lie. "It's one of my favorites."

He was almost as dark as George, with thick, shoulder-length, wavy hair. His lips were full but did not overpower his face. His eyes were as black as marcasite. Penny told him she thought he was a great singer. He blushed, turned to George, suggesting they help the band finish packing up the equipment. Penny and I waited for them to finish.

George was frenetic, always moving, always smiling, and always looking at Penny to make sure she had not left. Ricky was meticulous, concentrated. He rarely smiled. At ten feet away he seduced me with every lift of his arm, every shift of his hips, and with every glance in my direction.

In a few minutes the work was complete. The kids left the puppy on the porch panting, waiting for his next adventure. George hugged Penny. Ricky moved close to me. "So, your name is Donna, right?" I nodded, afraid to talk lest I say something stupid. "Do you want to go for a walk?"

I mumbled, "Sure."

Later that evening, after a walk around the base and much talk about ourselves, we returned to George's to find him and

Penny on the porch. It was past dinnertime. Penny and I had to go or my mother was going to have a fit. Ricky said he wanted to see me again. I nearly died.

My mother was not happy. "Where have you been? Do you know what time it is?"

"We were over at George's house listening to his band rehearse."

"All this time?" she asked. "And who the hell is George and where does he live?"

Maybe I did not tell her about George.

Penny went to my bedroom.

Prudence followed.

"I told you," I said. "He's a kid that goes to our school. Don't worry," I assured my mother, knowing she was the suspicious type, "his mom was there. His little brothers and sisters were there. We hung out on the driveway and listened to his band. No big deal." My mother did not like to be told what was and what was not a big deal.

"Oh, is that right. No big deal? Well, what if something happened and I needed you to drive me somewhere?"

I could not help myself. "Then why don't you learn how to drive so you don't have to worry about people carting you around anymore?"

She got up from the couch, put her finger in my face, and snapped, "Let me tell you something. You will take me wherever I want to go and like it. From now on I want to know where you are going, how long you're going for, and a phone number where I can reach you."

It was my turn. "Oh yeah. How come all of a sudden you care where I go? Now that Gail's leaving what I do matters to you?"

My mother was furious. "You know, you wouldn't be talking to me like this if your father was home."

"You're right. But guess what, Mom, he's not home. Maybe

he'll never come home. And if he does come home, he won't care anyway."

She was nearly speechless. "What's gotten into you?"

"Nothing's gotten into me, what's gotten into you?"

She threatened, "Keep it up little girl and you'll never leave this house until your father comes home."

"Does that mean I won't have to drive you around anymore?" A stupid thing to say since I rarely drove her anywhere.

"Keep it up and I'll put you on restriction for the next two weeks." The threat hit home. Most of the time when my mother put me on restriction I could talk her out of it after a couple of days, but I didn't want to chance it now that I had met someone who might turn into a boyfriend.

"Okay. Okay." I told her I was sorry but didn't mean it.

She said, "You'd better be."

"I am," I lied. "I am."

Bonnie

THE FORGOTTEN OF
THE FORGOTTEN
(1970–1972)

Bonnie and the children returned to Harbor Beach to spend the summer of 1970 with the family. All of them looked forward to going home, a place filled with love and the best summer camp in Michigan. As soon as they arrived, Bonnie signed them up for camp, and off they went every day to play with their friends as if they did not have a care in the world.

When they returned to Schilling in time to start school, around the same time my family moved from Japan to El Paso, many of their friends had moved without having had an opportunity to say good-bye. Bonnie felt even more certain that she would have to move from Schilling to give her children a sense of permanence. She thought about where they might live, deciding that Salina was a nice town. That way she could still be close to the commissary and to Colonel Miller, who had taken great care in seeing to her family's well-being.

After the children were settled into their school routines, Bonnie resumed her speaking engagements. Throughout the fall and early winter of 1970, while my father studied Vietnamese and we prepared to move to Schilling, she traveled locally and nationally, speaking out for the prisoners and the missing men and against the policies of the NLF, the North Vietnamese, and the Pathet Lao, another enemy faction said to have American prisoners within their borders.

When she wasn't speaking, or traveling to Washington with the National League of Families, or tending to her children, Bonnie attended a Bible study group at church, and as Christmas approached she began preparing for the Schilling Manor Christmas pageant.

Major McKain continued to call upon her whenever one of the wives needed help. Bonnie's skills as a nurse and as a waiting wife who understood the emotional strain of being alone without a husband to raise children had proved invaluable to the community. She was tireless, fueled by her faith and her unwavering belief that Bruce could walk through the door at any moment. Her goal until then was to make sure the public applied pressure on his captors to treat him according to the rules of the Geneva Convention. She also wanted the enemy to know that whether Bruce was in the jungle or in the highlands, in a cell or on an endless march, his family was waiting for him. Would wait for him forever.

My mother and Bonnie met during a meeting of the Waiting Wives Club in the spring of 1971. During the meeting my mother said that Bonnie did not give any of the wives time to feel sorry for her because she was calm, self-confident, and never even hinted that her situation was a pitiable one. Her message was more like, "Let's get to work ladies, there's a lot we can do to change things."

Bonnie attended the meeting to update the wives on the efforts being made on behalf of the POWs/MIAs and to ask them to become involved with a new petition drive launched by the National League of Families. The women readily agreed. While they sipped their coffee Bonnie provided them with the information they needed to launch a local drive in Salina. She assured the women that the city was one hundred percent behind the effort. In fact, she told her fellow waiting wives, Mayor Caldwell would be the first to sign a petition. She explained to the women, most of them willing to do what they could for their neighbors, "Salina is the first city to launch a local petition drive in a national campaign." The petition was on behalf of the forgotten of the forgotten and would be sent to Pham Hung, the first secretary of the Central Office for South Vietnam. The campaign pleaded the case for the American POWs and MIAs in South Vietnam. Bonnie handed out copies that read, in part, "Throughout the world, people regard the inhumane treatment of our POWs as an intolerable crime against humanity. We demand that the Viet Cong, Pathet Lao and other Communist forces cease immediately their brutal, sadistic treatment of our POWs."

Bonnie said that Salina churches would also help gather names on the one thousand petitions the League sent to the city. Along with unsigned petitions, Bonnie gave the women two different posters, one with a picture of a POW and the words *Won't You Please Help? He Is Your Brother*, that they could display around the petition signing tables.

Bonnie and the wives, the citizens of Salina, and most Americans had no idea how U.S. prisoners in South Vietnam were being treated. There had been rumors, but no real evidence of what went on in the secret hideaways of the enemy. Some politicians, those privy to the top-secret memorandums distributed by the Directorate of Intelligence at the Central Intelligence Agency, had been made aware of what the prisoners were subject to as early as June 28, 1965. Eighteen days after Bonnie's husband disappeared, a memo was distributed to select individuals in the upper echelons of the Johnson administration. The report entitled "Status of U.S. Prisoners of the Viet Cong in South Vietnam" provided details on the condition of POWs.

> *There are no formal prison camps and conditions are primitive. The prisoners are often kept in a single redoubt area for weeks at a time, but frequently travel with their captors as the latter move about. U.S. prisoners are kept under guard, usually with their hands bound and often tied to trees. Some have reported being literally caged at night. When they travel by foot with the Viet Cong, they are usually blindfolded, sometimes with ropes around their necks. We have received several reports of white prisoners being paraded in this fashion through rural villages for the purpose of impressing local population. We have also had reports of caves being used to hold prisoners. Seriously wounded captives are apparently shot rather than taken prisoner. In at least three instances, U.S. advisers have obviously been tortured and shot rather than taken prisoner.*

Years before Bonnie made her appeals in Paris, the VC thwarted all attempts made to find out the status of U.S. prisoners.

> *Private and official U.S. efforts to obtain the release of or information about U.S. prisoners of the Viet Cong have so far proved fruitless. These have been efforts made through the Red Cross channels and via third countries having diplo-*

matic relations with North Vietnam or accepting represen-
tatives of the Liberation Front itself. Through International
Red Cross efforts, some letters and a few packages have been
accepted for U.S. prisoners, but there is no evidence that they
have been delivered, and efforts to set up channels for
exchange of mail or delivery of parcels have foundered.

At the end of 1971, while my family awaited my father's return
from Vietnam, a representative from the Committee of Liaison
with Families of Servicemen Detained in North Vietnam, which
served as a conduit for mail from prisoners, had been given letters from 332 prisoners of war; a handful of them had been written by prisoners held by the Viet Cong in South Vietnam. The
letters were the first ever to be released by the National Liberation Front.

It was a Vietnam War milestone.

On December 23, eighteen families, including a friend of
Bonnie's who was a member of the National League of Families,
received their miracle. Bonnie's family was not among them.

When asked by a reporter from the Associated Press what she
thought of the release of letters she said, "The correspondence
was a great encouragement. It's real thrilling. Compared to the
last eight-year block of silence, it's a ray of hope."

Bonnie continued her holiday activities, once again disappointed, but determined to continue her efforts on behalf of her
husband. Before the year ended she made plans to return to Paris
on February 12 with two other wives from the National League
of Families. The League had found out that eight hundred delegates from Communist countries were assembling in Versailles
with a pledge to mount an international campaign to force the
United States to withdraw from Vietnam and to accept the Vietnamese Communists' terms for peace. The women would position themselves as neutral observers whose only purpose was to

meet with the Viet Cong delegates to obtain information about their husbands.

January's weather rarely rose above freezing. The crisp air made everything vital. Bonnie had hired a Realtor, and spent a few afternoons looking at houses on the south side of Salina, close to Schilling Manor and the new junior high school. My family left Schilling Manor on a clear, brisk afternoon around the same time Bonnie received a telephone call from an officer from the Department of the Army. The man asked if she could come to Washington right away. Although the details are long forgotten the conversation went something like this.

We have a film we would like you to look at.

A film. What kind of film?

One of our agencies confiscated it from the Viet Cong.

Why is it important that I see this film?

Because it's footage from the battle of Dong Xoia. Perhaps you can identify some of the Americans in the film.

Bonnie told the representative it was impossible for her to fly to Washington in the next few weeks, because she was preparing to travel to Paris.

Could they send the film to Kansas?

Yes, he told her, someone would bring it to her as soon as they could make the arrangements. Before he hung up the officer told Bonnie that the film was highly classified: Do not tell anyone about this conversation.

Beverly

WAR
(1971)

On July 1, 1971, the Twenty-sixth Amendment to the Constitution granted eighteen-year-olds the right to vote. When Gail left for school at the beginning of August she may have had the right to vote in the next presidential election, but I had control of the family car.

The day we took her to the airport was monumental for me. I am sure when my mother, Lynn, Prudence, and I left for the airport to see Gail off she was driving. I don't remember feeling much of anything about her walking the tarmac, or waving good-bye, or anything to suggest we might miss each other. What I do remember is that I was in the driver's seat on the way home and that even my mother's backseat driving—you're going too fast, put both hands on the wheel—did not spoil the power I felt. As far as I was concerned, for the next few months, if I played the good daughter, the big, gold Chrysler Newport was mine.

My mother let me take the car most of the time as long as I followed the rules: go where you say you're going and nowhere else, drive only Lauren or Penny around, don't speed, and the only rule that counted, don't be late coming home. As long as I was not late, nothing else mattered because she would not have a reason to question me about where I was or who I was supposed to be with.

One afternoon I came home to find my mother reading a letter from my dad by holding it at arm's length from her face. I asked, "What are you doing?"

"What does it look like I'm doing? I'm trying to read this letter from your father."

"Can't you see it?" I sat down next to her.

"I can as long as I hold it far away and squint a little," she said, wrinkles creasing her skin as she read my father's words.

"Do you want me to read it for you?" I offered.

"No, I can read it from here."

"Does he say anything about getting the Joan Baez tape I put in the package we sent for his birthday?"

"I don't know," she said, "I haven't finished reading it yet."

"Can I go to the drive-in tonight?"

"Who are you going with?"

"Lauren and her older sister."

"What's playing?"

"*Dr. Jekyll and Sister Hyde* and some other vampire movie."

"Why do you like to watch that junk?"

"Well, can I go?"

"Yes, you can go."

"Can I take the car?"

"Why do you always have to take our car? Can't someone else drive?"

"Lauren's mother won't let her take their car," I said. "She has to have it at home in case one of the little kids falls down and they have to go to the emergency room or something. I mean we're only going to the drive-in for crying out loud. It's not like we're joyriding around with nothing to do."

"All right. Take it, but you had better come home right after the movie lets out."

"Okay. Thanks." She was straining to read the letter. "Why don't you have your eyes checked if you can't see? I'll take off from school and drive you to the eye doctor if you want me to."

She said she'd think about it.

The next week she let her neighbor take her to the eye clinic while I was at school.

The doctor prescribed granny glasses. Not the cool, colored Beatle kind, worn for style. My mother's were colorless, meant only for seeing. Her diet of cereal and cigarettes had begun to show on her face, which appeared gaunt. Her wrinkles had deepened, her neck stretched and stringy. She had turned forty-two in August, but when she perched the tiny glasses on her nose, she looked sixty.

She had lost nearly twenty pounds.

My mother told us my dad did not like fat women. He would divorce her if she turned to blubber. At least that is what she always said. My mother took his comment as an incentive to continue her diet. Not that she considered what she was doing a diet—she just never felt like eating. Once in a while she would splurge and eat a bag of potato chips. Feel sick. Devour a Hershey bar. Suffer guilt. Cereal for a week.

George and I had become friends. It was convenient since we lived so close to each other. We got along, making each other laugh and talking about each other's sweethearts. We analyzed our relationships, questioned the motives of our best friends, and assured each other that everything was cool.

When George came to my house for the first time he disarmed my mother by walking in without knocking. "Hey Mom, got anything to drink?"

It was his way of breaking the ice—catch strangers off guard, act like you belong, give them big toothy smiles. He didn't care what people thought of him. He said whatever he wanted, whenever he wanted. In a way, my mother and George were alike, having both learned to cover their insecurity with boldness.

My mother met his challenge. "Well, who do you think you are, barging in like you own the place?"

"Didn't Donna tell you I was coming over?" George looked at me. "How could you not tell her? I'm your long-lost son, George."

"Oh, is that right?" My mother raised her eyebrows, but smiled a genuine smile that curled just short of a chuckle.

George played the jokester. "Say what? You mean to tell me you don't remember ordering me from the Sears Roebuck catalog?"

It was an eyeball-rolling exchange, but I laughed anyway and even Lynn, who had been sitting at the table, popped her thumb out of her mouth to let out a giggle.

I knew my mother liked George, because even though she held her arms akimbo, her foot tapping, when he was around, she never asked him to leave. It didn't hurt that he helped out when things needed to be done with tools. He mowed the lawn a few times. He was nice to Lynn. My mother let me ride with George to school. Lauren usually rode with us, but Penny did not. Her mother did not approve of George. He was black.

She was prejudiced. We were appalled.

Political and social issues rarely came up in our house. I never knew which candidate my parents voted for in presidential elections. If they even voted. My mother did not comment about the race riots or the women's movement. I don't know why. Maybe because we were not personally involved or knew anyone involved in the equal rights movement. I am not sure she even knew what was going on. Looking back, the military protected its families from what was happening in the civilian world. Rank was more important than sex or color. No matter what gender or shade his commanding officer was, a soldier had better obey orders or face disciplinary action.

I got a glimmer that race was an issue for my family when I brought Ricky home. After he left my mother announced, "He's colored."

"No, he's not. He's Puerto Rican," I corrected.

"I don't care where he comes from, he's as dark as George."

"You're prejudiced!" I accused. She denied.

"I am not, but for God's sake, Donna, he's as black as they come."

"Yeah, but his family comes from Puerto Rico, not Africa, so he can't be black." My mother didn't see it my way. "Are you crazy? How am I going to explain this to your father and the rest of the family?"

"What's to explain? It's none of their business, and besides," I reiterated, "I told you, he's not black, he's Puerto Rican."

"Stop being so dramatic."

"Well I'm not going to stop seeing him because you think he's black." I walked out of the room.

My mother did not prevent me from seeing Ricky as long as we went out in a group. Ricky didn't have a car, so unless we went for walks around the base, we hung out with George and Penny. The only time I thought my mother was truly conflicted about how she felt was when my grandmother came for a visit. When I introduced my father's mother to Ricky she smiled sweetly, offered a hello. Later, she approached my mother. "Don't worry, Beverly, I won't tell anyone."

My mother replied, "Gram, she's barely sixteen, it's not like she's going to marry him. And besides, he's Puerto Rican, not black, and he's very polite."

It was my mother's way of sticking up for me.

George was at my house more than any of my other friends, except Lauren. He'd amble in unannounced, and despite my mother liking George, it drove her crazy whenever he'd open the refrigerator and help himself to a soda pop without permission.

And it was my relationship with George, not Ricky, that broke the peace, starting one of the biggest battles that ever took place in our house.

One Saturday, when Penny wasn't around and Ricky had to work, George and I planned to go to the drive-in. I asked my mother. "No."

"What?"

"No." She was making fried rice for dinner. Lynn was flipping around on monkey bars out back with one of her friends. Except for Prudence we were alone.

"What do you mean, no?" I was astonished.

"I said no." The oil popped in the frying pan. She tossed in chopped bits of onions that began to sizzle.

"It's Saturday night," I reminded her. "You always let me go to the drive-in." The oil got so hot that it splattered my mother's apron when she dumped chicken in the pan. "Well you're not going this time." She held the pan away from the flame for a moment to cool down the oil.

I told her, "That doesn't make any sense. There's nothing else for us to do." She remained silent as she checked the rice simmering on another burner. I couldn't believe it. Out of the blue my mother was putting her foot down. Why?

I pleaded. "Come on. This doesn't make any sense."

"If you don't have anything to do then why don't you stay

home for a change?" she asked, gathering the rest of the ingredients.

"What? Are you kidding? Stay home on a Saturday night?" I
was incensed.

"I said no. And I mean no." She dumped the rice in the chicken
and onions. Steam rose from the pan, filling the kitchen with
moist air.

"Well I'm going anyway," I yelled, adding, "Besides, George
can take his car," thinking that my mother's issue was my taking
the car too often.

The rice pot sailed into the white porcelain sink, making so
much noise that Prudence ran from the room. She turned from
her cooking. "Oh no you are not. There is no way in hell that you
are going to the drive-in alone with George. Now don't ask me
again." She went back to the frying rice.

Shocked.

Confused.

What was she talking about? I asked, "Why? What's wrong
with George? You like George. We hang out all the time. We're
good friends."

She stirred, saying nothing. I turned away. What was going
on? George was at our house all the time. He helped her do stuff.
She liked him. Most of the time *no* did not mean *no*, so I persisted, determined to wear her down.

"Stir the food." She went to the door to call Lynn inside for
dinner.

I ignored her.

She hollered at Lynn to come in for dinner, then returned to
the stove. Soy sauce dribbled into the frying rice. We continued to
argue. She threw frozen peas in the pan. My mother showed no
signs of giving in and refused to explain anything beyond our
volley of "why nots" and "because I said sos."

Dinner was ready.

"Lynn is still outside. Call her in."

I walked away. "Why should I do anything for you when you never let me do anything?"

"Is that right? Keep it up. You'll never leave this house."

She went to the door, screamed at Lynn to come in the house or she wouldn't be able to go back outside after dinner. My younger sister ran home. I returned to the kitchen. Lynn came in the door to hear: "Just give me one good reason why you won't let me go to the drive-in with George."

Before my mother could respond Lynn said, "You can't go out with a black kid."

I looked at Lynn, who was eleven years old, had thick bottle-bottom glasses, and a nasally twang that went right through me. I was furious.

What a stupid jerk. What was she talking about?

I chased her down the hall to her room. She cried for me to leave her alone.

Slam went her door. *Lock it before I kill you.* My mother left dinner, demanding that I leave Lynn alone. I went to my room.

Slam went my door.

"Unlock that door right now, Lynn."

"No," she said, "I'm not coming out until she leaves and never comes back." My mother came in my room. "Tell your sister you'll leave her alone." I refused.

We were at war.

Was Lynn right? Did George's color have something to do with my mother's decision to not allow me to go to the movies?

I went back into the kitchen. My mother was scooping fried rice onto Lynn's plate. I sat down, "Is it true?"

She put the cover on the pan, opened the fridge, took out a beer, and pulled off the tab. She looked at me.

"Well?" I asked.

When she did not answer, I persisted.

"It's true, isn't it?" I was in disbelief. "George is a friend. He's dating Penny and I'm going out with Ricky." I kept at it. "And so what if George *was* my boyfriend? And so what if he *is* black? What's the big deal? Dad wouldn't care. Besides," I continued, "what about Ricky? He's sort of black. How come you don't say anything about me going out with him?"

She snapped, "I thought you told me he was Puerto Rican?"

"He *is* Puerto Rican."

She was confused. "You know, you've been nothing but a problem since you started hanging out with that group of kids." Pots were flying into the sink. "What happened to Lauren? You had better climb off of your high horse, missy, because your father's going to hear—"

I cut her off. "Hear about what? That you won't let me go to the movies with my friend because he's black? Oh. That'll sound great. And what makes you think he cares anyway? I never hear from him. He only writes Gail and sends her TVs and stuff." My father had sent Gail a TV for her dorm room. "And what do I care what he'll say anyway?" I huffed out of the kitchen, insisting that I was going to go to the drive-in no matter what she said. Slam went my door. I had lost the battle.

Where was my mother's perfect little baby? The one who never cried. Maybe only whined a little when she needed changing. She was so quiet. No trouble at all, really. Not like Gail the crybaby. Of course, Lynn was always sick. *I never had to pick Donna up. I never had to hold her. I never had to pay attention to her. She was such a good little girl, such a happy baby.* That little baby loved playing alone for hours in her crib, sometimes reaching through the bars for people when they passed.

My mother bragged about me for years. I felt proud.

Where was her perfect little child?

* * *

257

I loved my bedroom. I had decorated it with the things that mattered to me. Posters of Santana, Three Dog Night, and the Doors hung on my walls instead of the cheap five-and-dime pictures of wide-eyed, underaged, fantastical-looking ballerinas in pink and blue tutus my mother favored. I replaced the baby-blue pom-pom bedspread with a deep red bedcover.

A three-foot piñata of Topo Gigo dangled from my ceiling. Neon-pink flowers made with filmy plastic blossomed out of a Japanese vase placed on top of the reel-to-reel that sat on the nightstand. Orange sherbet–colored curtains hung out of sorts from the long, narrow windows. A multicolored shag rug lay matted on the floor, always in need of raking. The flower-power pattern on the trash can resembled the clothes in my closet.

I had a bookshelf filled with memorabilia: a wooden *kokeshi* doll from Japan, white sand from the White Sands Missile Range sparkled inside a baby-food jar. Tucked away in the back of the second shelf were five Day-Glo paint pots—pink, green, blue, yellow, and orange. My Aiwa amplifier and speaker were on top of the bookcase. At attention on top of the amplifier was a picture of my father in an iridescent orange frame. I positioned three candles in front of the picture, a pack of matches, with a Buddha-shaped incense burner to the side. Peacenik dolls and trolls were everywhere. Everything needed dusting.

I put on my Doors album, lit a piece of incense in the Buddha, and reached over my bed to close out the setting sun. I switched on the black light.

Peace.

There was no such thing as peace in my house.

Barely ten minutes had passed when my mother barged into my room without knocking. Prudence scuttled in behind her, jumping to the unmade bed. My mother's reaction was automatic: "Get off that bed." She stood in the door, a cigarette burned between two fingers, her head perched on a thin neck. She took a drag. The smoke poured into my room, overtaking the musky haze of the incense. I wanted a cigarette, too. Maybe if we were both smoking we could talk more easily. But I was not an adult. I was to do as she said, not as she did.

My mother opened the blinds. I waited for a barrage of ultimatums.

Another stream of smoke replaced the air in my room. It was early evening and the late September sun setting through the half-opened blinds cast a dappled light on the walls, on my mother. The intermittent glow highlighted motes of dust floating in the smoke. I could see the vocal cords move in her neck. "I'm calling your father. Maybe he can straighten you out."

"Yeah. And what do you think he can do to me? He's a million miles away and couldn't care less." Once more. "He probably won't come home anyway."

Where was my mother's perfect little baby?

It took a friend stationed at a communications unit in Guam, a couple of Military Affiliated Radio Relay Stations, the Red Cross, two Hamm radio operators—one at my father's unit in Vietnam and one in the States—and twenty-four hours before the white phone rang in our kitchen.

It was Sunday and my mother had forbidden me to go out. She threatened to hide the car keys until I turned eighteen if I so much as ventured beyond the front steps. Sometime in the morning Gail arrived from Chicago. Our mother had called her after I had sequestered myself in my room for the night. When she walked through the door I could not help but think how convenient it was for her to arrive on the only day, out of all the days my father was away, that we would speak to him on the telephone.

I was in my bedroom when the phone rang. The two of them,

co-conspirators against my happiness, were waiting at the kitchen table drinking coffee, a new addition to Gail's diet since she had become a coed. I waited for one of them to appear at my door. It took a minute. They had to explain the horrible things going on in his home, the things so bad that a phone call was required from twelve thousand miles away.

I imagined them taking turns telling my father how out of control I was: how I was such a jerk; how I wouldn't listen; how my dirty clothes were strewn all over my bedroom floor. I imagined them using the previous day's battle to indict me for every little wrong I had done while he was away.

Then there she was, standing at my door in the same position, cigarette in hand, as she had the day before.

"Your father wants to talk to you."

"I have nothing to say to him."

She wanted to put the cigarette out in my face. Her eyes squinted, her teeth clenched, then, in a voice so threatening that I could not help but pay attention, she said, "You had better get your ass off that bed. Now. Your father's calling from the goddamned war for crissake. What in the hell is the matter with you?"

I walked to the telephone. Gail was having a conversation with my father about school. She stopped talking about herself when I walked into the kitchen. "Okay, here she is, Dad. Talk to you later. Over."

She shoved the phone in my face. "You had better not say anything stupid. Don't forget to say 'over' when you're finished talking."

I put the phone to my ear. "Hello."

Gail yelled at me to say "over."

"Oh, yeah, okay. Hello. Over."

I heard static and clicking, a millisecond of silence and then my dad.

"This is your father. Over."

* * *

Our conversation was brief. I forgot to say "over" most of the time, but Gail was there to remind me. My father never yelled, always speaking in a calm and controlled voice. He understood about the George thing, but supported my mother's decisions. My father reminded me that my mother was alone. She needed all the help she could get from us girls.

Obey her rules.

My responses were simple: "Okay. Over," or "Right. Over," or "Uh huh. Over." He was giving me one of his lectures, which were monologues with little opportunity for dialogue. When he finished I asked him if he got the Joan Baez tape I had made and put in the package we sent him for his birthday. "Over."

A moment passed.

He might have. "Put your mother back on the phone. Don't worry. I'll be home soon. Over."

"Yeah, okay. Over." I handed the phone to my mother. I whispered, "I don't care if you ever come home."

Gail snapped, "What did you say?"

"Nothing."

As I turned to go back to my room she quietly said, so my mother could not hear, "I hope you didn't say what I thought you said."

Where did that perfect child go?

For the second night in a row I lay on my bed thinking about the letters I had written, the mailbox devoid of anything for me, and the random comments my father addressed to me on the tapes he sent home: *Do what your mother tells you. Be careful driving the car.* I remembered the handshake he had given me before he went back to Vietnam after R&R in July. The Joan Baez tape I had made for him that he had apparently never listened to. In my tape recorder was another tape I was making for him. I yanked the cassette out of the machine and began pulling the tape out of its case until a pile of brown, filmy ribbon curled up on the floor.

Five Day-Glo paint pots in the corner.

For the next hour I smeared my furniture with atomic pink, green, blue, yellow, and orange. I used every drop making flowers and circles and swirling lines on everything I owned. When I was finished my room exploded with color under the black light.

My mother went berserk. Gail rushed in when she heard her screaming, "You've ruined the furniture."

But it was done.

They stood in the doorway, stunned into silence. Prudence jumped on my bed—my mother did not tell her to get down. She walked out of the room without saying another word. Her perfect little baby was gone.

LEAVING

When I move from Schilling Manor
I will no longer be a part of the military.
My heart however will be.
All my energy will be spent working on
*   something that is now very special to me.*
That something is patriotism.
Let us all lead a protest in favor of the
*   United States and the job our husbands*
*   are performing, or have performed.*
It is the least we can do.

SCHILLING SUN, SEPTEMBER 13, 1969

EXCERPT FROM AN OPEN LETTER WRITTEN BY A
WAITING WIFE PRIOR TO HER DEPARTURE FROM
SCHILLING AND AFTER HER HUSBAND WAS KILLED
IN VIETNAM

The Committee

———

THE FASHION SHOW

Time went by fast the week before the fashion show and there had been so much left to do, especially since the lieutenant's wife had lost her husband, that the committee had to work well into the evenings. Luckily they had had a lot of help and the show was finally about to begin with Colonel Miller's entrance.

The audience took their seats.

The committee stood together. A profound sadness washed over them.

One of them was missing, gone forever from Schilling Manor in the middle of a waiting wives' nightmare come true.

Before Miller left the lieutenant's wife's home that afternoon he had pulled the colonel's wife aside and told her that when he received the casualty report on the lieutenant he knew the committee would be at her house so he hurried over with the chaplain before the women went their separate ways.

"I thought she might need some help getting over the shock. She was too young to handle the information by herself."

He was grateful the other wives were around, knowing they would help the new widow until her family arrived from the Midwest. He also asked the women to see if the lieutenant's wife was up to making a phone call home. The colonel's wife assured the commander that someone would make the call if the lieutenant's wife could not.

The lieutenant's wife had held on long enough to call home. A second after she hung up the phone she fell into deep, inconsolable despair. The women, fearing for her health, called the dispensary. One of the post's doctors arrived to sedate her.

Don't leave her alone.

The wives knew their friend was in no shape to care for herself or her children. They stayed with her in shifts. As word got around, other women on her block came over to help. Some took the children for a few hours at a time, while some brought over casseroles. Some simply sat with their friend while she slept away the agony of so many losses—a husband and lover, a father, and their dream for a happy future together—all of them lost in one of those dreaded minutes that, for her, would last an eternity.

Two days before the fashion show, the young wife and her daughters left with her mother and father, who had driven all day and night to rescue their child. Although still on a mild sedative the widow said good-bye to her friends, wishing them luck with the fashion show. *It will be a wonderful success. Send pictures of all the beautiful outfits.*

And then she was gone.

The remaining committee members held their breath as Colonel Miller took the stage.

"Ladies and gentlemen, thank you for coming and welcome to the first annual fashion show put on by the waiting wives of

Schilling Manor to raise money for the post's day-care center. We would like to dedicate the show to a committee member who can't be with us today. So with her in mind, let's see what's happening in the world of The Mix-and-Match Wardrobe: Adaptable Styles for Today's Busy Women."

Lorrayne

___

ONE YEAR LATER

(1966)

On June 6, 1966, Schilling Manor's pool opened its gates to the four hundred families that had moved to the community. Lorrayne had been determined, asking Fort Riley and local businesses to donate money and supplies. The Westinghouse Company had offered money to get the pumps and other pool mechanisms working. The local hardware store contributed all the painting and resurfacing supplies.

Fort Riley sent a maintenance crew to help with the restoration, and a dozen or so Salina citizens and a slew of Schilling women and kids volunteered to fix, wash, paint, and fill the pool. The Medina boys, the Klein kids, Robbie and Terry, and nearly every other preteen and teen worked after school and on Saturdays until the job was finished.

The Fort Riley housing office had so many requests for quarters from soldiers with orders to Vietnam that it hired John Kindlesparger, a recently retired Air Force pilot, to be the Manor's on-site housing manager. All requests for transfers were sent directly to him.

Lorrayne had also requested that the dispensary reopen with more than one doctor. After Dr. Nelson left, the Army had not replaced him. Women were running their kids to Salina's emergency room or transporting them the forty miles to Fort Riley when they were sick. It was a pain. Many women did not drive, including the foreign wives who were uncomfortable in the American civilian population. On July 1, thanks to Lorrayne's efforts and because of a study conducted by the Family Services Department of the Army, Fort Riley authorized reopening the clinic with two doctors, a nurse, and a couple of corpsmen to run a twenty-four-hour, seven-day-a-week operation for the families.

By midsummer over five hundred families with nearly two thousand children, and almost as many dogs, had moved onto Schilling. Dr. Scott Norton, Salina's superintendent, knew that the town's elementary schools could not handle the deluge of students expected to attend classes at the beginning of the school year. He worked with Schilling's commander to reopen the Schilling Elementary School and to build five new rooms, thus reactivating a plan that had been aborted when the air base shut down. The town was happy to see the population of Schilling explode because it meant more jobs for its citizens. The school alone would provide jobs for a principal, thirty-three teachers, three custodians, and two secretaries. If Schilling Manor thrived, so, too, would the town.

Schilling Manor had turned into a boon for military families, for Salina, and for Army public relations. The U.S. Army was now fully behind Schilling Manor. Many things were happening that Lorrayne did not know about. The doctors at the dispensary requested that Fort Riley provide Schilling with a psychiatrist. Some women needed more than medical attention. At the end of

August, while the children prepared to return to school, Major Elliot B. Samuels of the U.S. Army Engineers, the first permanent commander, was assigned to take over the base.

Schilling Manor was a success.

Lorrayne opened a letter from Bob in August. When he returned to the States in late September, the family would move to Fort Sill, Oklahoma.

She had one month.

Lorrayne phoned two of her friends and found out that both of their husbands would be home in two weeks. They'd be gone a week later. *Well, at least I have more time to clear these quarters than they will.* She had cleared military quarters enough times in her life to know what a nightmare it could be, especially if the inspector happened to be the white-gloved, persnickety type.

As far as she knew, no one had cleared quarters at Schilling. She wondered if the new housing manager would do it or if someone would come down from Riley. Either way she had a lot of scrubbing and packing and throwing out to do before Bob came home. She made one last attempt to get the PX opened. But military red tape had wrapped itself around the idea and Lorrayne had run out of time. One of the other wives would have to pick up where she left off.

Lorrayne and the boys met Bob at the airport. The next week the family packed, cleaned, and prepared to leave for Oklahoma. Terry and Robbie were blue about leaving their friends, even though most of them were gone or would be moving soon after. At the same time they were excited to meet new friends at Fort Sill.

Lorrayne had mentally moved on, thinking about what kind of housing Sill had, how the schools were, and how long it would take her to acquire a real estate license in Oklahoma. Bob would be home for a while, Robbie was doing fine, and she never worried too much about Terry. It made sense for her to go back to work.

On the day they were to leave, the boys asked Lorrayne if they could play one last game of ball in the field with their friends. *Okay, but keep tidy and take Tuffy with you.* Lorrayne and Bob waited for the inspector to arrive. She fussed around the house, scrutinizing the range she had spent nearly a day scouring, running her hands along the molding above the doors to make certain dust had not accumulated in the few hours since she had wiped them down, checking the bathroom for stray hairs, surveying the walls in case a hole had escaped being spackled, drinking cups of coffee that Pat and Cricket brought over, and wondering aloud when the guy would come so that they could be on their way.

It was time to go. Time to move on.

Clearing quarters put Lorrayne on edge. If the inspector did not like the way something was done, their departure could be delayed for hours while they fixed the problem. Pat felt the same way about housing inspections, but assured her best friend that she had never seen a more spotless house than Lorrayne's. *Don't worry. You'll pass with flying colors.*

Pat was correct. Lorrayne passed without so much as a frown from the housing officer.

The friends said their final good-byes, lamented their separation, and vowed to stay in touch no matter where or how far apart they lived. Lorrayne and Pat were certain they'd be assigned to the same post again at some point in the future. They never were.

The boys had played several innings before Lorrayne, in the Chevelle convertible, and Bob, in the Opel, drove to the field to pick them up.

Time to go, boys.

They said good-bye to their friends, called Tuffy, got in the car, and left.

Lorrayne passed through the Schilling Manor gates for the last time. For a moment, she wondered what would happen to the base. She followed Bob onto Highway 81 South, drove seven hours, and arrived at Fort Sill.

She never looked back at the home she had created for more than seven thousand waiting wives and their children.

Bonnie

GREATER LOVE HATH
NO MAN . . .
(1972)

Smoke floated like a supernatural fog over the battle, making it hard for Bonnie to see things clearly. Her eyes strained to see what was going on in the film. The images were grainy, like an old movie that over time had been exposed to dirt and dust and hours of replay.

So this was it. The battle that had taken place years before when she and her children were still so very young, still so very innocent.

Harvey Stewart, the pilot who tried to rescue Bruce, had described the battle to her in the first weeks after it had taken place. She had imagined it in her mind, had thought about it when she was alone, maybe even dreamt about it in the years of twilight sleep that followed Bruce's disappearance. But now, watching the battle in the dim, steel-gray setting of an Army audiovisual room, it did not seem real.

The officer asked if she could identify any of the bodies lying beside the helicopter. It was an American helicopter, a UH-1B, the one that Bruce jumped on when he heard the crew was going on a mission into Dong Xoia to rescue troops caught in an ambush at a rubber plantation.

He explained. Several government agencies had tried to identify the men. They could be sure of only two of the soldiers because their name tags were visible on their uniforms.

He pointed to the crumpled bodies.

That is Specialist First Class Owens.

And that one over there is First Lieutenant Hall.

Although the government was fairly certain that the other bodies were those of the Huey's crewmen, the footage was so gritty the agents were having a hard time making any conclusive determinations. Perhaps Bonnie could help.

He suggested to Bonnie that the other bodies in the film might be the remains of the other men who had flown into battle on the aircraft that morning. One of the bodies might be Bruce's, but, of course, he told Bonnie again, the images were so distorted they couldn't be sure.

He asked her to please study the film carefully.

Bonnie agreed, not really believing for an instant that she would see Bruce in the film, so confident was she that he was alive. He was Grapevine 6, the soldier who had transmitted that the chopper had gone down.

He was the only survivor.

Stewart told her mortar rounds exploded where Bruce was. Stewart thought Bruce had perished. He was surrounded.

But later reports suggested her husband had survived the attack. He was the big American being led away from a battlefield, the big American who spoke Vietnamese. The document had been in his file for years. She had read parts of it. A Viet Cong prisoner reported that he and his coworkers were on a rice procurement mission. They observed a U.S. Army officer being led away from the Binh Gia battlefield. *Binh Gia.* Around March of 1965. *March 1965.* The American had a rope tied around his upper arms, which were behind his back. The prisoner was about five feet nine, 165 pounds with blond hair. *Five feet nine, 165 pounds, blond.*

The battle was wrong. The date was wrong. Bruce was six feet one, 185 pounds, with light brown hair.

The government did not think the differences were significant. Bruce could have lost weight; his hair could have lightened in the hot Vietnamese sun. The Viet Cong might have mixed up the dates and the battle. The report went in Bruce's file.

What Bonnie's casualty officer did not tell her, or perhaps did not know himself, was that the same document had been placed in the files of two other soldiers who went missing during the first half of 1965. The final line on the evaluation report read, "because certain discrepancies exist in each case with the source's information, it is not possible to conclude which of the three is the best possibility." The analyst who filled out the paperwork added that the reliability of the information could not be judged and that the information was of moderate value. No conclusions could be made regarding who the Viet Cong prisoner had actually seen. As a result, three families would live with hope until the government could obtain more information.

Bonnie did what the officer in charge of the film asked. She scanned the images of the unidentified heroes who had died in the late spring of 1965. Up and down and sideways she looked for clues. For Bruce.

The quality was poor, like looking through a clouded window. Bonnie remained in the room for a long time—looking deeply into the shadows, filling in the slight tears, searching beyond the roughness of the film.

So much depended on her answer.

Her eyes focused on one of the bodies. Something had caught her attention. On his left hand was a wedding ring. Did she recognize the thin band of gold? No. It was not possible. Lots of husbands have rings similar to the band Bruce wore.

Bonnie turned to the officer and told him that she did not think her husband's body was in the film. She asked permission to tell Bruce's mother and father about the film, thinking they might see something she had missed. The officer agreed, reminding her that no one else was to know, that the film remained highly classified.

Bruce's parents chose not to see the film. It would be too much. She understood. Bonnie asked Bruce's cousin, a military man, to look at the film. He did not think it was Bruce, but he had not seen him since they were teenagers. Bonnie watched the film several times. Her eyes were drawn to the wedding band. It nagged at her.

How could he be dead when I have been with him all of these years?

"I cannot be sure."

Bonnie went to Paris in February as planned. Once there, she and her fellow wives met several representatives from the Viet Cong delegation. When she presented her case, one of the delegates said that "as one human being to another, I will do everything in my power to learn about your husband." Bonnie had discovered that the man had not heard from his wife and children for many years. In him she had found the kindest response she had ever received during all of the years she had appealed for information about Bruce.

The ring. Bonnie never stopped thinking about the ring. She had believed so strongly and for so long that Bruce was alive. A simple gold band was a harbinger of death? It was not possible.

No. I know in my heart that Bruce is alive.

When she returned home she asked to look at the film one more time.

"I cannot be sure."

Bonnie left the viewing room for the last time. She went home to her children. Afterward, maybe within an hour, or a day, or a week, something inside, something almost unnoticeable even to her, began to slip away. The body of the soldier with the wedding ring had shaken her confidence. Doubt seeped into her heart like slow poison.

Bonnie had missed Bruce while he was away, but believing he was alive kept her from feeling alone, no matter if she was speaking before Congress, the Waiting Wives Club, or to her children's teachers. He had always been with her. After seeing the film, no matter how hard she tried to hold on to her children's father, Bruce began to fade away. She was no longer sure. It was a subtle realization that she noticed when she walked into a room of friends and felt vulnerable, naked in her isolation.

Bonnie was not allowed to tell anyone about *The Flames of Dong Xoia*, the dead soldiers, the wedding band, or the uncertainty that invaded her thoughts. She kept everything to herself, continuing to live as if Bruce would walk through the door one day. After all, she was not sure that it was her children's father in the film. Unless she were one hundred percent positive she would not say anything about it to anyone. To her children, her friends, her family, and to the world at large, Bruce was and would remain missing in action until he came home, dead or alive.

Bonnie's one long day of certainty had ended. She alone would start the new day with doubt.

Bonnie bought a house in South Salina, near Schilling Manor. It was one she and the children could live in for a good long time.

They would move before traveling to Michigan for the summer. She gradually pulled away from her duties with the National League of Families. When it came time for elections she did not run for office. She rarely accepted speaking engagements, reasoning that other women were better able to speak out on behalf of their missing men. Although she continued working as an advocate for the POWs/MIAs, Bonnie remained close to home, meeting with the Waiting Wives Club, or helping to organize an art exhibit in Salina in honor of the prisoners and the missing men. Her Bible study group was more important than ever.

God's word gave her strength and the belief that no matter what had happened to Bruce, she could turn to God and find him faithful. When Bonnie thought about Bruce, she sometimes turned to the Gospel of John and found solace in the passage: "Greater love hath no man than this, that a man lay down his life for his friends."

Or his country.

On February 27, 1978, after being missing nearly thirteen years, the secretary of the army issued a Presumptive Finding of Death for Bonnie's husband, who had been promoted to Lieutenant Colonel while in MIA status. As of this writing, his remains have not been repatriated.

Beverly

TRUCE
(1971–1972)

A cool front raced southward across the Midwestern plains, bringing an end to a sweltering late-summer heat wave in Kansas.

An uneasy peace settled on our house after the phone call from my father. My mother and I were exhausted from days of battling. Gail went back to school with her new Sony color TV. Lynn stayed away, playing outside with a new friend who had moved in next door during the summer. Prudence skittered around the house like a diplomat, somehow knowing not to show more affection to one person over another.

My mother took me shopping for school clothes, insisting that I start buying things from the half sizes rack. They would fit better, she assured me. In the meantime she had lost so much weight that her friends wondered if she were sick. No, she told them, she simply wanted to be as skinny as possible when her husband came home.

Lauren and I spent my sixteenth birthday volunteering for the Jerry Lewis Muscular Dystrophy Telethon. We helped man the call center located in one of Salina's church basements. We were hooked on buying cards at the Hallmark store in town, so I wasn't surprised when she handed me two cards on the way to the church. The character was the same on each cover; a squat little cartoon girl carrying a hairless rag doll whose head hung toward the ground. One card was for my birthday and told me how wonderful I was, the other was a "please don't worry, everything will be okay" card. I appreciated her giving them to me; after all, we had been through a lot together.

Besides the telethon and the cards from Lauren, I can't remember anything else about by sixteenth birthday, nor can anyone in my family.

While the unrest in my family slowed to a simmer and Bonnie prepared her fall speaking schedule and for a third trip to Paris, instability surrounded South Vietnam's political elections. President Thieu was accused of rigging the outcome, causing his opponents to withdraw from the race. Students, militant Buddhists, and anyone against the war, against America, and against the reigning president took to the streets, demonstrating their unwillingness to participate in the fraudulent elections. As a result, violence flared. Buses were bombed and grenades were being tossed into any convenient opening, including the windows of American military vehicles.

No one was sure who the enemy was as South Vietnamese citizens were added to the list of opponents that already included the North Vietnamese, the Viet Cong, the Chinese, the Cambodians, and the Laotians.

We never knew exactly where my father was. Somewhere near Saigon? His letters and tapes never suggested that he was in any danger, unless he was flying in some sort of aircraft. He wrote that he was scheduled to return home a day or two before Christmas and would let us know as soon as he knew.

In the meantime, we should think about going through our belongings and throwing away things we did not need.

What?

Already?

Did we ever finish unpacking our stuff? Weren't there boxes in the garage that we never got around to opening after the last move?

We ignored his request for most of the fall. My mother wanted my father to come home, but the idea of having to pack, clear quarters, and move to who knew where was not something she was willing to confront until she had no other choice. I stayed away from home, too busy to clean my room let alone take it apart and pack it up. I rehearsed with the chorus after school a couple of days a week to prepare for the school's Christmas concert and when I wasn't at school, I was with my friends.

Another move.

I had a real boyfriend who was wild about me and I was crazy about him.

I was sixteen. Life stunk.

One afternoon I came home from school to find a new picture taped to the refrigerator door. Charles Schulz's Snoopy character, his doghouse, and his bowl were outlined in black and divided into one hundred little numbered squares.

"What's that."

"It's a short calendar."

"A what calendar?" I asked my mother, having never heard of it before.

She explained. "The girls give them out at the wives club

meetings when someone's husband has one hundred days left until he comes home."

"So what are we supposed to do with it?"

"Every day you and Lynn color in the blocks. It's a countdown until your father comes home," she said.

"Don't you want to color in any of the blocks?"

"I'll do it when you forget."

By the time Halloween arrived most of the friends my mother watched Walter Cronkite with in our living room had moved away. She had made new friends. They never came over for the news. She may not have invited them. News was something she avoided.

We were short.

As long as she heard from my dad every few days, she was all right. After four days she could not sleep. Terrible things happened to soldiers in the minutes and days before they were supposed to leave Vietnam.

Late at night I could hear my mother in the kitchen smoking cigarettes and boiling water to make instant coffee. I listened while she filled the kettle from the tap, placed it on the stove, and then turned on the flame. Her cup was always on the counter, within easy reach, the coffee never too far from the spoon that held the perfect amount of the black granules. She took long, deep drags on her cigarettes then released the smoke with an audible sigh while waiting for the water to boil.

I never knew if she was writing a letter, or reading a magazine, or simply sitting at the table with Prudence watching over her, making sure that while my mother sat alone, the shadows on the wall never crept beyond the rising or setting moon.

My father might be blown to bits in the next month.

In early November, President Nixon announced a U.S. troop withdrawal of forty-five thousand men by February. Defense Secretary Melvin Laird said many of them would be home for

Christmas. My father still did not know when he would be home.

By Thanksgiving the war in Cambodia was as vicious as it ever was in Vietnam. In a card my father wrote that it looked good for his return to the West Coast around December 20. *Beverly, plan to meet me at Travis Air Force Base. We'll return to Schilling together.*

My mother bought a new nightgown.

The Paris Peace Talks deadlocked during the second week in December; both sides announced that they would not show up even if a new date were set. It was the most divisive walkout in the history of the Talks.

We still had not heard from my father.

George came over and helped us put up our outside Christmas lights. My mother thought my father might appreciate seeing them aglow when he returned. Snoopy's head was the only part of the picture that needed color. Gail returned home about ten days before Christmas, around the same time we got a letter from my father, telling us he would arrive at Travis on the twenty-second. He wrote that he had booked my mother's ticket and that she should pack her bag to meet him because he was coming home. He also mentioned that we would not be moving very far, that the Army had agreed to let him bootstrap for a semester at the University of Omaha where he would finish up his bachelor's degree.

Gail and my mother put up our old aluminum tree for Christmas. The last time we had used it was when my father was on a hardship tour in Alaska during the early sixties. The scrawny faux tree had sparse, metal stems covered with tangled tinsel that stuck out of a six-foot aluminum pipe; round, metallic red ornaments hung on the tip of every shoot.

It was a monster. Instead of being lit by cheerful strands of lights dangling from its branches, a red, green, yellow, and blue wheel rotated in front of a white household bulb, lighting up the tree from about two feet away. No one liked the tree except Prudence, who sat with her ears perked and her head cocked sideways, watching the tree sparkle when we turned on the color wheel.

Besides the outside lights and the tree, the only other decoration on display was one of the nativity sets my mother and Gail had made during the summer. Why open any holiday boxes only to have to repack them the day after Christmas? We had too many other things to do if we were going to be ready to leave ten days after my father returned home.

On the evening of December 20, while I was singing in the treble choir at Salina High South's Candlelight Christmas Concert, and my dad was preparing for his return home, four F4 Phantom jets were shot down by Soviet MiG-21 fighters on the Laotian border. Only two of the eight Phantom crewmen were rescued, the others became prisoners of war. On the same day, two Viet Cong rockets hit Saigon. We held our breath when we heard the news, and then let it out when the newscaster reported no casualties. As a result of the attacks, the United States retaliated with massive raids over North Vietnam. Government officials reported that the ground war for Americans was over, but failed to mention to the public that the skies over Vietnam were on fire.

My father flew out of battle the next day.

While Vietnam heated up, cold winter winds from Canada caused the mercury in Salina to drop into the teens. On the day my mother left to pick up my father in California, the temperature never reached twenty degrees. She dressed in wool slacks that were at least a size too big, and though bundled up in a heavy coat she refused to cover her head, fearing that a hat or a scarf would ruin her hair.

It was so cold that when Prudence went outside, no more than a minute passed before she was crying to come back indoors. My sisters and I went to Scotties for lunch and to Lums for dinner.

We watched Christmas specials on TV.

We wrapped our presents.

We waited for my parents to return.

We waited.

A holiday truce in Vietnam went into effect the day after my father landed in the States. On Christmas Eve morning we put up a huge WELCOME HOME, DAD sign in the window. The three of us took a turn coloring Snoopy's nose then put the crayons away.

The picture was finished.

My mother made my father dress in multiple layers of wool and flannel as soon as he returned to Schilling Manor. She was not going to have him come home safe from war only to lose him to pneumonia. He willingly complied. My father was not accustomed to the frigid temperatures that had settled over Kansas during the holidays.

The curtains came down the day after Christmas. Sorting and tossing began in earnest. My mother had final cups of coffee with her friends. My dad dismantled stereo equipment, cleaned the lawn mower, removed curtain rods, and did all the things that fall into the realm of a handyman.

Gail was the first to finish organizing her bedroom for the packers. She helped Lynn with her room after my parents started yelling at each other over her lack of progress. A few days later Gail flew back to school.

She never looked back.

One afternoon when my mother went to her last Waiting Wives Club luncheon my father came into my room. He invited me to lunch at a Chinese restaurant. I said sure, but felt uncomfortable at the idea of being alone with him. I was fairly certain my mother had suggested that he spend some time with me.

Do your duty.

We ate moo goo gai pan and lo mein. My father asked me an endless list of questions, most of them having to do with my plans for the future. They were the same questions he had asked me before he left for Vietnam. It was as if the last year had not existed, as if there had not been a phone call, as if my mother had never told him how out of control I was while he was away. Neither was there any mention of the Joan Baez tape I had sent him or of the letters he never wrote me.

We were one year older with experiences that neither of us would mention but had changed us forever.

On our last night at Schilling Manor, a friend of my mother's hosted a buffet dinner to celebrate the end of her minutes as a waiting wife. Lynn went to her friend's house. I spent a final evening with my friends.

The next morning the movers came and took half of our stuff to storage and the other half to the little house my father rented in Omaha.

We would live there until June.

From there—Fort Hood, Texas, the home of electronic warfare.

In the afternoon Ricky, Lauren, Penny, and George came over as we loaded the trunk. We said our good-byes. I promised to return for a visit before everyone moved away. After all, I told them, Omaha wasn't that far away. We swore to stay in touch. They would write. They would call. One day we would be together again.

My father pulled out of the driveway where someone else's car would be parked in a few days. We drove down Phoenix Street. My friends, Lynn's friends, and several waiting wives waved good-bye until we turned the corner, losing sight of them forever.

It had taken much longer than my parents had anticipated to clear quarters. By the time my father turned the keys to our house into the housing office it was late afternoon and the winter sun was already setting in the west. We drove down Schilling Road listening to a Carole King song on the radio. My parents talked quietly about what it was going to be like to live in a civilian community for the next few months.

They never looked back when we passed the Schilling Manor sign.

Lynn sat behind my father in Gail's seat. She stroked Prudence who sat between us in the backseat.

She never looked back.

We drove off base. A full moon was rising. Lifeless trees swayed in the wind. I remember looking out my window thinking that the stars popping up in the sky represented all of the friends I had left in my life. I had forgotten most of them.

I missed all of them.

Before we turned off Schilling Road toward the highway, I looked back at the home I never forgot.

THE END

Schilling Manor
  The quiet almost hurts the soul.
  Where are the waiting wives?
  Where are the laughing children?
Schilling Manor
  Compassionate shelter
  To thousands of wives and children
  Of men in lonely far-flung patriots' service—
Schilling Manor
  Seems dead now.
  Ere long, it shall rise Phoenix-like to new challenges.
  But now its streets, its homes, stand empty,
  Brooding in silence on their memories.

ANONYMOUS,
SALINA JOURNAL, OCTOBER 2, 1977

735 Housing Units and 238.96 Acres of Government Property for Sale

From an eagle's view Schilling Manor resembled every other military fortress. On closer inspection, when squinted eyes focused the blur, what remained was no longer the fortress for brave men and their mighty machines. Nor was it any longer what it had been for over a decade, the sanctuary for thousands of fatherless families. The home for waiting wives was gone forever.

In its wake, the cold specter of military life was left one last time to bleed out on the prairie.

Rumors that the base might close began after the war. Then on April 1, 1976, the U.S. Army announced the proposed closing of nine military bases. At the bottom of the list was Schilling Manor, subpost of Fort Riley, the military's first and only family housing project.

The endnote would toll by the fall of 1977. Schilling Manor: Home of the Waiting Wives of the United States Armed Forces,

Lorrayne's salvation, then her legacy to a dying generation of military wives would close.

Schilling was a place constructed with steel and timber and given life with a million drops of tears. The streets were a double-edged sword—one side provided comfort, the other outrageous pain, where residents learned to live in the dual world of tragedy and joy, as was their duty as military wives.

What happened?

The base was no longer advertised in the *Army* and *Air Force Times* or in military base and post newspapers. Flyers ceased being printed and distributed to the men by battalion leadership. A rumor suggests that Schilling's last commander was disinterested in administering CPR to the base.

He wasn't alone. Keeping it alive for the next generation of wives and children was futile. Once the order from the Department of Defense came down, dismantling the operation was a matter of time. The home for waiting wives had run its course. After the war ended so did Schilling Manor. Apathy had replaced desperation, not unlike what had happened to America.

The town of Salina was resigned to the closing of the base. Salina had turned the potential catastrophe of the Schilling Air Force Base closing in 1964 into a "phoenix risen from the ashes." So when word came down that Schilling Manor was on the Department of Defense's hit list, the manager of the Salina Chamber of Commerce said he did "not expect any formal protest about the closing." He added, "What we probably will do is see that the General Service Administration handles the property to the best interest of Salina. I think a protest would be futile."

It was all so futile.

A few citizens tried to save Schilling. Lieutenant Colonel Norman Miller, who had retired and settled in Salina, and Sergeant

Elmer K. Denning, who was assigned to the base at the time of the announcement, wrote a letter to the editor of the *Salina Journal*. In it, the men made their appeal: "The concept developed in Salina of this military community was certainly sparked by the Schilling Air Force Base closure. But the real success story should not be reflected by today's declining population [of the base], but rather by the Army's inability to let prospective families know a Schilling Manor is available."

Then they directed their attentions to Salina.

Our Chamber of Commerce might have advertised in national publications much read by service personnel. It might have encouraged Ft. Riley command to allow such advertisement. To see this fine military community die because of local apathy is criminal to the needs of future military personnel being assigned on unaccompanied tours. Once closed this book is finished and we wager there will never be again such an installation providing so much for so many with a minimal expenditure of money by the military service.

Miller also wrote letters to Kansas's politicians.

The operation of Schilling Manor resulted in many plus services not readily apparent unless one was either involved or was one that gives a damn about military people and families. . . . In today's tight dollar market and the military quest for more dollars for troop support, many items will be deleted. To close a successful operation providing so many families with a safe haven when their father is on an overseas assignment is nothing short of criminal. Once this Waiting Wife operation is closed there will be many a cold day before an attempt is made to provide this caliber of services needed by many families.

The politicians expressed their shared concern over the closing of Schilling and the negative impact the closing would have on the military community at large, and that, unfortunately, the final decision rests with the Department of the Army. Little could be done once the decision was made.

Other considerations: America was at peace. Military personnel assigned to unaccompanied tours were greatly reduced. Women's roles changed in the seventies. The era of the hat-and-glove military wife who hosted or attended weekly officer or enlisted wives teas or coffees and who was expected to attend formal military functions waned in the years following the Vietnam War. Women had become more independent. Wives were going to work, establishing careers, leaving them less time for the day-to-day traditions of military life. Although many continued to follow their husbands from one assignment to another, others had become less tolerant of the transient life. They wanted to give their children stability, roots—at least for a few years at a time. The Community and Family Services division of the military accommodated them by allowing the families of servicemen assigned to hardship tours to remain on the base of deployment.

A reporter for the *Salina Journal* asked one of the wives what her feelings were after the Department of the Army announced that Schilling was on the chopping block. She said, "I have no big reaction, but it's a shame The Manor is closing. I've really enjoyed my time here—the Salina people have really been nice. I'm wondering, though, if I'm ever in this position again, where will I go?" After the April announcement, no other families moved to Schilling Manor.

Through attrition, the base slowly came to a standstill. Miller was right. Never again did a community as unique as Schilling Manor exist.

* * *

On September 26, 1977, almost twelve years to the month that Lorrayne, Terry, and Robbie moved to Schilling Manor, Sergeant Jack Vickery, his wife, and their children moved out of their quarters at 147 Hartford, the last home occupied by a waiting wife and her children.

One week later the natural gas supply was curtailed.

Days later the General Services Administration took official control of the property. Its mission: to prepare the property for transfer over to the town of Salina.

It didn't take long for inches-high weeds to take over the sidewalk. Once-green trees surrendered to autumn reds. The foliage rustled quietly as brisk winds heralded summer's passing, then fell to the ground, lifeless. Dead leaves piled up so high in patio corners that they looked like shivering hills unable to escape the onset of winter.

Monkey bars, tarnishing without little fingers to keep the metal polished, stood beside empty weatherworn swings. A dented slide remained unfixed, each nick and scratch open to an infection of rust, corroding quickly and alone.

Feral cats, the offspring of pets left behind by overburdened families who took pet care casually, strolled across the lifeless playground, leaving puddles to soak into the sand. Leftover candy wrappers tumbled across pockmarked lawns. Nameplates outside the front doors were empty. Every home, many that had at one time or another housed nine, ten, or even thirteen children, was uninhabited, slowly turning to shambles.

The Manor was empty of life, save for little creatures no longer threatened by the whack of a broomstick or the sole of a shoe. The critters, like the weeds, were free to take over when the people moved out. On August 16, 1978, Lorrayne's, Bonnie's, and our quarters, as well as the homes of nearly seven thousand military families went up for sale to the general public.

For several years Schilling Manor lay dormant, languishing

from disuse. Barricades stood sentry at every street crossing. Signs threatened visitors turning onto Schilling Road: RESTRICTED AREA, NO TRESPASSING, PROPERTY OF THE UNITED STATES— ENTRY BY AUTHORIZED PERSONNEL ONLY.

Highway travelers who had exited too soon in search of a meal had no choice but to turn back, to leave the ghostly neighborhood where every deserted house looked the same. Did the strangers wonder what had happened? No bikes parked on lawns. Disintegrating shades shuttered the windows. Mangled clotheslines were empty of clothes. Garages housed no cars. At the Sunshine Elementary School, children's art—puffy clouds, rainbows, flowers, and outlines of houses peopled with stick figure families—hung eerily on the windows. Crayola's most brilliant colors faded to pastels from years in the sun.

What happened to the people? the travelers might have asked one another. Had they fallen victim to some sort of Andromeda strain, something alien and lethal? Has the government been up to its old tricks and called for another cover-up of the truth?

No surprise there.

After the war even honest Democrat Jimmy Carter could not coax Americans back to national pride. Too much had happened. Americans had lost their innocence. Americans had grown up. From idealistic youngsters to cynics in a decade, the result of a realization that those in government, the elected officials we entrusted with our lives, did not necessarily have our best interest at heart.

Most Americans no longer trusted the government after living through a war that had lost its meaning, allowing it to spiral out of control.

After listening to years of accumulating death tolls on the nightly news.

After seeing epic numbers of flag-draped coffins.

After witnessing thousands of children weeping at the funerals of their dead fathers.

After living through years of teach-ins, sit-ins, takeovers, marches, riots, and assassinations.

After failing to close the widening gap between generations.

After suffering through the lies of one politician after another.

And after living through the revelations of the Pentagon Papers and Watergate and the resignation of a president.

The price America paid, its greatest fatality, American patriotism, the ultimate collateral damage for a proud country, was as dead as the 58,226 casualties of the Vietnam War.

On the way back to the main road, the wayward visitors might have seen a crew disassembling a decaying sign on the side of the road, at that place where the city of Salina began and Schilling Manor ended. A few words could be seen between the bodies of the workers—Schilling—Home—Wives—Forces. For a while they might wonder what the words meant. Eventually, they would turn up the eight-track, listen to some disco as they found their way back to the main road, and forget about their detour down Schilling Road while they moved forward on their journey.

The only thing they would think about was what kind of food they might find at the next exit.

Acknowledgments

I am extremely grateful to the many people who, over the last six years, have encouraged me to write *Waiting Wives*. My deepest thanks go to my parents, Donald and Beverly, and to my sisters, Gail and Lynn. All were eager contributors to the book and unwavering in their support of me. Thanks also to Leon Moreau, my uncle and fellow writer, who never minded sitting at the dinner table for hours discussing the process of writing a story, and to Julie Papageorge, my cousin and most dedicated cheerleader. I am especially thankful to my son, Mathew, and my sweetheart, Bobby, who lived with me during the years of travel, the hundreds of hours of writing alone, and all of the extremes that come with the creation of a book.

I give my deepest appreciation and respect to Kathleen Frisbie and Lorrayne Vogel. Thank you, ladies, for sharing your lives.

Waiting Wives might not have existed had it not been for the support I received from the teachers and writers I met through Columbia University's MFA program: Richard Locke took a chance on me, Lis Harris believed in me, and Patty O'Toole encouraged me, rallied behind me, mentored me, and willingly devoted time above and beyond what was required of her as a teacher. I am also grateful to Jenny Conant who took the time to read my early material, give me advice, and set me straight about life as a writer.

Thanks to Jill Berman, Lynda Curry, Jeanette Horn, and Dave Lane, my extraordinary writer's group. They were there before anyone else. Special thanks to my friend Tara Smith for her support and enthusiasm, to my oldest friends, Liza O'Keeffe and Bob Boulanger, to Sam, Ed, and Emily Kamanitzer who helped me in a million different ways, to Julie Lynch for making me look good, to my treasured friend Sarah Hollister, and to Bill and Peg Medina, whose door is always open.

Waiting Wives required years of research and the use of many sources. I am indebted to the professionals who shared their knowledge and gave me guidance: LTC Harold E. Allen, author of *Schilling Manor: A Survey of a Military Community of Father Absent Families;* Paul Archer of KSAL Radio; Jean B. Bischoff, Senior Archivist, Robert J. Dole Institute of Politics, University of Kansas; Harriet Black, Department of the Army/FOIA Program; Dorothy Boyle, Smokey Hill Museum, Salina, Kansas; Marc Curtis, Military-Brats.com; Tom Dorsey, the *Salina Journal;* William P. Fischer, National Archives and Records Administration; Toni Gavin, CBS News Archives; Ann Mills Griffiths, National League of POW/MIA Families; Ken Jennison, KSAL Radio; Judy Lilly, Kansas Room at the Salina Public Library; Bob Lind, *In-Forum,* Fargo, North Dakota; Sharon Montague, the *Salina Journal;* Marque Siegelman, NBC News Archives; and the staff at the Salina Chamber of Commerce. And many thanks to the Reference, Periodicals and Microforms, and Interlibrary loan staffs at Columbia University's Butler Library.

I interviewed hundreds of people during the writing of this book. Many of the stories and the details about Schilling Manor, Salina, Kansas, the Vietnam War, and American and military history came from conversations with a remarkable group of individuals who willingly gave up their time to talk with me about their lives and experiences. I am especially grateful to the following people, not only for their input, but also for their generous hospitality and kindness during my visits with them. Richard and Leah Blanchard; Caroline Burrows; Elmer Denning; Sue Dorffeld; John Dorffeld; Joseph Dorffeld; Robert Dorffeld; Judith Fitton; Lenore Fitton; Kathleen and Bob Frisbie; Dorothy Gallagher; Sharon Hauser; Bill and Rosemary Heaps; Jim Hughes; Bryan Johnson; John Kindlesparger; Gertie Klein; Liz Knittle; Virginia Knittle; Chief Master Sergeant of the Air Force (Ret.) Leo Knoblach; Barbara LaForge; Sharon Laurence; CDR Mary E. Lewellyn, USN; Barbara Lindsay; Larry Martin; Cathy Moze; Dave and Ann Nelson; Vicki L. Newton-Berry; Colleen Nunn; Tom and Wanda Payne; Ann Predaris; Wilma Ray; Pat and Ralph Reel; Gary B. Roush; Maggie Russell; Margaret Scanlan; Mary Shoultys; Sergeant Major Harold Smith; Lois Smith-Rohly; Madonna Stephens; Colonel (Ret.) Harvey E. Stewart; Mrs. Sybil Stockdale; Ruth Ellen Stout; Lorrayne and Bob Vogel; Robbie Vogel; Terry Vogel; Chief Warrant Officer Four Bruce Watts; Major General (Ret.) David and Nancy Watts; Chris Watts.

Sincere appreciation and big hugs go to Jerry and Mary Ellen McKain and Norman and Mary Lou Miller. They went above and beyond for me.

Special thanks to Senator Bob Dole for taking the time to share his memories of Schilling Manor with me.

And finally, I was lucky to have an agent who found *Waiting Wives* an editor who cared about the book as much as I do. Thank you, Jenny Bent at Trident Media Group for the gift of Brenda Copeland at Atria Books who shepherded the story of Schilling Manor and its women with heartfelt dedication from the beginning through to its completion. I am also profoundly thankful to everyone at Atria who championed *Waiting Wives* and transferred it to its final form: Judith Curr, Michelle Hinkson, Sarah Wright, Nancy Clements, Paolo Pepe, and Amy Tannenbaum.

Sources

ARTICLES

"The War in Kansas" by Calvin Trillin - 1967 *The New Yorker;* "Schilling Manor" by Colonel (Ret.) Jerry L. McKain - 1971 *Military Review;* "Military Induced Separation: A Stress Reduction Intervention" by William G. Black - 1993 *Social Work;* "Combat Casualties Who Remain at Home," by Edna J. Hunter - 1980 *Military Review;* "The Forgotten Americans of the Vietnam War" by Louis R. Stockwell - 1969 *Air Force and Space Digest;* "Waiting Wives: Women Under Stress," by Douglas R. Bey - 1974, *American Journal of Psychiatry.*

BOOKS

Uncle Sam's Brides: The World of Military Wives, Betty Sowers Alt and Bonnie Domrose Stone; *City on the Move: The Story of Salina, Kansas,* Ruby Bramwell; *The World Almanac of the Vietnam War,* Introduction, Fox Butterfield, John S. Bowman, ed.; *The Army Wife Handbook,* Ann Crossley and Carol A. Keller; *Army Wives: Veterans Without Glory,* Louise Lawrence Fuller; *Vietnam and America: The Most Comprehensive Documented History of the Vietnam War,* Marvin E. Gettleman, Jane Franklin, Marilyn B. Young, and H. Bruce Franklin, eds.; *The Sixties: Years of Hope, Days of Rage,* Todd Gitlin; *365 Days,* Ronald J. Glassner M.D.; *So Your Husband's Gone to War,* Ethel Gorham; *A Chorus of Stones,* Susan Griffin; *Dispatches,* Michael Herr; *American Tragedy: Kennedy, Johnson, and the Origins of the Vietnam War,* David E. Kaiser; *Vietnam: A History,* Stanley Karnow; *Vietnam Wives: Facing the Challenges of Life with Veterans Suffering Post-Traumatic Stress Disorder,* Aphrodite Matsakis; *In Retrospect: The Tragedy and Lessons of Vietnam,* Robert S. McNamara with Brian VanDeMark; *Dereliction of Duty: Lyndon Johnson, Robert McNamara, The Joint Chiefs of Staff, and the Lies that Led to Vietnam*, H. R. McMaster; *The Officer's Guide*—9th, 14th, and 22nd editions, The Military Service Publishing Company; *We Were Soldiers Once . . . and Young: Ia Drang–The Battle That Changed the War in Vietnam*, Lieutenant General (Ret.) Harold G. Moore and Joseph L. Galloway; *The Sorrow of War: A Novel of North Vietnam*, Bao Ninh, et al.; *RN: The Memoirs of Richard Nixon*, Richard Nixon; *A Bright Shining Lie: John Paul Vann and America in Vietnam*, Neil Sheehan; *Army Brat: A Memoir*, William Jay Smith; *In Love and War: The Story of a Family's Ordeal and Sacrifice During the Vietnam Years*, Jim and Sybil Stockdale; *The Vietnam War Almanac*, Colonel of Infantry Harry G. Summers, Jr.; *Brats: Children of the Military Speak Out*, Mary R. Truscott; *The Encyclopedia of the Vietnam War: A Political, Social, and Military History*, Spencer C. Tucker, ed.; *Military Brats: Legacies of Childhood Inside the Fortress*, Mary Edwards Wertsch.

DISSERTATION

Schilling Manor: A Survey of a Military Community of Father Absent Families, by LTC Harold E. Allen.

GOVERNMENT

Department of the Army; Department on the Army/Family Support Division; Department of the Army/FOIA Program; Department of Defense Office of Public Affairs and Office of Communications; Defense Prisoner of War/Missing Personnel Office; Fort Riley Library; Library of Congress; The Congressional Record—8/1/67 and 4/29/70; The National Archives and Records Administration; United States Army Center of Military History; The Veteran's Administration; Vietnam Veterans of America.

MEDIA

CBS News Archives; Erickson Archival; NBC New Archives; *The Air Force Times; The Army Times;* The Associated Press/News and Information Research Center; *The Fort Riley Post; In-Forum,* Fargo, North Dakota; *The Milwaukee Sentinel;* The Museum of Television and Radio; the *Salina Journal; The Schilling Sun; The Wichita Eagle;* Radio Broadcast: Paul Harvey "News and Comments" ABC Radio Network/March 1967.

REPORTS

American Prisoners of War in WWI, WWII, Korea, Vietnam, Persian Gulf, Somalia, Bosnia, Kosovo, and Afghanistan by Charles A. Stenger, Ph.D.; Status of US Prisoners of the Viet Cong in South Vietnam—Central Intelligence Agency Intelligence Memorandum, June 28, 1965.

QUESTIONS AND TOPICS
FOR DISCUSSION

1. Along with her family's story, why do you suppose—out of the thousands of women who called Schilling Manor home—Donna Moreau chose to tell Beverly's, Lorrayne's, and Bonnie's stories? How does each of these three accounts contribute something different to the narrative?

2. In the preface, the author says that for the women she interviewed, "Schilling Manor was a place of light during the darkest, most terrifying time of their lives." What did Schilling Manor provide for these women that other places, even living near family, could not?

3. What do the sections titled "The Committee" add to the overall picture of what life was like for the waiting wives at Schilling Manor? Why does the author refer to each woman on the committee not by name but by her husband's rank?

4. Along with Lorrayne's desire to turn Schilling Manor into a home for waiting wives and her determination to see it done, what other factors played a part in the founding and success of Schilling Manor?

5. Housing officer John Kindlesparger was advised by his superior officers not to allow MIA/POW wives residence at Schilling Manor because of the negative emotional impact it might have on the community of waiting wives. Did Kindlesparger make the right decision to let Bonnie and other MIA/POW wives live at Schilling Manor?

6. Discuss the role of the "military wife" as portrayed in *Waiting Wives*. How about Beverly in particular as a military wife and mother? When Lorrayne was diagnosed with endometrial cancer, she asked that her surgery be postponed so her husband would not have to be called from active duty. Why was she willing to risk her health and possibly her life for the sake of her husband's career?

7. During a committee meeting one of the women remarks, "I think, out of everything, this war is harder on the children than anyone else." What examples in the book support this statement, from the neighborhood children's fascination with playing war to Robbie's refusal to speak to Bruce, Jr., who was making a Valentine in class? How was the author, even as a teenager, affected by the absence of her father, the concern for his safety, and the continual waiting?

8. Some of the waiting wives would gather daily to watch the evening news for information about Vietnam. "The women waited for Walter Cronkite to explain the larger context of war during the evening news.... The women trusted Walter

to tell them the truth about Vietnam. He spoke to them in tones suggesting care and concern for them and their husbands." Why was the media—and their trust in Walter Cronkite—such a powerful influence on them? How did images of America's changing reactions to the war—including negative remarks and protests—impact these women, whose husbands were putting their lives at risk?

9. While in a way time stood still for the waiting wives, the world outside Schilling Manor continued. How did politics and the actions of the government play out as told in this book, particularly in the sections about Bonnie? After several years of waiting for news about Bruce's whereabouts, what galvanized Bonnie to actively seek information about his status? What impact did politics have on the daily lives of the women at Schilling Manor?

10. Bonnie had clung to her hope that Bruce was alive based in part on a record that went into his file stating witnesses had seen someone fitting his description being led away from a battlefield. What was your reaction to the revelation that the government put the same report in three different soldiers' files?

11. Nearly seven years after Bruce was declared missing in action, Bonnie was asked by the government to watch a tape of combat, but she was unable to confirm if her husband's body was among those on the tape. "Afterward, maybe within an hour, or a day, or a week, something inside, something almost unnoticeable even to her, began to slip away. The body of the soldier with the wedding ring had shaken her faith. Doubt seeped into her heart like slow poison." Why did the image of the wedding ring affect Bonnie so deeply? How was she changed by this experience?

12. Did reading *Waiting Wives* give you a greater understanding of the Vietnam War, its place in American history, and what it was like for the wives left behind? One of the memories Moreau shares is about a peace sign she had hanging in her room as a teenager. What is the significance of her taking down the emblem and, after her father's return from Vietnam, hiding it "deep inside a scrapbook, a memento never to lose, and never, ever to brag about"? How does this reflect her conflicted feelings about the war and her father's job as a soldier?

13. Does Donna Moreau's vantage point as an adult give her a different perspective on the time she spent at Schilling Manor, and on the Vietnam War? How about on her family and her relationship with them? What stands out the most for you about *Waiting Wives?*

14. The author says that the women of Schilling Manor were "members of the last generation of hat-and-glove military wives called upon by their country to pack without question, to follow without comment, and to wait quietly with a smile." The world has changed since the 1960s and early 1970s. America has changed. Society and technology have changed. How are the waiting wives and husbands of the current war different from the waiting wives of the Vietnam War? How are they the same?

15. At the end of the book the author suggests that most Americans no longer trusted the government after living through a war that had lost its meaning, after the revelations of the Pentagon Papers, after Watergate, and after the resignation of a president. Moreau states, "The price America paid, its greatest fatality, American patriotism, the ultimate collateral

damage for a proud country, was as dead as the 58,226 casualties of the Vietnam War." Why is this a true (or a false) assessment of America? Why (or why not) did Americans lose their patriotism? Is America a better country than it was before the Vietnam War era?

About the Author

DONNA MOREAU was born in Ft. Meade, Maryland, and raised on Army posts throughout the world. She now lives and writes in Leominster, Massachusetts. *Waiting Wives* is her first book.